SAY WHAT YOU DO

BUILDING A FRAMEWORK OF IT CONTROLS, POLICIES, STANDARDS, AND PROCEDURES

Dorian J. Cougias · Marcelo Halpern, esq
Rebecca Herold, CISSP, CISM, CISA, FLMI · Karsten Koop

Erikka Innes (research analyst) · E.L. Heiberger, CISA (ed.)
Steve Helwig, PhD, CISSP (tech ed.)
Jessica McCurdy Crooks (indexer)

Copyright information

The information contained in this publication should not be construed as legal advice. We encourage you to consult with an attorney experienced in these areas, if you need further analysis or explanation of the laws or regulations discussed herein.

Schaser-Vartan Books

US Offices: Feedback: info@netfrontiers.com
5620 West Dayflower Path
Lecanto, FL 34461   **For bulk orders: (650) 255-3552**

SAN # 255-2582   http://www.saywhatyoudo.com

Print version: eBook version:
ISBN   0-9729039-6-8   ISBN   0-9729039-2-5
ISBN13 978-0-9729039-6-7   ISBN13 978-0-9729039-2-9

Library of Congress Catalog Card Number: 2006906946
Printed in the United States of America
10 9 8 7 6 5 4 3 2 1

Contents

A quick note on our voice, tone, and the use of "I," and "we."

As you can tell from the inside cover, there are a lot of folks contributing to this book. As individual writers we all tend to use "I" when writing versus always using "we." And that's okay. The "I" here can refer to Dorian, Marcelo, Rebecca, Karsten, Erikka, Lynn, or Steve when they were writing, editing, and speaking in the first person. When you see a "we" it means that all of the writers *and* the editorial team agree completely. Hence, you'll be sure to see a lot more "I's" than "we's" in our writing.

Our tone is somewhat loose and informal. Because that's how we all talk. We aren't big on writer formality when penning our books and articles. We aren't Shakespeare and don't try to be. What we are big on is getting the message across in a way that you can understand it and use it.

We hope we've done that.

Let us know one way or the other.

Dorian and the rest of the writing team.

dcougias@netfrontiers.com

DEDICATION AND INTRODUCTION

This book is dedicated to all of those who have served, are serving, and will serve in the armed forces of their country. Why? Because you know, better than anyone on the planet, the *importance* of well written policies and procedures.

You know that lives are at stake if you spend more time reading than doing.

You know that if it takes you too long to understand your directions, you could miss an important deadline. You know the dire repercussions of that.

You know that the consequences of misunderstanding directions could be disastrous.

You know that if your procedures aren't well communicated and understood by the group, that the loss of the only person on the team who understands the procedure could mean the loss of the team itself. And that's a bad thing.

Sometimes we, in the business world, think of policies and procedures as an undue burden on our jobs. We tend to slough off writing them and even slough off following them. Maybe it is because the only repercussions are a monetary loss to the organization that we are a member of and not a personal loss to ourselves. But with regulatory compliance hovering over our collective heads, policies and procedures are becoming more and more important and the impact more personal. Policies and procedures are profoundly important to our organizations.

Why? Because it is the auditor's job to go through the remains of last night's dinner to figure out what was on the menu (that's a metaphor, and you can get as graphic as you want in your own head). And the only real way that the auditor knows whether or not we are *doing* our jobs and *being* compliant is to look at our policies and procedures to see if the direction has been set. And then look for evidence to see if we've been following our own directions. Simple as that.

So what makes a good policy and what makes a good procedure? And more importantly, can *you* create one? Sure you can. Below is a page from the US Army's famous "Woodchuck book," more formally known as Field Manual 5-34. It is a book that every combat engineer (even Special Forces engineers) carries in the field and is an indispensable tool for any engineering task at hand.

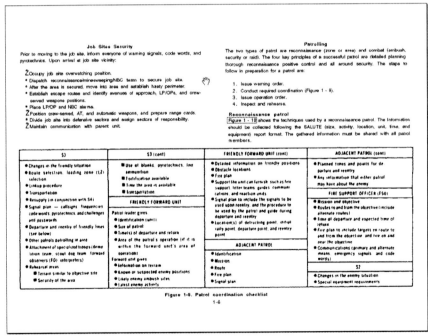

A sample page from the Woodchuck book

More importantly, it is a policy and procedure manual. A well written, easy to understand, easy to follow, policy and procedure manual. If you want to know how to stop tanks coming down the road by cutting down trees – it's in there. If you want to know how to blow up a bridge – it's in there. If you want to know how to build a bridge – that's in there too. The page that we show points out the four major things that have to happen when your group goes out on patrol. And because the second item involved coordination with multiple people, it breaks the steps down by group.

Easy to follow. Easy to understand. Gets the group moving because they are *doing* rather than *reading*. You can write like that.

Anybody who works within the organization, and who knows how it works in reality, can draw a process map that says "this is step 1 of what I do, that's step 2 of what I do."

Anybody who has a grasp of language can write bullet points about what should happen – bullet points to match the process map.

Once you understand the process that you've drawn and summarized in bullets, you can make a decision about the direction your staff should take. **That's a policy statement**. A policy statement describes your organizational management team's decision about the actions (processes) you are going to follow.

Anyone can then review those process documents for clarity (do you really understand it?) and conciseness (are they too wordy?). Anyone with a word processor that checks grammar and spelling can put the finishing touches on it. Anyone with common sense who tries to follow the steps can ensure that each step is in the right order. **That's a procedure document**. A procedure document lists, in order, the steps the team needs to take to complete the process.

You can do it.

This book will show you how.

Here's what to avoid

The biggest sin is to either hire a professional writer to do the job, or think you are a professional writer. Professional writers don't understand your business. You aren't Shakespeare. Keep everything as simple as if you were explaining your processes to your parents.

Avoid big words or words a ten year old can't understand. Not many people want to read Proust. Most people like reading the comics.

Avoid long sentences. If your sentences are longer than 12-15 words, they are too long. Shorter sentences are easier to understand.

Avoid messing with the chronology of a process. If a step should happen first, then place it first. If you have a prerequisite step that has to happen *before* the first step, then *place the prerequisite first.*

Avoid passive action descriptions or identifiers such as "the delivery agent will be instructed to pick up the backup tapes." That doesn't say anything about who is doing the instructing or which tapes. A better writing of this is "the delivery agent will be instructed by the administrator to pick up the backup tapes marked for off-site storage."

Avoid two or three word headlines (Log review). Instead, provide a summary of the section (The administrator will review logs weekly).

Avoid writing policies before you understand the process. Too many times organizations write policies that *can't* be enforced because they've never worked out the process their staff needs to follow in order to support the policy. The development order is simple — 1) decide which rules you have to follow, they will give you a direction; 2) attempt to follow the course by working out and documenting your processes (and change course if necessary); then 3) formalize your direction in a policy statement and your method in a set of procedures.

And most importantly, avoid too much of anything. Too much of anything is a bad thing.

DEFINING A UNIFIED COMPLIANCE FRAMEWORK

Before we can seriously discuss the Unified Compliance Framework, we have to ensure that we are on the same page with a few definitions. We need to have a joint understanding of what it means to "comply," and what the rules are that we are complying *with*.

Say what you Do

What does it mean "to comply?"

Compliance is ensuring that the requirements of laws, regulations, industry codes, and organizational doctrines are met. This also applies to contractual arrangements to which the business process is subject, i.e., externally imposed business criteria.

In other words, it simply means following the rules that are set by people other than ourselves.

Because of human nature, if we were left to ourselves to comply with all of the rules and regulations foisted upon us, do you really think that we would? Of course not. At least not all of the time. No one reading this (and us as writers) can say that we have always complied with all laws and regulations. Who among us *hasn't* driven over the speed limit, cheated in solitaire, or broken/bent the rules? Not one of us.

And because we are apt to break the rules, we need to have measurable organizational compliance programs put in place to ensure that we do follow the rules. Compliance programs aim to prevent, and where necessary, identify and respond to; breaches of laws, regulations, codes, or organizational requirements occurring in the organization. They should promote a culture of compliance within the organization. The organizational compliance program is instilled through the use of compliance controls.

Compliance control is a process, effected by management and other personnel, designed to provide reasonable assurance that transactions are executed in accordance with 1) laws governing the use of budget authority and other laws and regulations that could have a direct and material effect on the financial statements or required supplementary stewardship information and 2) any other laws, regulations, and government wide policies identified in audit guidance. How the organizational leadership makes this process of compliance control known to its staff is through the publication of policies, standards, and procedures that must be followed unless a formal exception has been granted.

Documented organizational controls, in the form of policies, standards, and procedures guide organizational staff when conducting day-to-day operations. The reason that these policies, standards, and procedures are called controls is that they *do* guide and limit the actions of users abiding by them.

Therefore, when we say that an organization is in compliance, or complying, we are saying that they are following all of the rules and guidelines set before them by creating a compliance program that outlines and documents specific controls in the form of policies, standards, and procedures that must be followed.

Authority documents: regulations, principles, standards, guidelines, best practices, policies, and procedures

When we say that we are "complying," we are saying that we are complying with authoritative rules that are not of our own creation. (OK, so some of you reading this are, in fact, responsible for creating these rules – that's why you bought this in the first place. But when you're creating these rules you are not you, but rather you are your organization. So you, as yourself, are obligated to comply with the rules created by you as your organization. Got it?) These authoritative rules can come in the form of regulations, principles, standards, guidelines, best practices, policies, and procedures. Which is which, and what makes one authoritative body a regulator and another a best practice author? Let's start with regulations and move from there.

- Regulations are rules of law that, if not followed, can result in penalties. Regulations state *that* something must be done. Regulations are promulgated by governmental agencies to interpret or expand the reach of statutes.

- Standards are rallying points created by well organized groups or are generally accepted within the industry. Standards rally the affected entities around *what* must be done.

- Guidelines are detailed outlines and plans for determining a course of action. Guidelines *prioritize and direct* the course of action.

- Best practices are programs, initiatives or activities which are considered leading edge or exceptional models for others to follow. Best practices *set the example* of *how to do* something the best way.

Collectively, we refer to these as **authority documents** throughout this book and throughout all of the other documentation within the Unified Compliance Framework.

Regulations

To regulate is to bring under *the force of law* or a *governing authority*. Everyone in his or her own country falls within the realm of the national, regional, and local laws. Hence, traditional regulators are those within the levels of government just mentioned. When governmental agencies create their acts, they are codifying legal documents that resulted from deliberations of their legislative bodies. Often, however, the acts passed by those legislative bodies establish broad principles rather than detailed prescriptions for the behavior of people and companies and delegate to regulators responsibility for filling in the details and gaps. The regulators are empowered to interpret how the laws are to be implemented and to establish rules for following those laws. Those rules are then documented as **regulations**, such as the <u>Code of Federal Regulations</u> that we have in the United States. These acts and regulations, therefore, *must* be followed under penalty of law.

Regulations are enforceable by law. Failure to follow regulations will result in penalties.

Contractual and self-regulatory structures

There is much confusion between "regulations" promulgated by government regulators as discussed above and the rules, standards and, yes, "regulations" promulgated by other so-called regulatory bodies and other organizations that *can* and *do* emerge to reign in our actions. Variously known as "self-regulatory bodies," "standards bodies," or by similar names, these organizations are not part of the government and do not have the force of law behind their requirements, but failure to comply with those requirements may well disqualify an entity from participating in certain businesses. The promulgators of these rules may be industry-based organizations that band together to address a concern that is common to industry members. For example, the credit card companies (Visa, MasterCard, American Express, etc.) have banded together to create the <u>Payment Card Industry Security Standard</u>. They may also be self-appointed watchdog organizations that have gained sufficient acceptance, prominence and/or moral authority over time that people turn to them as authorities in the field. For example, the ability to display the BBBOnline and TRUSTe seals in online commerce has achieved this type of prominence that makes it worthwhile to comply with those standards. Certain membership based organizations promote similar types of rules as a condition of membership. The unifying principle is that they all have something you want and you're willing to *contractually* commit to play by their rules to get it.

We'll get to the definition of a standard in a moment, but just because this one is *called* a standard (it can't be called a law, Act, or regulation because it does not come from the government), doesn't mean that it can be ignored without consequences. Compliance with these types of contractual standards are, legally speaking, optional. If a company is not interested in accepting credit cards as a form of payment, it is not obligated to comply with the PCI standards. However, anyone wanting to accept credit cards is required to *contractually* agree to comply with the PCI standard. Similarly, anyone wanting to display the BBBOnline seal must contractually agree to follow certain guidelines and processes. Failure to comply with these obligations creates a breach of contract and, depending on the contract terms, may result in a variety of fines and, potentially, the loss of valuable contractual rights – losing the ability to accept credit cards in the case of the PCI standards could have grave consequences to just about any merchant. Losing the right to use the BBBOnline or TRUSTe seals may not have as severe an effect on a merchant as being unable to accept credit cards, but it could drive customers away to competitor sites – particularly if the contractual breach is widely publicized. The payment card industry has already fined a great many organizations and affected the closure of at least one organization that we know of for not properly following their standard. Because the payment card industry *can* exercise *authority* over its user body, and that user body is so large, in this instance they can be compared to regulators even though they haven't been given the statutory mandate of a regulator. However, there is one big difference between the payment card industry and true regulators – while the payment card industry may be able put you out of business, they can't put you in jail.

Contractual standards promulgated by self-regulatory bodies are enforceable under contract. Failure to comply carries with it the remedies established by the contract which may include fines and/or loss of valuable contract rights and such consequences are enforceable under contract law.

Principles

A principle is a widely accepted rule, norm, doctrine, or assumed truth. A set of principles form the basic foundation for a specific set of guidelines. A good example of general principles are the seven principles of the OECD Guidelines for the Security of Information Systems and Networks (awareness, responsibility, response, risk assessment, security design and implementation, security management, and reassessment principles). Principles, then, are fundamental beliefs that set the course for the rest of the thinking on the subject at hand. Principles can be combined with a semi-detailed set of controls which flow from them, such as the <u>Generally Accepted Internet Security Principles</u>.

Many principles will find their way into standards and guidelines and even regulations as they serve as general behavior directives that drive standards discussions in the first place. One example of a principle directly creating standards are the Generally Accepted Accounting Principles found within the world of finance which have spawned the SAS 91 accounting standard.

Principles are not enforceable by law. Failure to follow principles may result in actions that are not within keeping of the rule of law or proper conduct.

International standards and control models

We love the origination of the term standard. Originally a standard was a conspicuous object (a tall pole with a banner, flag, or symbol on top) that was used to mark a rallying point in battle. Today, a standard is a criterion, a means of determining what rules, principles, and measures established by an authority should apply to a given situation in order to improve efficiency and compatibility. Control models are very much the same thing but tend to focus more specifically on certain aspects of implementation. In contrast to the original definition, a standard today comes into existence *because* people rally around it rather than the other way around. International standards and control models are consensus models that are generally accepted by the user community (or at least by the community creating the standard), such as the <u>Control Objectives for Information Technology</u> created by Information Systems Audit and Control Association (a control model) or the International Organization for Standardization's (ISO) various standards such as their ISO 27001:2005 <u>Information Security Management System</u>.

Formal international standards begin as draft documents which are then published as a Request for Comments (RFC) document. As these RFCs mature through the editing process, they become proposed standards, draft standards, and ultimately the final published standard.

Does your organization *have* to follow any given standard? Not if the standard's author isn't a regulator or a body with contractual authority over you – meaning that they can't *force* your organization to use their standard under threat of legal action or penalty. Some might think defacto standards must be followed, but that isn't true.

In the world of regulatory compliance for information services, the CobiT audit standard comes pretty close to being *the* defacto standard. We've seen presentations in which the speaker mistakenly told the audience that this or that regulation *called for* the use of CobiT as the measuring stick against which they must judge whether they were following the regulation. That just isn't so (though see our section "A note about Safe Harbors" that follows). There isn't one regulation that mandates the use of CobiT. However, the Sarbanes-Oxley Act did create the Public Company Accounting Oversight Board which created and mandates the use of its own auditing standards. The Payment Card Industry Association also mandates the use of its PCI-DSS standard as the audit standard that must be followed when proving that you've met their guidelines. Of course regulators are certainly free to require the use of a particular standard, but that hasn't happened yet and we think it unlikely to happen any time soon – the government tends to avoid ceding its authority to non-government groups and will, instead, plagiarize the standard and incorporate it directly into the text of the regulation.

*Standards are not enforceable by law. However, failure to follow standards may result in actions contrary to regulations which **are** enforceable by law.*

Guidelines

A great example of a guideline is The Business Continuity Institute's Business Continuity Management Good Practice Guidelines. This guideline doesn't attempt to provide every answer for business continuity planning. However, it prioritizes the steps that should be followed when creating, developing, and testing the plan.

The hallmark of a guideline is that it will have a set of general principles followed by a set of procedures which direct the user through the necessary steps that should be followed with respect to the given topic under consideration.

*Guidelines are even less enforceable than standards. However, failure to follow guidelines may lead to certain aspects of a standard or regulation being skipped or missing the mark, which in turn may result in actions contrary to regulations which **are** enforceable by law.*

Best practices

Best practices are leading edge models of methods or actions for others to follow. These are combinations of activities, processes, policies, or procedures that document the *best possible* way of doing something.

Are they enforceable? Nope. As a matter of fact, many times they aren't even *desirable* – in their fullest sense, the "best" way to do something is often also the costliest. Too many times we've seen people spending $1,000 to fix a $100 problem by using an industry "best practice." Best practices must always be viewed in context, weighing the cost vs. the benefit, and then adapted to the particular situation in which they may be applied.

Controls

Organizational controls (especially compliance controls) are the activities that comprise and are carried out by policies, standards, procedures, and practices designed to provide reasonable assurance that certain business objectives will be achieved and undesired events will be prevented or detected. These control activities help ensure that management directives are carried out by providing a description of what physical, software, procedural, or people related conditions must be met or be in existence in order to satisfy a core requirement.

*Following properly structured and validated organizational controls is **the** essential prerequisite to compliance, and failure to follow controls will directly lead to whatever fines or penalties the regulatory body can mete out.*

Organizational policies

A policy is a definitive plan or method of action to guide decisions and actions. Policies should be selected from the various possible alternatives in the light of organizational conditions and the impact that they will have. Policies are meant to limit individual discretion to make decisions about which choices and actions (or behaviors) can be taken regarding the topic in question. Because of this, a policy's intended purpose is to influence and guide both present and future decision making to be in line with the philosophy, objectives, and strategic plans established by the organization's management teams. In addition to policy content, well structured policies describe the consequences of failing to comply with the policy, the means for handling exceptions, and the manner in which compliance with the policy will be checked and measured.

In practice, an organizational policy is a formal document describing the organization's position on a particular aspect of compliance with regulations, standards, and guidelines. Therefore, it acts as an official statement of a position, plan, or course of action established by an identified sponsoring authority, which is designed to influence, to provide direction, and to determine decisions and actions with regard to a specific topic. Organizational standards, procedures, and guidelines flow from policies. Policies come in two basic forms; high-level policy statements and detailed policies.

Many times the high-level policy statements will have direct links to organizational standards and procedures, such as an organizational policy for the destruction of electronic media (tapes, drives, etc.) that would then point to the organizational degaussing standard and associated step-by-step procedures for more explicit information.

Detailed policies provide more in-depth information such as purpose, authority, and detailed definitions of sub-topics. Detailed policies often have direct links to individual procedures for follow-through methods. A good example of a policy-procedure pairing is an organizational records retention policy that details various definitions of record types and then links each type to the procedures that need to be followed to carry out that specific portion of the policy.

Policies, because they are mandatory within the organization, are enforced by the organization under the auspices of the Human Resources and/or Legal departments and failure to comply with a policy is generally punishable by disciplinary action that could include suspension or even termination to the extent permitted by law.

Organizational standards

Standards are definitional and clarifying in nature and established either to further understanding and interaction or to acknowledge observed (or desired norms) of exhibited characteristics or behavior. Organizational standards are used to define the commonality of parts and processes. A standard can be:

1. An object or measure of comparison that defines or represents the magnitude of a unit.

2. A characterization that establishes allowable tolerances or constraints for categories of items and parameter settings.

3. A degree or level of required excellence or attainment.

Thus, organizational standards may specify minimum performance levels, describe best practices within the company, or serve as the list of controls (or their parameters) that the organization must follow in order to attain compliance within a given area. In general computing terms, a standard is a set of detailed technical guidelines used as a means of establishing uniformity in an area of hardware or software development.

Standards can be put in place to support a policy, a process, or as a response to an operational need. Like policies, well structured standards will include a description of the manner in which noncompliance will be detected.

Because standards directly support organizational policies, they should be enforced with the same level of authority as the organizational policy they clarify.

Organizational procedures

A procedure is a step-by-step description of tasks required to support and carry out organizational policies. Therefore, a procedure can be thought of as an extension of a policy that articulates the process that is to be used to accomplish a control.

More formally, procedures are the step-by-step documentation of the course of action to be taken to perform a given task as a series of steps, followed in a definite regular order, ensuring the consistent and repetitive approach to accomplish control activities.

Because procedures directly support organizational policies, they should be enforced with the same level of authority as the organizational policy they support.

A note about "Safe Harbors"

Nothing muddies the waters better than a good "safe harbor." While a safe harbor is intended to make laws and regulations easier to follow, oftentimes the safe harbor is co-opted by consultants, speakers, and other well-meaning (or not so well-meaning) folks to support their position that a particular standard, guideline, procedure, or control is required under the law and that failure to adopt that particular standard, guideline, procedure, or control will subject the organization to legal action. Nothing could be further from the truth.

A safe harbor in a law or regulation is a shortcut used by the regulators to make it easier for people to determine whether they are in compliance with the law without requiring an in-depth analysis of each particular case. Thus, the safe harbor provides that *if* you take the steps required to be within the safe harbor, *then* you will (more or less) automatically be considered to be in compliance with that particular aspect of the law or regulation. However, the converse is not true – if you do *not* fall within the safe harbor, that does not necessarily mean that you are not in compliance with the law. What it *does* mean is that you will have to show that the steps you chose to take are *also* in compliance with the law.

Let's use our previously mentioned CobiT standard as an illustration. Supposed some regulator enacted a regulation requiring that certain types of organizations conduct annual audits of their information services systems that adhere to auditing standards that are reasonable and customary in the industry. Suppose further that our helpful regulator adds a statement along the lines of "The CobiT audit standards are reasonable and customary standards in the industry." This safe harbor offers organizations the opportunity to reduce compliance risk by adopting the CobiT audit standards. However, there could be many reasons why the CobiT standards are inappropriate for the particular organization – cost, complexity, etc., may simply not warrant the use of that standard. Is the organization bound to use CobiT anyway? (If you've read this far, you probably already know the answer.) The answer, of course, is **no** – the organization is free to use whatever auditing standard it chooses *provided* it meets the two-prong test of "reasonable" and "customary in the industry." However, if the organization chooses to use a standard other than CobiT and the regulator doesn't like it, the organization may have an uphill battle to convince the regulator (and, perhaps ultimately, the court) that the chosen standard is, in fact, reasonable and customary in the industry.

Safe harbors tend to be very conservative and avoid gray areas. If a safe harbor is available, it's always good to know – even if you choose not to follow it, it can provide valuable guidance and insight into the regulator's mindset. However, the needs of the organization may dictate that it leave the safe harbor and enter riskier waters.

The authority documents tracked by the UCF

To give you a scope of the authority documents that we've used to form this material, and all of the other material within the Unified Compliance Framework, here is a listing of all of the authority documents that we are currently tracking and referencing. Please know that this is an ever growing list and is subject to change as the documents themselves change. For the most up-to-date listing, along with URL links to each of the documents we track, see the Unified Compliance Framework website at www.unifiedcompliance.com.

Sarbanes Oxley

- Sarbanes-Oxley Act (SOX)
- PCAOB Auditing Standard No. 2
- AICPA SAS 94
- AICPA/CICA Privacy Framework

- ⚡ AICPA Suitable Trust Services Criteria
- ⚡ Retention of Audit and Review Records, SEC 17 CFR 210.2-06
- ⚡ Controls and Procedures, SEC 17 CFR 240.15d-15
- ⚡ Reporting Transactions and Holdings, SEC 17 CFR 240.16a-3
- ⚡ COSO Enterprise Risk Management (ERM) Framework

Banking and Finance

- ⚡ Basel II: International Convergence of Capital Measurement and Capital Standards - A Revised Framework
- ⚡ BIS Sound Practices for the Management and Supervision of Operational Risk
- ⚡ Gramm-Leach-Bliley Act (GLB)
- ⚡ Standards for Safeguarding Customer Information, FTC 16 CFR 314
- ⚡ Privacy of Consumer Financial Information, FTC 16 CFR 313
- ⚡ Safety and Soundness Standards, Appendix of OCC 12 CFR 30
- ⚡ FFIEC Information Security
- ⚡ FFIEC Development and Acquisition
- ⚡ FFIEC Business Continuity Planning
- ⚡ FFIEC Audit
- ⚡ FFIEC Management
- ⚡ FFIEC Operations

NASD NYSE

- ⚡ NASD Manual
- ⚡ NYSE Rules
- ⚡ Recordkeeping rule for securities exchanges, SEC 17 CFR 240.17a-1
- ⚡ Records to be made by certain exchange members SEC 17 CFR 240.17a-3
- ⚡ Records to be preserved by certain exchange members SEC 17 CFR 240.17a-4
- ⚡ Recordkeeping SEC 17 CFR 240.17Ad-6
- ⚡ Record retention SEC 17 CFR 240.17Ad-7

Healthcare and Life Science

- HIPAA (Health Insurance Portability and Accountability Act)
- HIPAA HCFA Internet Security Policy
- Introductory Resource Guide for HIPAA NIST (800-66)
- CMS Core Security Requirements (CSR)
- CMS Information Security Acceptable Risk Safeguards (ARS)
- CMS Information Security Certification and Accreditation (C&A) Methodology
- CMS Info Security Business Risk Assessment
- CMS Business Partners Systems Security Manual
- FDA Electronic Records; Electronic Signatures FDA 21 CFR Part 11+D1

Energy

- FERC Security Program for Hydropower Projects
- North American Electric Reliability Corporation Critical Infrastructure Protection Cyber Security Standards

Payment Card

- PCI DSS (Payment Card Industry Data Security Standard)
- PCI DSS Security Scanning Procedures
- VISA CISP: What to Do If Compromised
- American Express Data Security Standard (DSS)
- MasterCard Wireless LANs - Security Risks and Guidelines

U.S. Federal Security

- FTC Electronic Signatures in Global and National Commerce Act (ESIGN)
- Uniform Electronic Transactions Act (UETA)
- FISMA (Federal Information Security Management Act)
- FISCAM (Federal Information System Controls Audit Manual)
- FIPS 140-2, Security Requirements for Cryptographic Modules
- FIPS 199, Standards for Security Categorization of Federal Information and Information Systems

- FIPS 191, Guideline for the Analysis of LAN Security
- Clinger-Cohen Act (Information Technology Management Reform Act)
- The National Strategy to Secure Cyberspace
- GAO Financial Audit Manual
- Standard for Electronic Records Management Software, DOD 5015.2
- CISWG Report on the Best Practices Subgroup
- CISWG Information Security Program Elements
- Appendix III to OMB Circular No. A-130: Security of Federal Automated Information Resources
- NCUA Guidelines for Safeguarding Member Information, 12 CFR 748

U.S. Internal Revenue

- IRS Revenue Procedure: Retention of books and records, 97-22
- IRS Revenue Procedure: Record retention: automatic data processing, 98-25
- IRS Internal Revenue Code Section 501(c)(3)

Records Management

- Federal Rules of Civil Procedure
- Uniform Rules of Evidence
- ISO 15489-1, Information and Documentation: Records management: General
- ISO 15489-2, Information and Documentation: Records management: Guidelines
- The DIRKS Manual: A Strategic Approach to Managing Business Information
- The Sedona Principles Addressing Electronic Document Production

NIST Publications

- Generally Accepted Principles and Practices for Securing Information Technology Systems, NIST SP 800-14
- Developing Security Plans for Federal Information Systems, NIST SP 800-18
- Security Self-Assessment Guide, NIST SP 800-26
- Risk Management Guide, NIST SP 800-30

- Underlying Technical Models for Information Technology Security
- Contingency Planning Guide for Information Technology Systems, NIST SP 800-34
- Creating a Patch and Vulnerability Management Program, NIST SP 800-40
- Guidelines on Firewalls and Firewall Policy, NIST SP 800-41
- Recommended Security Controls for Federal Information Systems, NIST SP 800-53
- Guide for Mapping Types of Information and Information Systems to Security Categories, NIST SP 800-60
- Computer Security Incident Handling Guide, NIST SP 800-61
- Security Considerations in the Information System Development Life Cycle, NIST SP 800-64

International Standards Organization

- ISO 73:2002, Risk Management - Vocabulary
- ISO 13335, Information Technology - Guidelines for Management of IT Security
- ISO 17799:2000, Code of Practice for Information Security Management
- ISO 17799:2005, Code of Practice for Information Security Management
- ISO 27001:2005, Information Security Management Systems - Requirements
- ISO/IEC 20000-12:2005 Information technology — Service Management Part 1
- ISO/IEC 20000-2:2005 Information technology — Service Management Part 2
- ISO/IEC 15408-1:2005 Common Criteria for Information Technology Security Evaluation Part 1
- ISO/IEC 15408-2:2005 Common Criteria for Information Technology Security Evaluation Part 2
- ISO/IEC 15408-3:2005 Common Criteria for Information Technology Security Evaluation Part 3
- ISO/IEC 18045:2005 Common Methodology for Information Technology Security Evaluation Part 3

IT Information Library

- OGC ITIL: Planning to Implement Service Management
- OGC ITIL: ICT Infrastructure Management
- OGC ITIL: Service Delivery
- OGC ITIL: Service Support
- OGC ITIL: Application Management
- OGC ITIL: Security Management

General Guidance

- CobiT 3rd Edition
- CobiT 4.0
- ISACA IS Standards, Guidelines, and Procedures for Auditing and Control Professionals
- Disaster / Emergency Management and Business Continuity, NFPA 1600
- ISF Standard of Good Practice for Information Security
- ISF Security Audit of Networks
- A Risk Management Standard, jointly issued by AIRMIC, ALARM, and IRM
- Business Continuity Institute (BCI) Good Practice Guidelines
- ISSA Generally Accepted Information Security Principles (GAISP)
- CERT Operationally Critical Threat, Asset & Vulnerability Evaluation (OCTAVE)
- The GAIT Methodology
- IIA Global Technology Audit Guide (GTAG)

U.S. Federal Privacy

- Cable Communications Privacy Act Title 47 § 551
- Telemarketing Sales Rule (TSR), 16 CFR 310
- CAN SPAM Act
- Children's Online Privacy Protection Act (COPPA), 16 CFR 312
- Driver's Privacy Protection Act (DPPA), 18 USC 2721
- Family Education Rights Privacy Act (FERPA), 20 USC 1232

- Privacy Act of 1974, 5 USC 552a
- Video Privacy Protection Act (VPPA), 18 USC 2710
- Specter-Leahy Personal Data Privacy and Security Act
- Amendments to the FTC Telemarketing Sales Rule
- Children's Online Privacy Protection Act
- U.S. State Privacy
- Arkansas Personal Information Protection Act AR SB 1167
- Arizona Amendment to Arizona Revised Statutes 13-2001, AZ HB 2116
- California Information Practice Act, CA SB 1386
- California General Security Standard for Businesses CA AB 1950
- California Public Records Military Veteran Discharge Documents, CA AB 1798
- California OPP Recommended Practices on Notification of Security Breach
- Colorado Prohibition against Using Identity Information for Unlawful Purpose, CO HB 1134
- Colorado Consumer Credit Solicitation Protection, CO HB 1274
- Colorado Prohibiting Inclusion of Social Security Number, CO HB 1311
- Connecticut law Requiring Consumer Credit Bureaus to Offer Security Freezes, CT SB 650
- Connecticut law Concerning Nondisclosure of Private Tenant Information, CT HB 5184
- Delaware Computer Security Breaches DE HB 116
- Florida Personal Identification Information/Unlawful Use, FL HB 481
- Georgia Consumer Reporting Agencies, GA SB 230
- Georgia Public employees; Fraud, Waste, and Abuse, GA HB 656
- Hawaii Exempting disclosure of Social Security numbers HI HB 2674
- Illinois Personal Information Protection Act IL HB 1633
- Indiana Release of Social Security Number, Notice of Security Breach IN SB 503
- Louisiana Database Security Breach Notification Law, LA SB 205 Act 499
- Maine law To Protect Maine Citizens from Identity Theft, ME LD 1671

- Minnesota Data Warehouses; Notice Required for Certain Disclosures, MN HF 2121
- Missouri War on Terror Veteran Survivor Grants, MO HB 957
- Montana bill to Implement Individual Privacy and to Prevent Identity Theft, MT HB 732
- New Jersey Identity Theft Prevention Act, NJ A4001/S1914
- New York Information Security Breach and Notification Act
- Nevada Security Breach Notification Law, NV SB 347
- North Carolina Security Breach Notification Law (Identity Theft Protection Act), NC SB 1048
- North Dakota Personal Information Protection Act, ND SB 2251
- Ohio Personal information - contact if unauthorized access, OH HB 104
- Rhode Island Security Breach Notification Law, RI HB 6191
- Tennessee Security Breach Notification, TN SB 2220
- Texas Identity Theft Enforcement and Protection Act, TX SB 122
- Vermont Relating to Identity Theft, VT HB 327
- Virginia Identity theft; penalty; restitution; victim assistance, VA HB 872
- Washington Notice of a breach of the security, WA SB 6043

EU Guidance

- EU Directive on Privacy and Electronic Communications, 2002/58/EC
- EU Directive on Data Protection, 95/46/EC
- US Department of Commerce EU Safe Harbor Privacy Principles
- Consumer Interests in the Telecommunications Market, Act No. 661
- OECD / World Bank Technology Risk Checklist
- OECD Guidelines on Privacy and Transborder Flows of Personal Data
- UN Guidelines for the Regulation of Computerized Personal Data Files (1990)
- ISACA Cross-Border Privacy Impact Assessment
- Information Technology Security Evaluation Manual (ITSEM)
- Information Technology Security Evaluation Criteria (ITSEC)

➤ Directive 2003/4/EC Of The European Parliament

UK and Canadian Guidance

➤ FSA Combined Code on Corporate Governance

➤ Turnbull Guidance on Internal Control, UK FRC

➤ Smith Guidance on Audit Committees, UK FRC

➤ UK Data Protection Act of 1998

➤ IT Service Management Standard , BS 15000-1

➤ IT Service Management Standard - Code of Practice, BS 15000-2

➤ British Standards Institute PAS 56, Guide to Business Continuity Management

➤ Canada Keeping the Promise for a Strong Economy Act, Bill 198

➤ Canada Personal Information Protection Electronic Documents Act (PIPEDA)

➤ Canada Privacy Policy and Principles

Latin American Guidance

➤ Argentina Personal Data Protection Act

➤ Mexico Federal Personal Data Protection Law

Other European and African Guidance

➤ Austria Data Protection Act

➤ Austria Telecommunications Act

➤ Bosnia Law on Protection of Personal Data

➤ Czech Republic Personal Data Protection Act

➤ Denmark Act on Competitive Conditions and Consumer Interests

➤ Finland Personal Data Protection Act

➤ Finland act on the amendment of the Personal Data Act (986/2000)

➤ France Data Protection Act

➤ German Federal Data Protection Act

➤ IT Baseline Protection Manual Germany

➤ Greece Law on the Protection of Individuals with Regard to the Processing of Personal Data

- Hungary Protection of Personal Data and Disclosure of Data of Public Interest
- Iceland Protection of Privacy as regards the Processing of Personal Data
- Ireland Data Protection Act of 1988
- Ireland Data Protection Amendment 2003
- Italy Personal Data Protection Code
- Italy Protection of Individuals Other Subject with regard to the Processing of Personal Data
- Lithuania Law on Legal Protection of Personal Data
- Luxembourg Data Protection Law
- Netherlands Personal Data Protection Act
- Poland Protection of Personal Data Act
- Slovak Republic Protection of Personal Data in Information Systems
- Personal Data Protection Act of the Republic of Slovenia of 2004
- South Africa Promotion of Access to Information Act
- ORGANIC LAW 15/1999 of 13 December on the Protection of Personal Data
- Sweden Personal Data Act
- Switzerland Federal Act on Data Protection

Asia and Pacific Rim Guidance

- Australia Better Practice Guide - Business Continuity Management
- Australia Spam Act
- Australia Spam Act 2003: A practical guide for business
- Australia Privacy Act
- Australia Telecommunications Act
- Hong Kong Personal Data (Privacy) Ordinance
- India Information Technology Act (ITA-2000)
- Japan ECOM Guidelines Concerning the Protection of Personal Data in Electronic Commerce in the Private Sector (version 1.0)
- Japan Handbook Concerning Protection Of Personal Data
- Japan Personal Information Protection Act (Law No. 57 of 2003)

- Korea Act on Promotion of Information & Communication Network Utilization and Information Protection, etc
- Korea Act on the Protection of Personal Information Maintained by Public Agencies 1994
- Korea Act Relating to Use and Protection of Credit Information
- New Zealand Privacy Act 1993
- Taiwan Computer-Processed Personal Data Protection Law 1995
- India's Information Technology Act, 2000

The process of building your framework of IT controls, policies, standards, and procedures

Now that we've covered what it means to comply, let's take a brief moment to put the whole thing in perspective. You'll need to begin by collecting all of the authority documents that are going to influence your efforts. You'll then assimilate and harmonize the controls that they call for and create your overall control framework. From that framework you'll then develop your policies, the standards to enumerate various parameters set by the policies, and the procedures to carry out each policy's call to action.

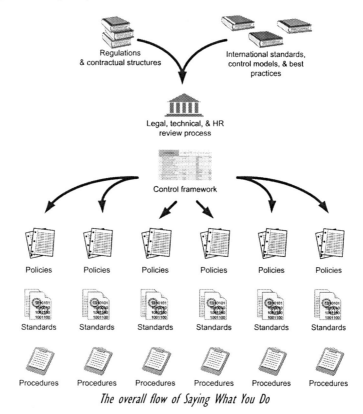

The overall flow of Saying What You Do

As these documents are being created and put into place, you'll then add training, measurement, and change management to the process to complete the picture.

How process maturity models relate to compliance

A maturity model is a structured collection of elements that describe characteristics of effective processes. They provide a place to start, a structure for prioritizing actions, and a way to define what improvement means for an organization.

Whether or not an organization fulfills a control's objective isn't a Boolean answer – there is no real way to determine simply if we are or aren't complying by providing a yes or no answer. It's a matter of levels of maturity. No auditor would say that your organization has complied with a required objective if your staff at one point in time executed a control (such as "tested for security of a system") but then never repeated the process nor measured its success.

There are six more or less agreed upon and defined levels of process maturity for an organization within the frameworks we've studied. Some frameworks such as CMMI ignore level zero while others such as CobiT include zero. In addition, CobiT adds seven qualitative attributes in order to better identify an organization's level of maturity. These seven attributes are awareness and communication; policies, standards, and procedures; tools and automation; skills and expertise; responsibility and accountability; goal setting; and measurement. For goal setting and measurement, we have combined the CobiT attributes with the CMMI general goals for each level. Here are the levels and their associated attributes and goals as we apply them within the Unified Compliance Framework.

0. **Nonexistent** (complete lack) There are no recognizable processes that fit this particular control, nor does the organization recognize that there is an issue to be addressed regarding this control.

1. **Initial** (chaotic, ad hoc, individual heroic efforts) There is evidence that the organization has recognized that the issue exists and needs to be addressed. Without standardization, there are ad hoc approaches to each issue that are either applied person-by-person or situation-by-situation. In other words, processes are unpredictable, poorly controlled, and reactive.

⚡ *Awareness and communication* – recognition of the need for the process is emerging, but there is sporadic, often confusing communication of the issues.

⚡ *Policies, standards and procedures* – There are ad hoc approaches to processes and practices and policies are as yet undefined.

⚡ *Tools and automation* – While tool usage might exist, there is no planned approach.

⚡ *Skills and expertise* – Required skills are not identified and no training plan exists.

⚡ *Responsibility and accountability* – Ownership is based upon personal pride without any definition of accountability and responsibility.

⚡ *Measurement* – At this point, metrics cannot provide a trusted baseline because the baseline either does not exist or is being developed.

⚡ *Goal setting* – The overall goal is to be able to perform the base practices without any real measurement by

　　o *Identifying and involving relevant stakeholders*

　　o *Perform the base practices*

2. **Repeatable** (project management, process discipline) The process is used repeatedly. Similar procedures are followed by different groups or people when undertaking the same task. However, there is no formalized standardization, documentation, communication, or training of procedures. All intellectual property of the process is locked inside each person's mind.

⚡ *Awareness and communication* – Management are aware of the need to act and are able to communicate their basic issues.

⚡ *Policies, standards, and procedures* – Informal documentation and understanding of policies, standards, and procedures exist. Intuitive common processes are emerging based upon individual expertise.

⚡ *Tools and automation* – Individuals within the organization have created tool based automation that may or may not have become common usage among their peers.

⚡ *Skills and expertise* – For critical areas, minimum skill requirements have been identified. On the job training is provided in response to specific needs only, without a formal training plan being developed.

⚡ *Responsibility and accountability* – Individuals are assuming responsibility and are being held informally accountable. However, there is confusion about responsibility when problems occur, leading to the finger pointing and blame.

    ✦ *Measurement* – At this point metrics are binary – either the process is being performed or not. Baselines are now being established and defined.

    ✦ *Goal setting* – The overall goal for this phase is to institutionalize a managed process through

- *Establishing an organizational policy*
- *Documenting processes and procedures*
- *Providing the necessary resources*
  - *Assigning responsibility*
  - *Training the staff*
  - *Managing configurations*
- *Monitoring and controlling the process*
  - *Objectively evaluating adherence*
  - *Reviewing the status with higher level management*

3. **Defined** (institutionalized) The process is defined/confirmed as a standard, documented course of action. Existing practices have been formalized into policies that have been documented and communicated. Standards have been created to regularize key parameters within policies. Procedures that carry out these policies have been harmonized, documented, communicated, and staff trained. However, there is no continuous monitoring and measurement that the processes are being followed according to procedure.

    ✦ *Awareness and communication* – Management is formal and structured in is communication of their understanding of the need to act.

    ✦ *Policies, standards, and procedures* – The policies, standards, procedures, and processes are defined and documented for all key activities. Usage of good practices has emerged.

    ✦ *Tools and automation* – A plan has been defined for the use and standardization of process automating tools. However, individual too usage may not be integrated with other related tools.

    ✦ *Skills and expertise* – Skill requirements are defined and documented for all areas. A formal training plan has been developed, but the actual training that takes place is based upon individual initiative.

✦ *Responsibility and accountability* – Process owners have been identified with process accountability and responsibility defined and documented. However, process owners are unlikely to have full authority to exercise their initiatives.

✦ *Measurement* – Tolerances of change for metrics are being established.

✦ *Goal setting* – The overall goal for this phase is to institutionalize a defined process through

    ○ *Ensuring full dissemination of defined procedures and processes*

    ○ *Collecting improvement information*

4. **Managed** (quantified) Process management and measurement takes place. Through the monitoring and measurement of compliance with organizational policies, standards, and procedures the organization is able to intervene and take actions where processes are not effective.

✦ *Awareness and communication* – Management is able to maturely use techniques and tools to communicate their understanding of their full requirements.

✦ *Policies, standards, and procedures* – All aspects of the process are documented and repeatable. Policies are approved by management and documented. Standards for developing policies and procedures are adopted and followed.

✦ *Tools and automation* – Tools are implemented according to a standardized plan and some have been integrated with other related tools. Tools are being used in main areas to automate management of processes, as well as monitor critical activities and controls.

✦ *Skills and expertise* – Skill requirements are routinely updated for all areas with proficiency being ensured for all critical areas. Mature training techniques are applied according to a training plan with knowledge sharing being encouraged. Internal domain experts are involved in training. Effectiveness of the training plan is routinely assessed.

✦ *Responsibility and accountability* – Process owners have full authority to exercise their initiatives with accountability and responsibility fully accepted by management. A reward culture has been put into place.

✦ *Measurement* – Metrics are now statistically valid with an increase in their breadth and interconnectedness.

- *Goal setting* – Effectiveness and efficiency are linked to business goals and the overall IT strategy. Root cause analysis is being standardized through institutionalizing a quantitatively managed process by
  - o *Establishing quantitative objectives for procedures and processes*
  - o *Stabilizing sub-process performance*

5. **Optimizing** (process improvement) Process management includes deliberate process optimization/improvement. Processes are being continuously refined to a level of best practice.

- *Awareness and communication* – Management is able to integrate tools and techniques when proactively communicating their forward-looking understanding of issues and requirements based upon trend analysis.

- *Policies, standards, and* procedures – Process documentation has evolved into automated workflows. Policies and procedures are standardized and integrated to enable end-to-end improvement.

- Tools and automation – Tools are fully integrated with other related tools to enable end-to-end support of processes, automatically detect control exceptions, and improve the process. Standardized toolsets are used across the enterprise.

- *Skills and expertise* – Based upon organizational goals, continuous improvement of skills is formally encouraged. Training and education support best practices and use leading-edge concepts and techniques. Knowledge sharing and knowledge-based systems have been formalized.

- *Responsibility and accountability* – Process owners are encouraged to make their own decisions and take action on their own accord. The acceptance of accountability and responsibility has been cascaded throughout the organization in a consistent manner.

- *Measurement – Metrics* are used adaptively, depending upon the current need.

- *Goal setting* – An integrated performance measurement system links IT performance to business goals. Exceptions are globally and consistently noted by management through root cause analysis. Continuous improvement has been inculcated into organizational culture through
  - o *Ensuring continuous process* improvement
  - o *Correcting root cause analysis of problems*

WHAT ARE THE FRAMEWORKS FOR COMPLIANCE?

A framework is nothing more than a structure, a set of underpinnings that you can use to ease the burden of creating a system for your policies and procedures. Is there a magical "one size fits all" compliance framework out there? Nope. That's why we created the Unified Compliance Framework – to stitch all the rest of the frameworks together into a fabric that can be tailored to each and every organization as the organization sees fit.

The major frameworks used for establishing IT controls

In its simplest terms, a framework is an arrangement of parts that provides a form, or structure, to the whole. A control framework is a structured way of categorizing controls to ensure the whole spectrum of control is covered adequately. The framework can be informal or formal. A formal approach will more readily satisfy the various regulatory or statutory requirements for organizations subject to them[1]. Some frameworks focus solely on process maturity analysis and others focus more on standardized policies and checklists for IT controls.

The major control frameworks

Some of the frameworks mentioned here are publicly available and others are for purchase. There is no single framework that is all encompassing and "complete" in every sense of the word. The major players in the IT framework arena are:

1. AICPA/CICA Trust Services, Principles, and Criteria

2. Carnegie Mellon University Software Engineering Institute (CMU/SEI) OCTAVE

3. CICA CoCo – Criteria of Control Framework

4. CICA IT Control Guidelines

5. CMMI – Capability Maturity Model Integration

6. CobiT – Control Objectives for Information and related Technology

7. COSO – Internal Control Integrated Framework

8. GAISP – Generally Accepted Information Security Principles

---

1   The Language of Compliance, as referenced by CobiT, Institute of Internal Auditors, ISO/IEC 27001:2005.

9. ISF Standard of Good Practice for Information Security

10. ISO 17799:2005

11. ISO 9000

12. ITIL – the IT Infrastructure Library

13. Malcolm Baldridge National Quality Program

14. Organization for Economic Cooperation and Development (OECD) Principles of Corporate Governance

15. OPMMM – Organizational Project Management Maturity Model

16. Six Sigma

17. Organization for Economic Cooperation and Development (OECD) Guidelines on the Protection of Privacy and Transborder Flows of Personal Data

This explanation of these various frameworks is derived from what we've read ourselves in the creation of the Unified Compliance Framework and also from what others have written specifically about IT frameworks[2].

AICPA/CICA Suitable Trust Services, Principles, and Criteria

The American Institute of Certified Public Accountants (AICPA) Assurance Services Executive Committee and the Canadian Institute of Chartered Accountants (CICA) Assurance Services Development Board developed the Trust Services Principles and Criteria. The principles are broad statements of objectives with specific criteria to be achieved in order to meet each principle. The principles and criteria are broken down into 1) policies, 2) communications, 3) procedures, and 4) monitoring.

---

[2] Gary Anthes (2004). Quality Model Mania, Computerworld; Bob Violino (2005). IT frameworks demystified, Network World; Judith Myerson (2006). Managing compliance: An overview of IT frameworks, IBM.

Strengths

The Trust Services Principles and Criteria can be used to deliver branded SysTrust and WebTrust engagements which are assurance services designed for a wide variety of IT-based systems.

Weaknesses

The principles don't address all operational issues. Although system availability, functionality, and usability are connected, the availability principle does not address system functionality (the specific functions a system performs) and system usability (the ability of users to apply system functions to specific tasks or problems).

Carnegie Mellon University Software Engineering Institute (CMU/SEI) OCTAVE

Operationally Critical Threat, Asset, and Vulnerability Evaluation (OCTAVE) is a massive self-directed, risk-based, strategic assessment and planning framework for organizations that want to understand their information security needs.

Strengths

OCTAVE focuses on organizational risk and strategic, practice-related issues, balancing operational risk, security practices, and technology.

Weaknesses

It is massive. Huge. Gigantic.

CICA CoCo – Criteria of Control Framework

The Canadian Institute of Chartered Accountants (CICA) produced the Criteria of Control Framework (CoCo) in 1992. This framework provides the groundwork for making organizational judgments about control effectiveness. In 1995, the same body produced the *Guidance on Control* in order to focus the organization toward a clear sense of shared purpose, collective commitment to achieve that purpose, the resources it needs to do the job, and the ability to learn from experience.

Strengths

CoCo's objectives are very similar to those of COSO, however CoCo adds the reliability of internal reporting and compliance with internal policies.

Weaknesses

CoCo's sweep is broad and its requirements for reporting are low.

CICA IT Control Guidelines

The *IT Control Guidelines* (currently in its 3rd edition), is published by the CICA, and is a reference source for evaluating IT controls. Information Technology Control Guidelines provides a practical means of identifying, understanding, assessing and implementing information technology controls in all types of enterprise.

Strengths

Very easy to follow, very easy to read.

Weaknesses

Not many people know about it and use it compared to the other frameworks.

CMMI – Capability Maturity Model Integration

A process improvement approach developed by the software engineering institute (SEI) of Carnegie Mellon University. CMMI provides organizations with the essential elements of effective processes. It can be used to guide process improvement across a project, a division, or an entire organization. CMMI helps integrate traditionally separate organizational functions, set process improvement goals and priorities, provide guidance for quality processes, and provide a point of reference for appraising current processes. CMMI measures process maturity which progresses through five levels: 1) initial, 2) managed, 3) defined, 4) predictable, and 5) optimizing.

Strengths

The strength of CMMI is its focus on continuous improvement from one level to the next.

Weaknesses

The problems with the CMMI model come into play almost immediately. It doesn't address IT operational issues such as security, configuration and change management, continuity, capacity planning, incident response, etc. It also doesn't provide specific guidance on *how* to meet the goals at each step of the improvement cycle.

CobiT

A framework, control objectives, and audit guidelines developed as a generally applicable and accepted standard for good practices for controls over information technology. Developed in 1996 by the Information Systems Audit and Control Association (ISACA) and IT Governance Institute as a standard for IT security and control practices, with the most recent version 4.0 released in November 2005, CobiT provides a reference framework for IT, security, auditing managers, and users. CobiT addresses four domains: planning and organization, acquisition and implementation, delivery and support, and monitoring and evaluation. In assessing an organization's stage of implementation of each of these domains, it relies upon a six level maturity model derived from CMM; 1) nonexistent, 2) initial, 3) repeatable, 4) defined, 5) managed, and 6) optimized.

Strengths

It has solid high-level checklists for information professionals and it can integrate well with CMMI, ITIL, ISO, COSO and other frameworks and standards.

Weaknesses

It is comparatively high level and therefore doesn't reach down into the organizational policy and procedure level of control definition. It focuses more on what an auditor should be looking at, and so generally ignores control details for software development, IT services, and has scant information for continuity.

COSO

The Committee of Sponsoring Organizations of the Treadway Commission (COSO) Internal Control – Integrated Framework (1992) is accepted by the U.S. Public Company Accounting Oversight Board (PCAOB) for the purpose of reporting compliance with financial reporting provisions. However, it is not specific to most areas of information technology.

Strengths

It is a suitable and recognized framework for Sarbanes-Oxley compliance because it covers all area of IT implementation (at a high level of abstraction) for financial reporting and auditing.

Weaknesses

COSO is written at a very high level of abstraction for most organizations and most IT shops will not be able to translate the controls to actionable IT activities.

GAISP – Generally Accepted Information Security Principles

Developed in 1991, the Generally Accepted Information Security Principles (GAISP) culls best practices from similar frameworks. It divides principles into pervasive principles, broad functional principles, and detailed principles.

Strengths

The GAISP is now in the hands of the Information Systems Security Association which has many members, and it should be developed more fully in the future with this backing.

Weaknesses

The principles are high level and the GAISP needs an overhaul in a bad way.

ISF Standard of Good Practice for Information Security

The standard prepared by the Information Security Forum (ISF) global working groups is developed from research based on the actual practices of, and incidents experienced by, major organizations. This publicly available document is split into five key areas: 1) security management, 2) critical business applications, 3) computer installations, 4) networks, and 5) systems development. Each area is further broken down by areas and sections.

Strengths

It is comprehensive and easy to read, providing great detail in its lists of objectives.

Weaknesses

Objectives are limited to individual sentences such as "re-route network traffic automatically should critical nodes or links fail" without providing information about *how* to achieve the objective.

ISO 17799:2005

ISO 17799:2005 is the code of practice for information security management from the International Organization for Standardization (ISO) and was updated in 2005. ISO 17799:2005 is a detailed security standard organized into major areas: business continuity planning, system access control, system development and maintenance, physical and environmental security, compliance, personnel security, security organization, computer and operations management, asset classification and control, and security policy.

Strengths

ITIL's security management guidelines are based on ISO 17799. It is currently the de facto standard in the IT world. It is also comprehensive, independent, and an evolving body of knowledge. It is a great fit with ITIL and CobiT.

Weaknesses

It is not prescriptive, but rather, broad in its reach. It is also unclear about who owns IT governance in the organization.

ISO 9000

ISO 9000 is a high level, customer-focused, auditable standard for quality management systems developed by the International Organization for Standardization (ISO). ISO 9000, 9001, and 9004 are all intended to ensure the control, repeatability, and solid documentation of organizational processes.

Strengths

Well established and mature, ISO 9000 can be applied across the entire organization, covering development, services, operations, and the documentation of policies and procedures.

Weaknesses

ISO 9000 focuses on repeatability and consistency, not on quality. Its focus is broad and sweeping and not really adaptable for spotlighting issues in the way that Six Sigma does. It is not an analysis tool like ITIL that can focus on root-cause analysis. It is not specific to information security or IT.

ITIL

Published by the UK Office of Government Commerce (OGC), the IT Infrastructure Library is a set of guides on the management and provision of operational IT services. ITIL is owned by the OGC and is developed in conjunction with the IT Service Management Forum (itSMF). ITIL consists of a series of publications giving guidance on the provision of quality IT services and on the processes and facilities needed to support them. The itSMF, a global organization consisting of several thousand corporate and government members, is responsible for advancing IT best practices through the use of ITIL. One of its strengths is tracking problems and facilitating root-cause analysis in IT service areas such as help desk, applications support, software distribution, and customer-contact system support. It overlaps CMM in certain areas such as configuration management. ITIL is divided into two main areas, Service Support and Service Delivery. Included in Service Support are incident management, problem management, configuration management, change management, and release management. Included in Service Delivery are service level management, financial management, capacity management, availability management, and continuity management.

Strengths

ITIL is well established, mature, detailed, and focused on IT production and operational quality issues. For many, it is the tool of choice for modeling IT operations and infrastructure planning. It is quickly increasingly being used within U.S. organizations.

Weaknesses

ITIL doesn't address quality management or software development. While ITIL defines repeatable, auditable and verifiable practices, it does not provide a maturity model. The information security concepts are high-level, lacking prescriptive detail.

Malcolm Baldridge National Quality Program

Sponsored by the National Institute of Standards and Technology, the Malcolm Baldridge National Quality Program is a high-level quality framework. It focuses on seven areas across the organizational spectrum, rating them from 0 - 100 in terms of approach, execution, and results; 1) company leadership, 2) strategic planning, 3) customer and market focus, 4) information and analysis, 5) human resources, 6) process management, and 7) business results.

Strengths

The scope of this program is broad and results focused. It can bring IT into the strategic arena and give the CIO a seat at the leader's table.

Weaknesses

It doesn't provide prescriptive focus to which processes, policies, and procedures should be applied to the organization and doesn't focus on continuity or tie into any regulatory guidelines.

OECD Principles of Corporate Governance

Published in 1999 and amended in 2004, the OECD Principles of Corporate Governance set out a framework for good practice that has been agreed to by all 30 OECD member countries and has become a generally accepted standard. Although the OECD principles do not provide specific guidance on IT controls, other OECD units provide further guidance and research on information security and privacy.

Strengths

The OECD Principles of Corporate Governance are actively used by governments, regulators, investors, corporations, and stakeholders in both OECD and non-OECD countries and have been adopted by the Financial Stability Forum as one of the Twelve Key Standards for Sound Financial Systems.

Weaknesses

The OECD Principles of Corporate Governance addresses the actions required to align IT with enterprise objectives and ensure IT investment decisions and performance measures demonstrate the value of IT towards meeting these principles – which means that the principles are not very prescriptive in terms of actual controls and procedures that should be met.

OPMMM

The Organizational Project Management Maturity Model, developed by the Project Management Institute (PMI), is a staged maturity model like CMMI but focused primarily on project management. It is used to analyze organizational strategies and execution of multiple projects across the organization by examining activities that align projects to strategic priorities as well as the organizational infrastructure that enables project management. OPMMM encompasses four types of projects; 1) strategic, 2) operational, 3) capital expansion, and 4) product and market-related projects. OPMMM's maturity model has five phases like CMMI; 1) initial process, 2) repeatable process, 3) defined process, 4) managed process, and 5) optimized process.

Strengths

It is outstanding for analyzing an organization's project management capability.

Weaknesses

Its sole focus is project management.

Six Sigma

Developed by Motorola, Six Sigma is a statistical process improvement methodology that uses the lens of the end user to focus on quality. It defines service levels and measures variations in those levels through moving projects through five phases; 1) define, 2) measure, 3) analyze, 4) improve, and 5) control.

Strengths

Six Sigma uses a data-driven approach when analyzing the root cause of problems, taking into account the cost of quality. It is best applied to repeatable activities. Six Sigma and CMMI could easily complement each other.

Weaknesses

It is difficult to apply Six Sigma to processes that aren't already well defined with measurable quantification methods. It is only focused on improving existing processes and not on defining the correct processes that should be in place. It is not a maturity model, and does not include a process maturity model.

OECD Guidelines on the Protection of Privacy and Transborder Flows of Personal Data

Published in 1980 the OECD Guidelines on the Protection of Privacy and Transborder Flows of Personal Data have continued to represent international consensus among the 30 member countries and 70 participating countries on general guidance concerning the collection and management of personal information. This publication has accompanying documents that serve as the foundation for privacy protection at the global level: the 1980 OECD Privacy Guidelines, the 1985 Declaration on Transborder Data Flows and the 1998 Ministerial Declaration on the Protection of Privacy on Global Networks.

Strengths

The OECD Guidelines on the Protection of Privacy and Transborder Flows of Personal Data establish the core principles around which most international data protection laws have been established. They are actively used by governments, regulators, investors, corporations, and stakeholders in both OECD and non-OECD countries.

Weaknesses

The OECD Guidelines on the Protection of Privacy and Transborder Flows of Personal Data represent broad prescriptions for the issues organizations must address to help ensure the privacy of personally identifiable information, but do not address the specific actions necessary to align IT with enterprise objectives and ensure IT investment decisions and performance measures incorporate these principles. So, these principles, while providing the goals of good privacy governance do not provide the details for how to implement the actual controls or procedures to meet those goals.

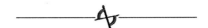

There is no single framework that covers all aspects of providing the information services and management team with the tools and direction they need to move from regulatory requirements to implementing policy, procedure, and process controls that meet those requirements. That's why Network Frontiers and Latham & Watkins have created the Unified Compliance Framework.

The Unified Compliance Framework (UCF)

There are two ways to read this section. The first is to read it from front to back so that you can learn more about the Unified Compliance Framework, how it came to be, and what our thinking is behind it. The second way to read this section is to skip to the very end where we discuss the components of the UCF under the heading of the same name, read what's in the components and how to use them, and then come back to read the rest when and if you care to learn more about how we came up with the material.

Compliance is defined as the act of following, or acting, in accordance with *someone else's* rules. And we know that those rules can be delivered in the form of regulations, contractual obligations, principles, standards, guidelines, best practices, policies, standards, and procedures.

But which rules should you choose from? Ahh, that's the question of the day, and where the Unified Compliance Framework comes in. Most organizations are under *multiple rulesets* from multiple authoritative bodies. Network Frontiers has to follow state and federal rules assigned to us by the U.S. government. We also have to follow rules set by the credit card companies when selling online. We have rules for how to plan our systems continuity framework and disaster recovery plans that are set for us by our insurance agency. And we have privacy rules for data that are set for us by our clients. Similarly, Latham & Watkins has to follow rules of legal practice set by various state and international bar associations, data privacy and client confidentiality rules, rules set by the SEC, and so forth and so on.

When we began researching this work about two years ago, there were *approximately* three or four major regulatory organizations within the U.S. that you had to worry about. Sarbanes-Oxley, Gramm-Leach-Bliley, HIPAA, and for folks who take credit cards, VISA joined the group. With the addition of all of the new security, operational management, and privacy regulations, there are now over 150 security auditing standards that have to be taken into consideration, as well as more than 100 privacy auditing regulations (not counting the too many to count standards) that have to be taken into consideration.

The problem with having to be compliant with so many rules is the amount of overlap found within each of the rulesets' frameworks. It wouldn't be a problem if the relationship between regulations, frameworks, and organizational policies and procedures were one-to-one. But that isn't the case. In today's overly regulated universe we have multiple regulations and multiple standards used to interpret them. Maintaining a one-to-one relationship between each regulatory requirement, each standard or guideline, and organizational controls would quickly prove to be rife with inefficiencies.

The problem is in actuality worse because, more often than not, multiple rules beget overlapping requirements. Which beget overlapping standards and guidelines, which makes creating organizational controls a nightmare.

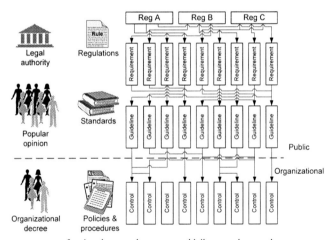

Overlapping requirements, guidelines, and controls

You can't handle the problem by creating a different compliance team for each regulation and standard. If your organization were to deploy multiple regulatory compliance teams, those teams would be dealing with multiple regulations, overlapping standards, and overlapping control objectives. They would also be competing for the same budget and resource and on the same timeframe for completion. It can't work that way.

Other than just the numbers (personnel costs, equipment costs, time lost due to stupid audit tricks), the leadership implications of having multiple audit teams would leave the internal auditors trying to take charge of the situation or risk total havoc. That doesn't work either.

So your organization, like ours and everyone else's, needs a consolidated framework that takes into account *all* of the compliance rules you have to follow, and consolidates them as much as possible. Hence, a **Unified** (consolidated, normalized) Compliance Framework as shown in the following diagram.

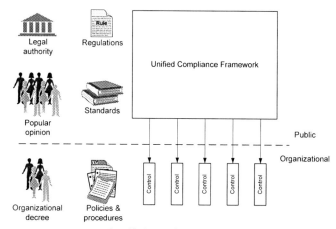

A unified compliance framework

Who developed the Unified Compliance Framework?

The Unified Compliance Framework (UCF) represents original research by Network Frontiers and Latham & Watkins together with input from our field editors worldwide. The IT Compliance Institute (ITCi), through their associated Unified Compliance Project (UCP), provides complementary research, publishing media, and financial support for each of the IT Impact Zones that has been identified within the UCF.

UCF Development methodology and core findings

Our methodology began by defining key terms, and we'll list them here. They differ slightly from those published by other groups such as the Information Systems Audit and Control Association's (ISACA) various mappings of their Control Objectives for IT (CobiT) against other standards, the various publications from the National Standards Research Board (NSRB), the Workgroup for Electronic Data Interchange (WEDI), the Centers for Medicare & Medicaid Services (CMS), and the Information Systems Security Association's (ISSA) Generally Accepted Information Security Principles (GAISP).

Generally accepted

The UCF's roots lie in many standardization projects already underway by a variety of organizations. As we've just stated above, ISACA calls its effort harmonization, WEDI calls it crosswalking, and ISSA calls it cross-referencing. This is where Network Frontiers and Latham & Watkins started its research for the UCF. The unification documents from CobiT, ISSA, GAISP, CMS, WEDI, and a few others all reference ISO 17799.

We have drawn the line in the sand of what to accept into the framework and what not to accept into the framework through the definition of material that is "generally accepted" in practice and publication. In other words, we've not formalized a definition other than through general usage and knowledge. This allows us to exclude individual authors' works (such as Network Frontiers' own "Backup Book" and "Compliance Book") as authoritative sources, and therefore leaves us with the following:

- Regulations from countries, states, and regulating bodies (such as the case with VISA, MasterCard and American Express for the credit card industry).

- Documentation from expert practitioner groups (CobiT, COSO, ISO, BCI, AICPA, NSA's IAM/IEM project, the Center for Internet Security, or the IT Process Institute) that follow a due process procedure and broadly distribute their information for public comment.

- Documentation from internationally recognized authorities, such as the United States' National Institute of Standards and Technology, the Australian DIRKS committee for records management, or the ITIL group.

In limiting our document sources to these authoritative bodies, we cast the broadest net and eliminate having to chase after individual authors who fade into and out of the picture.

During the process of assimilating these documents, we have come to characterize several key definitions.

Information

Information applies to any knowledge asset such as facts, data, opinions, numbers, graphics, narrative forms, communications, video, reports, etc. maintained in any medium.

Information processing

Information processing describes the organized collection, initial storage, processing, transmission, dissemination, and long term storage of information in accordance with defined procedures that could be automated or manual.

Information systems

Information systems describe the collected systems and technologies used in information processing.

Information technology assets

Information technology assets are the individual elements of an information system and are classified into the staff, documents and records, applications and databases, operating systems, storage components, firmware and hardware, network, power and cooling, and facilities.

The four properties of information assurance

Throughout our readings we found that there are four basic properties of information, information processes, and information systems.

- **Confidentiality** is the characteristic of information being disclosed only to authorized entities, processes, or persons; only at authorized times; and only in authorized manners.

- **Integrity** is the characteristic of information, information processes, and information systems being complete and accurate.

 ⚡ **Availability** is the characteristic of information, information systems, and information technology being accessible and usable on a timely basis.

 ⚡ **Accountability** is the characteristic of responsibly interacting at a level commensurate with the sensitivity and criticality of information, information processes, information systems, and information technology.

Furthermore, we found that in order for information assurance to be guaranteed, these four properties must co-support each other. Loss of one characteristic can lead to loss of the other characteristics.

Pervasive principles

Pervasive principles are aimed at information governance, information systems governance, and information technology governance. Pervasive principles address the four core properties or characteristics of information assurance. We have found that there are seven pervasive principles[3] strewn throughout the corpus of the foundational documents:

1. **Awareness** – Everyone who has a need to know should have access to the framework, policies, *and* procedures that your organization is using as a basis for confidentiality, integrity, availability, and accountability.

2. **Ethics** – Information should be used in an ethical manner. Security and privacy operations and management should be conducted in an ethical manner.

3. **Multidisciplinary** – Information governance from top to bottom should be addressed from the viewpoint of all interested parties and not just the interests of the information management department.

---

[3] A slightly different set of principles for information assurance can be found at (2005). Principles of Information Assurance, National Standards Registration Board. Carnegie Mellon University also released a set of "Principles of Survivability and Information Assurance" that overlaps most of the principles we show here.

4. **Proportional** – Information security and privacy controls should be proportionate to the risks the organization faces. These risks should include risks to availability, integrity, confidentiality, and even risks to accountability.

5. **Integrated** – The organization's information framework should be coordinated and integrated. This means that not only do the systems need to work together, but the policies and procedures need to be coordinated among all stakeholders, whether they are internal or third party stakeholders.

6. **Timely** – All stakeholders and those held responsible and accountable need to act in a timely (as well as integrated) manner to either prevent or respond to threats or actual breaches of availability, integrity, confidentiality, and accountability.

7. **Reassessment** – All threats and risks should be assessed periodically in order to ensure that the framework is as up to date and complete as possible.

Broad functional IT impact zones

While it might be nice to understand the pervasive principles, they don't really help us to determine the scope of each of the audits we are undergoing. For instance, CobiT and the ITIL library provide a massive span that covers a great deal of control objectives – everything from security through operational issues and even leadership objectives. Most of which can be ignored if the audit you are going through is an HR audit on hiring practices for your IT department. So for our first attempt to set boundaries for what should be "in play" during any particular audit, we searched for broad functional IT impact zones and came up with twelve of them. By using existing cross-references as a key, we were able to build our first table of impact zones and summaries of requirements for control objectives within each IT impact zone.

The next step was standardizing the terms to be used within the key IT control objectives. For example, we use the common moniker "confidential information" to refer to HIPAA's "electronic Protected Health Information (ePHI)", VISA's and GLB's "customer information," multiple privacy regulations' "client information," as well as Microsoft's "privileged information." Through this methodology we are able to determine when a yellow tomato and a red tomato should be simply referred to as tomatoes. And to ensure that we don't get confused ourselves, we maintain a full working glossary of all terms and their reference sources[4].

The final step in the process was to examine the commonalities of major impact zones and unify control objective definitions and labels. CobiT divides the world into sections labeled PO, DS, etc. ISO 17799 divides its material differently, as do all of the other standards. While this might seem confusing, what they are all doing is really talking about the same 12 information management impact zones:

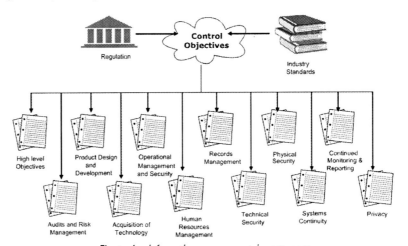

The twelve information management impact zones

1. **Leadership and High Level Objectives** ensures that your organization's top echelon leadership is coordinating strategy with your IS staff's tactics.

2. **Audits and Risk Management** ensures that you are actively conducting threat and risk audits to assess your vulnerabilities and create a triaged gap plan to fix the problems that could turn threats into reality.

3. **Product Design and Development** asks much tougher questions than most of us are used to asking when we are creating custom applications.

---

4   This can be found at http://www.glossarybook.com

4. **Acquisition of Technology** asks the same type of questions when the organization is putting customized systems into place through acquisition. The complex equation of scoping, assessing, sourcing, and implementing acquired technologies are covered in this impact zone.

5. **Operational Management** is, as it sounds, dealing with the day-to-day activities of most information management needs.

6. **Human Resources Management** focuses on the areas of identity management, background checks, separation of duties (and when it doesn't make sense), considerations for outsourcing and consulting services, supervision strategies, team development and communication, budgeting, recruiting, job definitions, performance discipline, and more are covered here.

7. **Records Management** isn't thought of much by most information management leaders, but needs to be brought to the forefront. Paper records have been professionally managed for years. But something happened when organizations moved to electronic records. We'd hazard a guess that most organization's electronic records management systems are no where near as professionally managed as they should be. And that includes e-mails, instant messages, and unstructured information as well as formal documents.

8. **Technical Security** has always been at the front burner of most IT staff members' minds and continues to play a dominant role in information governance. Access management, identity verification, data protection within and across networks, within databases and records archives, and down to individual computers and their software are all covered within this impact zone.

9. **Physical Security** is the touch-it-feel-it counterpart to technical security.

10. **Systems Continuity** has evolved out of the disaster recovery world. Organizations today have learned that it is much better to ensure an organization's continuity rather than waiting for a disaster to happen.

11. **Monitoring and Reporting** is one of the key regulatory compliance impact zones as it is fundamental to being able to collect data and report on the condition of the systems being monitored.

12. **Privacy** is becoming one of the most critical issues for information management – especially for organizations that are in multiple states or multiple countries.

By looking at the corpus of standards and regulations through the lens of unification and along the lines of the 12 impact zones we just discussed, we created a unification matrix *for each impact zone* that takes into account regulatory and standards bodies, doctrines, and language[5]. A small cross sampling of one of the matrices is shown in the following diagram[6], demonstrating how the control objective of "establishing the need to define high level objectives" is defined in the SOX regulations and standards several times, as well as the NASD/NYSE standards.

	SOX					Combined Code		17 CFR (SEC)			NASD/NYSE		
Bold = Required Normal = Addressable Underline = Link	Sarbanes-Oxley	PCAOB Rel. 2004-001 Audit section	SAS 94	AICPA/CICA Privacy Framework	AICPA Suitable Trust Services Criteria	Combined Code on Corporate Governance	Turnbull Guidance	240.15d-15 Controls and Procedures	240.16a-3 Website Reporting	Public Companies Checklist	NASD	NYSE	240.17a-1 Recordkeeping Rule
Establish need and define high level objectives	Implied		18-13	P10	¶11	A.1	¶16			X	Implied	Implied	Implied
Analyze organizational objectives, functions, actvities, and tasks	Implied						Implied			X			

A sampling of one of the twelve Impact Zone Matrices from the ITCi website

Matrices segregate authorities by type (Public Companies, Healthcare, General Standards, etc.). Within each type, authorities are listed by name (Sarbanes-

---

5   We've started with the most obvious regulations and standards and will continuously add to, and update the matrices as we process information, changes are made to standards and regulations, or new standards and regulations emerge.

6   The matrices can also be found online at http://www.unifiedcompliance.com

Oxley, NIST, Basel II, etc.), and, where appropriate, by specific publication (SAS 94, AICPA/CICA Privacy Framework, NIST 800-14, etc.). Relevant authorities are listed in a single row across the top of each matrix, and referenced against a hierarchical list of control objectives, set out in the leftmost column of the matrix. By looking at control objectives across the matrix, you can see which authorities provide recommendations for the objective. Moreover, we reference the specific section or paragraph that is relevant for each cited authority.

The next step was double checking our references. For each of the impact matrices within the 12 impact zones, we created a series of control-objective summaries. These helped us to check the context of each of the cross referenced items and rearrange accordingly. For each matrix, we re-read each of the references in each cell to ensure that the quoted selection truly fit the rest of the material present. If the material fit, the reference remained intact; if it did not, it was marked and referenced to a more appropriate position within the matrix.

Each impact matrix also contains original information: regulations and standards that were not a part of any other group's standardization project. The new material was read, indexed, and marked for matrix insertion. In most cases, we integrated the information into the existing list of control objectives. On rare occasion, it was added as a new row in the matrix.

Multiple editors reviewed and edited each proposed addition prior to insertion. When new terminology was encountered, it was added or assimilated into the existing glossary. The next step was integration of the new information into the impact zones' control-objective summaries.

Finally, once the master matrix, control-objective summaries, and glossary items were updated, the material was sent to our extensive list of "field-editors" (trusted friends and colleagues that work with these issues on a regular basis) for vetting and approval.

This process gives us as complete a list of control objectives as we can find[7]. What it doesn't provide is a way to decide which controls are material to your organization and which controls should be material to a framework that works for you. That's why you'll need to determine which controls we present to you are material for you, and the way your organization is set up.

We also should point out that, while this research is ongoing and updated as often as possible, you should never lose sight of the fact that this is a moving target. Governmental, regulatory, and industry groups around the world are actively working in this area to create new and different rules, regulations, and control objectives that promote their particular agendas and interests. At any given moment, this list is merely a snapshot of the compliance environment at that time it was posted. Particularly if your organization is involved in any type of heavily regulated industry or environment (e.g., healthcare, financial, government contracting, public securities) it is crucial that you actively monitor regulatory developments that most directly impact you and your business.

The Unified Compliance Project (UCP)

The Unified Compliance Project (UCP) published by the IT Compliance Institute (www.itcinstitute.com/ucp), has its foundation in the compliance matrices of the Unified Compliance Framework, and is a collection of tools and resources designed to help you standardize, simplify, and align your IT processes associated with corporate compliance. The key components of the UCP are:

↛ Introductory Webinars describing the Impact Zone's value, goals, and structure

↛ Custom IT Impact Matrix mapmaker: an interactive tool that shows you how regulations and IT standards you specify impact major IT functional areas

---

7   Many organizations have begun following the same model since our initial publication of the Unified Compliance Framework at the ITCi website. One nice example is Ross Carter, John Cobb, Lana Earhart and Anthony Noblett (2006). Microsoft Solutions for Security and Compliance: Regulatory Compliance Planning Guide.

⚡ The twelve IT Impact Matrices, instant cross-referencing of IT control objectives, regulatory requirements, and guidance offered by popular governance standards and frameworks

⚡ News and analysis, broken down by major IT impact area

⚡ Links to abstracts of specific regulations, including IT impact overviews

Below is a screenshot from the UCP's Leadership and High-Level Objectives Impact Zone. We've detailed where you can find information about the zone itself, the zone's Webinar, and how to launch the IT Impact Zone Matrix for the zone. We also show additional links for navigation to the other impact zones and a link to the "how to use the UCP" page.

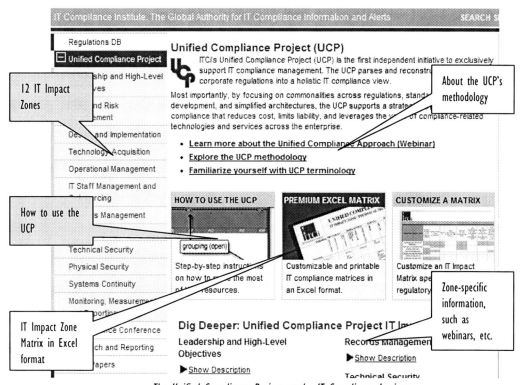

The Unified Compliance Project at the IT Compliance Institute

Each Impact Zone has its own HTML table, PDF table, and editable spreadsheet to make it easier for you to conduct your research and document your findings because helping compliance professionals to identify opportunities for alignment and unification of various compliance efforts is the primary goal of the UCP.

Available as HTML table or downloadable and editable files, the twelve IT Impact Matrices cross-reference Authority documents with IT controls related to each of the IT Impact Zones. The UCP's simple, tabular comparison of IT control objectives, regulatory requirements, and implementation guidance makes it easy to identify how regulations overlap with each other, as well as with established IT standards and governance frameworks. The IT Impact Matrices reveal how multiple regulatory requirements – such as Sarbanes-Oxley and HIPAA – overlap each other at the IT control level. This list of simplified control objectives can help you identify where your existing IT processes might already fulfill a part of your compliance obligations.

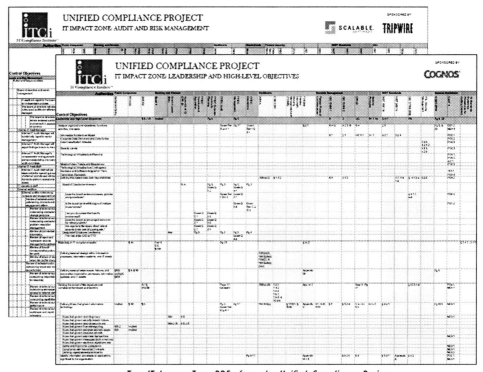

Two IT Impact Zone PDFs from the Unified Compliance Project

Reading and working with each of the tables is simple. The left-most column is the IT impact zone's control name. The top-most rows list each of the guideline documents categorized according to the industry or country category that they belong to. The individual cells within each of the matrices contain the section, page, or paragraph of the control's guideline reference that correlates the control name with the control guideline document. In the diagram that follows we show a sample of the Leadership and High Level Objectives IT Impact Matrix. The call-outs for our example show the control name (Board of Director Involvement), guideline document name (FFIEC Business Continuity Planning), and control guideline reference (Pg 3, and Exam Question 3.2).

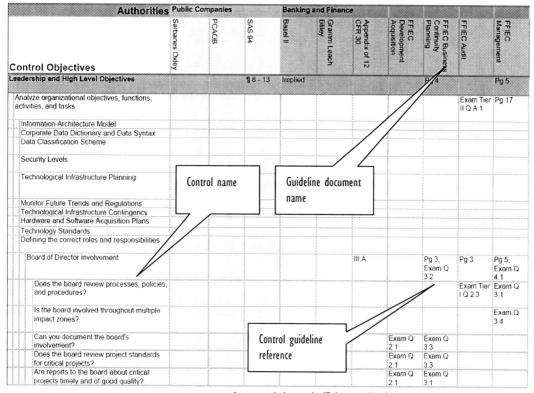

An expanded sample IT Impact Matrix

You can also tell from this example how the same control overlaps the Appendix of 12 CFR 30 (§ III.A), the FFIEC Audit Guide (Pg 3), and the FFIEC

Management Guide (Pg 5, and Exam Question 4.1). Without the Unified Compliance Framework and the IT Impact Matrices of the UCP you might think that each of those controls required different policies and procedures. With the UCP's IT Impact Matrices you can plainly see that they can all be covered by the same policy and procedures.

The Center for Internet Security

The **Center for Internet Security (CIS)** is a non-profit enterprise whose mission is to help organizations reduce the risk of business and e-commerce disruptions resulting from inadequate technical security controls.

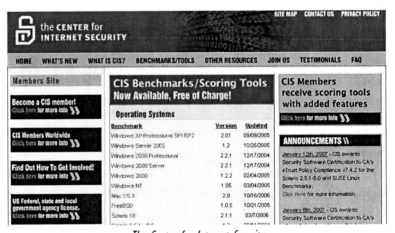

The Center for Internet Security

CIS members develop and encourage the widespread use of security configuration benchmarks through a global consensus process involving participants from the public and private sectors.

The practical CIS Benchmarks support available high level standards that deal with the "Why, Who, When, and Where" aspects of IT security by detailing *how* to secure an ever widening array of workstations, servers, network devices, and software applications in terms of technology specific controls.

CIS Scoring Tools analyze and report system compliance with the technical control settings in the Benchmarks. The CIS Benchmarks and Scoring Tools are available for download free of charge to the Internet community. In a joint partnership arrangement with the Center for Internet Security[8], we are working together to ensure that the CIS configuration Benchmarks and Scoring Tools dovetail into the UCF matrix methodology.

Components of the UCF

The Unified Compliance Framework's components are broken down into five distinct areas that provide the UCF with its form and structure:

1. The control matrices that we've been showing you in this section. These are available either through the IT Compliance Institute, or the Unified Compliance Framework's website[9]. Each of the matrices available on the Unified Compliance Framework site has a built-in process maturity reporting methodology for you to use when assessing your own capabilities.

2. In-depth control commentaries, also which are available on both the IT Compliance Institute's and Unified Compliance Framework's websites.

3. Along with standardized forms for policies, standards, and procedures, the Unified Compliance Framework's website has model policies, standards, and procedures for many of the controls mentioned in the UCF.

4. The Unified Compliance Framework site also has a well documented Change Management methodology that includes all of the forms you'll need, a model set of documentation, and an audit matrix of its own[10].

5. Finally, the UCF has its own working glossary that is kept up-to-date as changes in the authority documents happen[11].

---

8   http://www.cisecurity.org

9   http://www.itcinstitute.com/ucp or http://www.unifiedcompliance.com

10   http://www.unifiedcompliance.com/books_and_toolkits/change_management.html

11   http://www.glossarybook.com

Say what you Do

CREATING YOUR INFORMATION MANAGEMENT FRAMEWORK

This is the part where we help you build your *own* compliance framework. This section provides you a detailed, nuts-and-bolts method for moving through the process of creating a framework to fit *your* organization.

Creating a framework of controls defines how to create a framework for your controls by providing guidance on how to limit your selection of controls, a selection methodology based upon the Unified Compliance Framework's control list, and how to set the development goals for moving from control statements to fully trained policies and procedures.

From initial to repeatable assumes that some of the processes you'll need to put into place to support your controls are still being formed. And there's nothing wrong with that. Therefore, we provide you with the information you'll need to test, structure, and document your processes before turning them into policies and procedures.

From repeatable to defined assumes that some of your processes are refined enough to be molded into policies and procedures. Therefore, this chapter focuses on the writing and editing mechanics of turning repeatable processes into formal policies and procedures.

From defined to managed assumes that your policies and procedures are written. Therefore, the chapter focuses on best practices for communicating your policies and procedures to your staff and other interested parties.

From managed to optimizing assumes that your policies and procedures are in place and are communicated to the staff. Therefore, the chapter focuses on how to quantify each procedure's effectiveness and how to stabilize the sub-performance of any given procedure.

Finally, we'll wrap up this section with a self-audit guide for analyzing your compliance framework.

CREATING A FRAMEWORK OF CONTROLS, A HIGH LEVEL OVERVIEW

This chapter covers information you need to know about scoping your control framework, gives you a rough process map to follow, and helps you set your goals.

A guideline for scoping controls

Before you begin your decision process about which controls you want to add to your organizational framework, you should have a clear understanding and agree within your team about the rules of engagement for deciding which controls can be ignored, which controls should be based upon risk management, and which controls *must* be implemented.

In order to determine if a mandated compliance control is reasonable and appropriate for your organization, you need to be able to document what "reasonable and appropriate" means to you. This is called "scoping" the control, meaning that you are defining which controls you should leave in and which you should take out of your framework. You'll want to set the groundwork for scoping before you begin your project.

The best document we've read to date on scoping controls is from the United States' National Institute of Standards and Technology. NIST 800-53 is the Recommended Security Controls for Federal Information Systems, and it provides a baseline set of security controls that it mandates all United States federal organizations employ. With that aside, § 3.3 also has the best definition for the tailoring and scoping of controls that we've seen.

As NIST 800-53 points out, there are six considerations that can impact whether or how controls are applied. These considerations are related to 1) technology, 2) infrastructure, 3) public-access, 4) scalability, 5) common security control, and 6) risk. While NIST 800-53 speaks directly to security controls, we've modified the language to fit *all* controls.

Technology related considerations

Controls that refer to specific technologies (e.g., wireless, cryptography, public key infrastructure) are only applicable if those technologies are employed or are required to be employed within the information system.

Controls are only applicable to the components of the information system that typically provide or support the capability addressed by the control. In other words, if the system in question doesn't have the processing capability dealt with in the control, the control can be ignored. As an example, a single user system wouldn't need any networking controls because they don't apply to that system as everything is already self-contained.

For off the shelf products, if an automated mechanism isn't built in to support a control, it doesn't necessarily need to be developed. For example, if the control states that after three failed password attempts the user should be kicked out of the off-the-shelf application, but the application doesn't have that capability already built into it, you can ignore the control for that application because there's nothing you could develop to make the control work. However, you still need to document this fact including an explanation of why you made the decision to purchase the product despite the fact that it did not have this required control.

Infrastructure related considerations

Controls that refer to organizational facilities (e.g., physical controls such as locks and guards, environmental controls for temperature, humidity, lighting, fire, and power) are applicable only to those sections of the facilities that directly provide protection to, support of, or are related to the information system (including its information technology assets such as electronic mail or web servers, server farms, data centers, networking nodes, controlled interface equipment, and communications equipment) under consideration. That said, in a modern networked environment, that could include networked workstations sitting on people's desks, not just locked in a server room.

Public access considerations

Controls associated with public, customer, or third party access information systems should be carefully considered and applied with discretion since some controls (e.g., two-factor identification and authentication, personnel security controls) may not be applicable to users accessing information systems through public interfaces. For example, you might not want users to have to sign in when obtaining certain publicly available information while ensuring that they do so in order to change their account information.

Scalability related considerations

Controls must be scalable to match the system under consideration's size and complexity as well as its level of impact to the organization. Organizations should use discretion in scaling the controls to the particular environment of use to ensure a cost-effective, risk-based approach to control implementation. In other words, don't spend $10,000 protecting a $1,000 risk. Be careful not to equate the value of the risk with the value of the equipment and software, but rather the value of the risk is it's potential impact to the organization if breached – a $20 unsecured flash drive could easily contain enough valuable information to bring down an entire company. See risk related considerations for downgrading controls.

Risk related considerations

Controls that uniquely support the confidentiality, integrity, or availability objectives may be downgraded to the corresponding control in a lower baseline (or appropriately modified or eliminated if not defined in a lower baseline) if, and only if the downgrading action: 1) is consistent with the categorization for the corresponding objectives of confidentiality, integrity, or availability before moving to the high water mark; 2) is supported by an organizational assessment of risk; and 3) does not affect the relevant information within the information system.

Common control related considerations

Controls designated by the organization as common controls should be managed by an organizational entity other than the information system owner. As an example, access controls that support the entire network and all systems in it should *not* be managed by an information system manager responsible for a single system. Organizational decisions on which controls are viewed as common controls may greatly affect the responsibilities of individual information system owners with regard to the implementation of controls in a particular framework. This does not exempt the organization from implementing the control (i.e., letting it fall through the cracks). Every control in the framework must be addressed either by the organization *or* the information system owner.

Creating your own compliance framework

As we've seen, a framework is nothing more than a model or structure. It is the way the organization frames and formulates plans for explaining their goals and objectives. The goal for your organization is to translate the regulatory requirements *that your organization faces* into an effective toolset for defining controls and then creating policies and procedures to support those controls. Therefore, part of creating the organizational compliance framework will be to justify the selection of rules to follow and to define the complete set of rules that the organization will follow in order to be compliant.

This means that the framework itself needs to be documented. The framework must document the structure used to select the rules to follow as well as how those rules become the organizational compliance policies, standards, and procedures. What does a compliance framework look like? It can be as simple as the framework structure that we've listed in the following diagram.

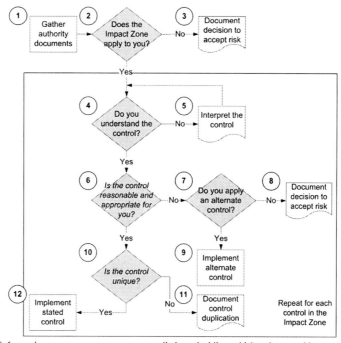

The information governance process as applied to deciding which rules to add to your rules

We'll go through each of these steps as a high level overview. First, you must understand a few things about our selection methodology.

What's the selection methodology and scoping process based on?

Our ideas behind creating an organizational framework are born out of the research we've conducted creating the UCF tables that compare regulations to standards and best practices controls. While the UCF is outstanding in providing a methodology to show the relationship between what the regulators say must be done and what the standards and best practices authors offer up as control sets, it doesn't provide a way to winnow, scope, or glean those controls down to the absolute minimum that make sense for any given organization.

So we turned to other scoping methods and documents such as the one from NIST SP800-53, Recommended Security Controls for Federal Information Systems, and a key document that we use, the Institute of Internal Auditor's GAIT scoping documents[12]. While the GAIT document focuses on risk assessment and scoping for Sarbanes-Oxley §404 assessment, its authors have stated that their intention is that it be used for other compliance controls as well.

Therefore, our methodology is loosely based upon the methodology used by GAIT v.3, but we've expanded the scope to be able to examine all regulations, standards, and best practices in a way that fits any organizational culture and structure.

What is the rule of measurement we are using to eliminate a control from being in scope?

Materiality is an auditing concept regarding the relative importance of an amount or item. The omission or misstatement of an item in a financial statement

---

12   We are currently working with a beta copy of version three of their document. Thanks to Gene Kim and Norman Marks for their continued support.

is "material" if, in the light of surrounding circumstances, it is probable that the judgment of a reasonable person relying on the information would have been changed or influenced by the inclusion or correction of the item (FASB Statement of Financial Concepts No. 2). An item is considered not to be material when it is not significant enough to influence decisions or have an effect on the financial statements. Therefore, materiality is an expression of the relative significance or importance of a particular matter taking into account the context in which such matter is considered.

With that said, only the financial regulations directly utilize this narrow a definition of materiality. What about privacy regulations; continuity regulations; or quasi-regulatory standards with a broad scope, such as the Payment Card Industry's PCI-DSS that covers privacy, security, and continuity? Because our scope is as broad as it is, reaching out to these and other types of authority documents, we must also widen the definition of materiality to fit our needs. The UCF definition of materiality is:

> *A material deficiency exists when the omission or commission of one or more actions results in an inability to maintain adequate levels of confidentiality, integrity, availability, and accountability for information, data, systems, or processes as defined by the authority document against which compliance is measured.*

This definition allows the *measurement* of materiality to be defined authority document by authority document. Therefore, if the authority document in question states that *no* confidential files may be accessed without proper authorization and permission, then a material breach has occurred when *one* record has been breached.

It's worth noting that materiality, both in the financial accounting context described at the beginning of this section and in our UCF definition of materiality, is very often a judgment call. In certain circumstances it is very easy to determine that a matter is material – an entire data center has been compromised. However, when the authority document speaks in terms such as "significant risk" or "substantial likelihood" or "reasonable expectations," someone is going to have to make that judgment call and the organization's framework documents, policies and procedures should document who will have the authority and responsibility to make that call.

Top down or bottom up?

The second principle for our methodology that we must discuss here is the approach to scoping. Approaches are either bottom up or top down. Bottom up controls start with system and information specific controls and then eventually focus on broader organization-wide and business process controls. A top down approach starts with the business process and then examines the information, data, systems, and IT processes that support it. We agree with the GAIT methodology that scoping should be a top down process that:

1. begins with the compliance assertions of confidentiality, integrity, availability, and accountability *for the organization as a whole and for each system in question*,

2. continues with the identification of the organizational processes and supporting information and systems affected by the compliance assertions,

3. identifies the objectives necessary to support the compliance assertions, and

4. provides the logic for determining which individual controls can be labeled out of scope because either the asset in question can be eliminated or the control can be eliminated.

Let's explain that in more detail, starting with the first point, using a generic version of one of the US state privacy breach notice laws as an example[13].

---

13   As of December 2006, there were 35 states with privacy breach notice laws and more forthcoming. The reason for not choosing a single state is that they are all slightly different. Therefore, for our example we'll use a fictional privacy breach law that addresses generically the *intended purpose* of these statutes.

The compliance assertions of the organization

In our example, the ultimate goal of privacy breach notice laws is to protect the personal information of people's records when they are in digital or digitally accessible format. Let's assume, for purposes of this illustration, that this applies to the organization as a whole, and therefore also applies to any system within the organization that holds information of this type.

The organizational process and supporting information and systems

For our example, privacy is the rule that must be complied with and adhered to. Therefore, any organizational process, such as manufacturing parts or supply chain management that do not involve personally identifiable information (PII), and thus have no privacy needs, automatically fall outside of the scope of compliance, as would all of the information and technology systems that support non-privacy related functions.

There are other organizational functions, such as the HR function, that *do* have privacy concerns. Therefore, the *function* falls within the compliance obligation, but not necessarily all of the information, data, and supporting systems fall within this compliance obligation.

All systems are combinations of IT assets that act together when handling specific input, processing, and output. The generic list of IT assets is listed below.

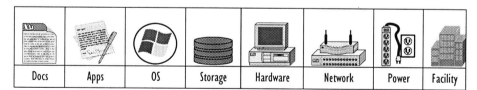

| Docs | Apps | OS | Storage | Hardware | Network | Power | Facility |

IT assets

To put this into context, let's walk through a simplified form of a typical HR system, annotating IT assets from documents through facilities.

⚡ A typical HR system might include three levels of documents - reports, the underlying database that lives on the server, and any user generated documents that might be leveraged during the process of creating those reports. This gives us three document types that are potentially "in scope."

A⛉ Both the reports and the underlying database tie directly to the HR application. The user files on the user's workstation tie to whatever local interface or local application that created and manipulates them. This gives us two applications that are potentially in scope.

A⛉ Because both the user's workstation and the server have operating systems and environments, those two operating systems are potentially in scope.

A⛉ Both the user's workstation and the server have storage locations where the reports could potentially be stored.

A⛉ Both the user's workstation and server have hardware environments (the compilation of cards, peripherals, etc. that hold everything together) that have to be analyzed.

A⛉ The network for the user runs throughout the cubicles in the facility. The network for the server is behind a firewall on a rack in the data center.

A⛉ The power (and air) for both the user and server have to be taken into question.

A⛉ And the office or cubicle where the user sits as well as the data center where the server is located also need to be taken into account.

Reports / Database	HR app	Server OS	DB storage	HR server	Rack network	Rack power	Data Center
User files	Local interface	User OS	User storage	Workstation	Cube cable	Cube power	Cube

HR system

That gives us seventeen individual assets in our simplified example. This doesn't take into account at least two key general support systems that provide access and boundary control for the HR system, namely the directory server and the appropriate firewalls (shown below). Because these general support systems provide boundary and compensating controls for the HR system, they are also in play.

	Directory Services	Server OS	Server storage	Directory server	Organizational network	Facility power	Facility
	Firewall	Device OS		Device	Organizational network	Facility power	Facility

General support system

What the top down approach allows us to do is eliminate assets that do not affect the warranted assurance of compliance for the system. In other words, we can ask the question "does the failure of one asset in the system affect the compliance assurance of the overall system." And if the answer is "no, the failure of these assets does not affect the warranted compliance assurance of the system," those assets can be eliminated from scope.

In our example, we are dealing with questions of **access regarding Personally Identifiable Information (PII)**. Beginning with the left-most assets, we can ask "if this asset were compromised (accessed without authorization in this case), would PII also be compromised?"

- The reports and underlying database would remain in scope, but the user files could be eliminated as they contained no private information.

- Because both the user and server applications have access to the private information, they both remain in scope.

- Even if either of the OSes were compromised, the only way to access the private information is through the applications, which have their own access controls. Therefore, the OSes are out of scope. Unless the OS is used to access the stored reports (see below).

- If the storage systems were accessed, the reports that aren't encrypted could be accessed, but the database which is encrypted can't. Therefore, the storage systems, insofar as they store un-encrypted reports, are in play.

- The configuration files for the computing devices (HR server, workstation, and directory server), insofar as they need to be tested for known access vulnerabilities, have to remain in play.

- Even if the reports can be printed by the end users and stored in their work area, because the breach notice laws apply only to electronic PII, work cube assets can be removed from scope.

- All other assets, because they have nothing to do with accessing private information, can be eliminated from scope.

- Because the access list of the directory system controls access to the system, it needs to be put into play.

- And because the configuration of the firewall controls access from outside the firewall, the access configuration file for the firewall has to be put into play.

By taking the top down view, we can eliminate whole assets or groups of assets from scope quickly, which will allow us to spend quality time applying relevant controls. Following is a complete list of all IT assets in scope and those that are out of scope (they have been stricken through).

Reports Database	HR app	~~Server OS~~	DB storage	HR server	~~Rack network~~	~~Rack power~~	~~Data Center~~
~~User files~~	Local interface	~~User OS~~	User storage	Workstation	~~Cube cable~~	~~Cube power~~	~~Cube~~
	Directory Services	~~Server OS~~	~~Server storage~~	Directory server	~~Organizational network~~	~~Facility power~~	~~Facility~~
	Firewall config	~~Device OS~~		~~Device~~	~~Organizational network~~	~~Facility power~~	~~Facility~~

IT assets in and out of scope

Identifying pertinent control objectives

The regulatory guidance for our example deals exclusively with the need to protect confidential access of information that has already been deemed to be "personally identifiable private" information. Now we have to determine the affected impact zones.

All frameworks, the UCF inclusive, are broken down into several impact zones. CobiT divides its framework into Plan & Organize, Acquire & Implement, Deliver and Support, and Monitor & Evaluate. The Unified Compliance Framework divides its impact zones into Leadership & High Level Objectives, Audit & Risk Management, etc. The point we are trying to make here is that if your regulatory guidelines required *only* that you focus on one subset of a framework, then there is nothing that says you *must* apply the controls from the other areas of the framework.

By taking the top down approach, you can eliminate whole categories of impact zones that don't apply to the guidelines you have to follow. In our example, we are left with the Technical Security impact zone, and its nine control objectives.

Simplified Control Objective	Ignore Control (X)	Control ID	Sarbanes-Oxley	Banking and Finance	NASD / NYSE	Health Care and Life Science	Energy	Credit Card	Federal Security	IRS	Records Management	NIST	ISO	ITIL	General Guidance	US Federal Privacy	US State Privacy	EU Guidance	UK Canadian Guidance	Latin American Guidance	Other European Guidance	Asia and Pacific Rim Guidance
Technical Security		508	X	X	X							X	X	X	X							
Establishing a security and access classification scheme		509	X	X	X				X			X	X	X			X	X				
Establishing overall access and security classification policies and procedures		512	X	X	X		X	X	X	X							X	X				
Network Access		529	X	X					X			X	X	X				X				
Operating system access		551	X	X									X			X		X				
Application and object access enforcement		558		X					X			X	X	X	X							
Remote access		559		X					X			X	X					X		X		
Encryption		570	X	X	X			X	X			X	X		X			X	X	X		
Malicious code		574	X	X	X			X	X			X	X	X	X							
Intrusion detection and response		579	X	X	X			X	X				X		X			X		X		

The core data of the Technical Security impact zone spreadsheet

Provide the logic for including or eliminating individual controls from scope

Once we know which control objectives are in scope for which assets, we need to provide the logic by which to examine the controls to determine their applicability to the situation. Before we can define the logic, we have to define what is behind the logic; namely the relationship between vulnerabilities, threats, controls, and risk.

Vulnerability means an opening for an attack or mistake. Vulnerabilities are weaknesses in information systems, system security practices and procedures, administrative controls, internal controls, implementation, or physical layouts that could be accidentally triggered or intentionally exploited (i.e., by a threat) to gain unauthorized access to information or disrupt processing and result in a violation of the system's compliance policy.

A *threat* is an expression of intention, an indication of something impending. It is any circumstance or event that has the potential to cause harm to a system (whether intentional or unintentional) in the form of destruction, disclosure, modification of data, interruption, and/or denial of service.

But just because our systems have vulnerabilities doesn't mean that they are open to threats becoming reality. And that is what *risk* is — the measurement of the likelihood of loss and its consequences. Risk is the combination of the likelihood and severity of impact that results from successfully exploiting a vulnerability by a threat. It is the chance of an act or event occurring that would have an adverse effect on the organization, its information systems, and/or its customers. Or to put it another way, risk is the possibility of suffering harm or loss.

*Likelihood of Occurrence * Severity of Impact = Risk*

Therefore, controls should only be put into place if they reduce the likelihood of occurrence, or the severity of, threats *and* cost less than the potential harm or loss. Notice that both the rate of occurrence and severity are required to properly measure risk. To put the likelihood of occurrence in perspective, we recently heard an in-house lawyer at a major consumer services company react to the concept of a remote "one-in-a-million chance" of something happening by pointing out that his company has 67 million customer interactions per day, which means that particular one-in-a-million risk would be realized *67 times each day*!

Because our example states that *any* breach equals 100% severity, we have to conclude that *any* potential for occurrence could affect the level of severity. Let's take a look at three of the controls listed under Technical Security and see which can automatically be eliminated because of low risk.

> Remove inactive user accounts at least every 90 days or sooner as defined by the organization
>> Immediately revoke accesses of terminated users
>> Control the addition, deletion, and modification of user IDs, credentials, or other identifier objects through automated methodologies

The common threat expressed in all three of these controls is that unauthorized users will gain access to currently idle accounts and use them as an entrance for breaching confidentiality.

The first risk-based question can be framed as "what is the likelihood of occurrence that someone will know of *any* inactive user account, using that account as an entrance method for breaching confidentiality?" Is the potential for occurrence there? Sure. Your access logs (if you have them) could show you the history of anyone using inactive accounts for however long you've kept the logs. If the logs show that no one in ten years has ever accessed an inactive account, then the chance of it happening with your current staff is probably very low. If, however, your logs show that people routinely access systems using inactive accounts, then the chance is very high. So your probability can be based on history.

 You'll notice that of the three controls we've listed, two are indented. That's because the indented controls are subordinate to those that aren't indented. If you can eliminate the first control we've listed from your scope, you can eliminate the subordinate controls below it.

The second risk-based question can be framed as "what is the likelihood of occurrence that someone will know of, and gain access to, a terminated user's account before the regularly scheduled sweep of idle/terminated accounts?" This now couples past history with timing. Can your team manually eliminate terminated user accounts more quickly than the knowledge of these open accounts finding their way to those staff who are likely to exploit the vulnerability? If they can, there is no threat and therefore the control can be eliminated.

The third control assumes that either manual coordination between HR and IT is nil, or that the timeframe it takes presents a threat, as it implies that automated, immediate controls are necessary. Therefore, you can frame your question as "what is the likelihood that miscommunication or non-communication between HR and IT results in someone gaining access to inactive accounts before the regular manual sweep by IT?"

By coupling likelihood with severity you can determine the level of risk that the control seeks to mitigate. However, **this doesn't mean you have to apply the control listed**. It simply means that you have to control that specific threat. You are free to apply alternate, or compensating controls of your own. You are also free to state (and document) that you are willing to accept the risk.

Compensating or alternate controls

Let's go back to that first control which asks you to remove inactive user accounts. A compensating control within the organization can easily be a policy and procedure for monitoring the policy that states "if you sign in to the system as anyone but yourself, you will be terminated – and we will know because we tie the logs of sign-ins to individual computers." If that control, the policy and its measurement procedure, stops your staff from utilizing inactive accounts it has indeed reduced the rate of occurrence from your authorized users for the threat to zero.

However, if the inactive user account was for an individual with systems or security administrative access to the network, thus perhaps also having knowledge of how to get into the network using a wide range of methods, then the compensating control to terminate employment may not be an effective control. In this case an alternate compensating control for such administrative user IDs can be to disable them immediately upon termination of the employee that would present an elevated threat to the network.

Accepting risk

For argument's sake, let's say that the logs show about once a month someone logs in using an inactive account in a way that you can't trace it back. So the threat is real and the risk is there. Let's say that the severity could lead to fines of about $5,000. Your normal control of manually sweeping the system every 90 days now creates a material deficiency because unauthorized access could happen at least 3 times before a sweep. However, software that ties your HR records to your directory records would cost you $15,000 in total cost of ownership. The remedy costs more than the sickness. At this point you might want to roll the dice and accept the risk.

Now that you understand the method behind our madness, let's walk through how to accomplish this in a step-by-step technique.

The step-by-step methodology

The preliminary step is to define the organizational business units, and who your main contacts are. You can do this in a spreadsheet, Word document, or even on a napkin as far as we are concerned[14]. The goal is to have a listing of all of the people you are going to need to talk to *who run processes* within your organization because they are the decision makers you are going to need to rely on.

1. The first step is to gather all of the authority documents applicable to your organization and that your organization *must* support, such as regulations, contracts, and service level agreements. That should be followed by gathering all of the standards, guidelines, and best practices that you *should* support, such as the ISO 27001 security standards or the OECD privacy principles. Once you have

---

14   In our example, we are starting with one of the framework spreadsheets available at our unifiedcompliance.com website.

your listing of authority documents, you can compare that list to the one found in the UCF at the unifiedcompliance.com website.

You'll notice in the spreadsheet below that there are only major headings and Xs. That's because in the spreadsheet you can collapse and expand each major guideline realm to see individual documents (such as all of the FFIEC examination booklets under banking and finance) and their citations. We've also designed the spreadsheets so that you can add your own authority documents on the right side to ensure that you are covering *all* of your compliance guidelines.

Simplified Control Objective	Ignore Control (X)	Control ID	Sarbanes-Oxley	Banking and Finance	NASD / NYSE	Health Care and Life Science	Energy	Credit Card	Federal Security	IRS	Records Management	NIST	ISO	ITIL	General Guidance	US Federal Privacy	US State Privacy	EU Guidance	UK Canadian Guidance	Latin American Guidance	Other European Guidance	Asia and Pacific Rim Guidance	Internal Guidance	Add your own guidance documents, beginning here...	...and filling rows to the right >>>
Technical Security		508	X	X								X	X	X	X										
Establishing a security and access classification scheme		509	X	X	X				X			X	X	X				X	X						
Establishing overall access and security classification policies and procedures		512	X	X	X		X	X	X	X	X							X	X						
Network Access		529	X	X					X			X	X	X					X						
Operating system access		551	X	X									X		X					X					
Application and object access enforcement		558		X					X			X	X	X	X										
Remote access		559		X					X			X	X		X				X						
Encryption		570	X	X	X		X	X				X	X		X				X	X					
Malicious code		574	X	X	X		X	X				X	X	X	X										
Intrusion detection and response		579	X	X	X		X	X				X			X				X						

Typical IT impact zone spreadsheet

2. The next step is to ask whether each of the impact zones within the UCF pertains to your organization and the controls you are currently focusing on. For instance, at Network Frontiers we don't develop our own software. Therefore, the Design and Implementation IT Impact Zone would not apply to us. However, we do have a systems continuity plan; therefore that IT Impact Zone does apply to us.

3. For each impact zone for which you answered "*no*" in the previous step, you'll want to document why you've chosen to ignore the controls that fall within that impact zone. The documentation could be as simple as "this organization does not develop hardware or software."

4. For each impact zone for which "*yes*" in step 2, you'll need to go through the entire list of controls and make sure that you understand each one. Embedded in

each of the control statements is a policy statement and Unified Compliance Framework ID number. Each of the IT Impact Zone spreadsheets within ITCi's UCP, and our guidebooks in the Unified Compliance Series, has a complete listing of all of the controls and their policy statements for that particular impact zone, such as the one that follows.

> **Create Systems Continuity Plan Strategies:** The continuity management process will include the key element of formulating and documenting a systems continuity strategy consistent with the agreed business objectives and priorities. [UCF ID 00735]

If you understand this control from reading the control statement, you can proceed to step 6. If not, you'll need to dig further, which is step 5.

5. If you didn't understand the control by reading it within the impact matrix, don't worry about it. Each of the controls is also tied to an in-depth analysis document that can run multiple pages, depending upon the amount of input from the authority documents. The format of each analysis document follows the structure of control title, policy statement, guidance from each of the regulatory group categories (banking and finance, international guidelines, NIST, etc.) explaining the citations found within each authority document, and then everything is wrapped up with over-arching commentary from our editorial team.

In-depth analysis of a UCF control

Each of these documents can be found online at the Unified Compliance Framework's website[15]. They are listed by the UCF Control ID and can be searched for quite easily.

6. Once you understand the control, the next step is to determine whether it is reasonable and appropriate for your organization and your circumstances. This is called *scoping the control*. Defining what is reasonable and appropriate for your organization is a much deeper topic than can be covered here. Let's just say that your organization should have its own documented definition of how to determine if a control is both reasonable and appropriate. If the control *is* reasonable and appropriate, you'll want to proceed to step 10. If it *isn't* reasonable and appropriate, you'll need to proceed to step 7.

7. If the control as stated by the authorities isn't reasonable or appropriate, do you at least apply an alternate control of your own? There are many explanations for why a control might not be reasonable or why it may not be appropriate to your organization – and one reason might be that the control itself is deficient and you

---

15   http://www.unifiedcompliance.com

have implemented a stronger control. Or it might be that the control is "over the top" and you don't need (or can't afford) that much protection in your organization. As a case in point, one of the controls within the overall framework is that of separation of duties. A field editor of ours simply couldn't afford to have additional people in their offices in order to comply with a complete separation of duties. It would have bankrupted the operations. Therefore, they came up with alternate means to the same end and documented their justification for it. If you do apply alternate controls, then proceed to step 9. If not, move on to the next step.

8. If the control is not reasonable and appropriate *and* you choose not to apply an alternate control, then you'll want to document your decision to accept the risk. As a case in point, within the Systems Continuity Impact Zone there's a control that states the need to take the organizational mainframe into consideration. If you have a mainframe that is kept in service purely for occasional access to legacy data from a system that is no longer in use, a mainframe outage may have little impact on business operations and therefore not be worth the time, money and effort to incorporate into a systems continuity plan.

    You are now done analyzing the control. Proceed to the next control by going back to step 4.

9. If, in step 7 you decided to apply an alternate control, then you'll need to implement and document that control as a policy and procedure or a set of procedures. You are now done analyzing the control. Proceed to the next control by going back to step 4.

10. You have reached this step having determined that the control is both reasonable and appropriate for your organization and your circumstances. You now have to decide if the control is *unique,* meaning that it isn't duplicating an existing control mandated by another authority. Within the realm of authority documents within the Unified Compliance Framework, we've already taken most of the guesswork out of it for you, as each of our impact matrices shows the overlap and duplication. What we don't (and can't) cover are the contracts, Memorandums of Understanding (MOU), and Service Level Agreements (SLA) that you have in place. Or even your own pre-existing policies, standards, and

procedures. If the control *does* overlap, proceed to the next step. If not, proceed to step 12.

11. By the time you've reached this step, you've determined that you might already be implementing this control (in whole or in part) by some other title. As they say, "a rose by any other name is still a rose," and if you already have a policy, standard, or set of procedures that fulfill the function of this control you can identify your policy, standards, and procedures that address this control. Note that you may have to tweak or supplement these existing policies in order to ensure complete coverage of these overlapping control objectives. This is where you'll need to extend our matrices to add your own authority documents in order to show the overlap (or lack thereof) in the controls that they state and that you already have in place. In addition to the self-paced audit guidelines we also have an Excel spreadsheet (if you don't already have it) for you to use as a baseline impact matrix of your own (see below under the section on "Documenting your compliance framework"). Or you can copy the contents of the IT Impact Zone PDFs and create your own matrix, adding your own set of authority documents and annotating the overlap of their controls with the base Unified Compliance Framework controls. Once you've done all that, proceed to the next control by going back to step 4.

12. If you've arrived at this final step, that means that the impact zone applies to you, you understand the control, the control is reasonable and appropriate, and it is not a duplicate of one you have already employed. That leaves you with one choice: implement and document the control as stated. In short:

⚡ If the rule applies to your organization (you might even want to state explicitly the types of systems it applies to),

⚡ and the rule is reasonable and appropriate,

⚡ and you don't already have this as a part of your repertoire,

⚡ then you'll need to create a control statement (also known as a policy statement) for it. You'll follow up your policy statement with an appropriate procedure or set of procedures.

Once you've done all that, proceed to the next control by going back to step 4.

Documenting your compliance framework

If you've been following our technique and using the spreadsheets that we make available to you, your documentation should be your filled out spreadsheet and any associated notes.

Simplified Control Objective	Ignore Control (X)	Control ID	Acceptance	Accept risk	Not applicable or too costly	Duplicate control	Implementing alternate or compensating control	Implement as stated	Awareness	Policies and Procedures	Tools and Automation	Skills and Expertise	Responsibility and Account	Measurement
Remove inactive user accounts at least every 90 days or sooner as defined by the organization		517	Yes					X	0	0	0	0	0	0
Immediately revoking accesses of terminated users		516	No	X					0	0	0	0	0	0
Controlling the addition, deletion, and modification of user IDS, credentials, or other identifier objects through automated methodologies		515	Yes				X		0	0	0	0	0	0

Sample documentation from the UCF spreadsheets

Your acceptance of each control or risk should take the form of one of five possible conditions:

1. You accept the risk of not applying the control. (Make sure to document why it is appropriate to take the risk.)

2. The control is not applicable to your situation, or it is too costly for your situation. (Make sure to document why this is the case.)

3. The control that is stated by the regulation/framework is a duplicate of a control that already exists (you shouldn't need to worry about this if you are using the UCF spreadsheets, as we've already taken the duplicate controls out for you by harmonizing all of the controls together). (Make sure you cross reference to the duplicate control(s).)

4. You are implementing an alternate, or compensating control. (Make sure to document the alternative or compensating control.)

5. You are implementing the control as stated.

    This brings you to the level of documenting the controls you are going to have in your framework. As the rest of the above spreadsheet shows, you'll then need to move on to creating your policies, procedures, and awareness campaigns.

Setting framework development goals

In order to get "there" from "here" you have to pass a few milestones. There's no such thing as moving directly from identifying that your organizational needs of adopting certain controls to optimizing those controls. Capability maturity doesn't work that way. From what we know about capability maturity, there is a six step process, with certain goals that must be achieved at each step as shown in the following diagram.

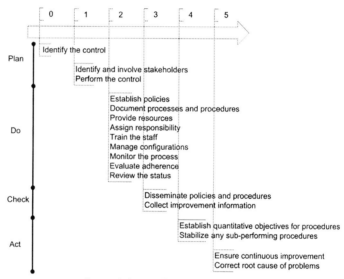

Key goals in compliance capability maturity

Given any list of regulatory controls, your organization is bound to be at different levels of maturity for each of the different goals. Some controls you might have already been implementing under another title for quite some time – and therefore you might need to focus on establishing quantitative objectives for measurement and collecting improvement information. Others, no doubt, you probably didn't even know about and therefore weren't focusing on at all – meaning that there are no organizationally defined and mandated policies and procedures to support them. Those controls can't even be documented until you've tested performing them a few times.

None of this should be new to any of us as business writers such as W. Edwards Deming and others have been talking about the "Plan-Do-Check-Act" (PDCA) cycle of quality development since the 1930s. And looking at the previous diagram, it should be plain to see that compliance capability maturity fits easily into this PDCA cycle. So how do we set our goals appropriately?

1. We start where the process of scoping left off – with the decision to either implement controls stated in the guidelines we must follow, or *not implement* the controls for one reason or another. This is the first step in the diagram that follows.

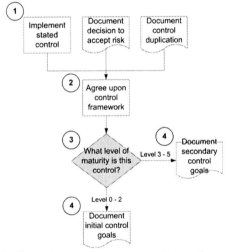

The process flow for setting compliance control goals according to their maturity

2. Once you've made your basic decisions whether to implement the goals or not, you'll want to gather your key stakeholders around the campfire and get a "harrumph" from them. The reason we list this as a discreet step is that most folks don't drag their **key** stakeholders through the process of deciding upon controls. They only involve them after the initial cut has been made.

3. After you've settled on your list of controls to implement, you'll need to ask yourself about your level of maturity for implementing those controls. As you examine each control, you'll need to decide the level of maturity your organization is at relative to the control. The best thing is to start with the highest level and ask if you meet the criteria for the level. If you do, then that's

the level you are at. If you don't, then go to the level below it and continue moving down the scale to level 0 if you've decided that you aren't even implementing the control in an ad-hoc manner. Here are the levels:

L5   We are continuously optimizing the policies and procedures for this control

L4   We measure the effectiveness of our policies and procedures for this control

L3   We have created policies and procedures for this control

L2   We repeatedly perform this control without formalized procedures

L1   We perform this control only in an ad-hoc way

L0   We do not perform this control, but should

This should give you a complete list of controls that you want to implement, arranged from maturity level 0 through 5.

4.   Your final step is to divide and conquer. If you have the staff, have one group focus only on those controls which are at level 0 through 2 – meaning that they are in the "plan" (0 and 1) or "do" (2) stage. These two stages are designed to prepare you to create policies and procedures to match the controls that you have to implement.

For those controls that fall into category 3 through 5, you can have a second group begin the analysis of monitoring your implementation of the controls (stage 3, or the "check" stage), or improving the controls (stages 4 and 5, or the "act" stage).

Your goals will be determined by the various levels of compliance capability maturity you've already developed. This isn't a "yes we are doing it" or "no we aren't" kind of thing. It's not Boolean. It's about levels of maturity.

Monty Python not withstanding, being alive or dead is a Boolean attribute. You are either alive, or dead. Your health is *not* a Boolean attribute. There are many levels of healthy and unhealthy. Same thing with your maturity level of implementing compliance controls – there are five levels of process maturity within six categories of control capabilities (awareness, policy and procedure development, tools and automation, skills, responsibility and accountability, and measurement). You need to document those levels before you can set your goals.

The second tab of the IT Impact Matrix spreadsheets has a built-in maturity index table. All you have to do is run through each control and list where you think you are at regarding your level of maturity for each category and the spreadsheet will list your maturity level for that category as a 1-5 for each.

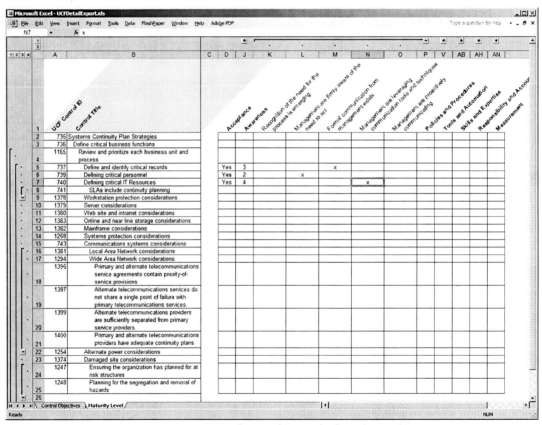

Documenting maturity for each control

FROM INITIAL (1) TO REPEATABLE (2)

At this stage your organization recognizes the need for this control and sporadic (at best) communication is taking place.

You might or might not have ad hoc approaches to the control, but there are no defined policies and procedures.

You don't have any planned automated tool usage for making the control tasks easier.

The skills needed to perform the control have not yet been identified.

No ownership has been codified in terms of accountability and responsibility.

And you can't measure how well you are performing this control because there is nothing defined to measure.

Therefore, your goals are twofold — get the right people involved and take an initial stab at performing the base practices that you think the control calls for.

Why you have to document your processes before you create your policies, standards, and procedures

Policies are high level plans that describe the *goals* of the procedures that your organization is going to follow. They describe management's decision regarding a direction and course of action. If you haven't attempted the process that will ultimately become the documented procedure (i.e., the method you will follow to support management's direction) – how will you know what goals and directions are realistic? How will you know which parameters of your policies and procedures should become harmonized into standards? While this might seem obvious, many clients of ours ask to skip the process testing and documentation stage and want to go directly to grabbing off the shelf policies, standards, and procedures, change a few words here and there, and then implement the documentation. It doesn't work like that because it *can't* work like that. What they end up with is a ripped-off version of ISO 17799 (or some other "base" authority document) that they *call* a policy – when in reality it is just a jumble of "you should" statements that don't make sense.

You can't just write policies and then write procedures to follow them – because you haven't **tested** what is possible in *your* organization with *your* staff, budget, and the other constraints of reality that you face.

True, policies do *not* contain implementation specifications. But how could you create an e-mail policy that states "all business correspondence sent and received in e-mail will be treated and protected as vital business documents" without knowing the implications of the policy? By implications, we mean

- the need to know the specific regulatory requirements for records retention;
- the difference in storing *all* e-mail, storing *some* e-mail, and storing *no* e-mail;
- the type of software necessary to parse and categorize the information;
- the hardware necessary to collect and store those records; and
- the significance in the cost (time and materials) to implement the policy.

In short, it's the homework that matters. If you are going to have policies that are enforceable and monitorable, then you are going to have to base those policies on real-world procedures that you've tested and validated as reasonable and effective. And if you are going to harmonize various parameters (such as password length and type, log sizes, etc.) into standards, you'll want to know what is going to work for *your* organization.

Remember at all times that policies, standards, and procedures are the harbingers of discipline and control. None of the three are natural to us. If you want to write policies (and later, standards and procedures) that *work* and are *accepted*, write them based upon reality.

Establishing the team

Who should be on the team? This isn't a game of dodge ball where you get to pick your buddies and exclude the geeks. Most authority documents will begin with, or at least describe somewhere, a defined set of roles and responsibilities for their controls. Even if they don't define roles and responsibilities for *each* control, most authority documents define an overarching set of roles and responsibilities. So you should start there for your listing of whom should be involved.

For example, one of the controls within the Unified Compliance Framework is to establish the roles and responsibilities for systems continuity (UCF Control ID 00733). This single control is cited by the following authority documents:

> AICPA Suitable Trust ¶ 24 (3.18), ¶ 20 (3.2); FFIEC Business Continuity Planning handbook Pg 3, Exam Q 1.3 and 5.6; FFIEC Management handbook Pg 10, Pg 30; NYSE Rules R 446 (g); NIST 800 26 Q 9.2.1; NIST 800 34 § 3.4.4; ISO 17799:2000 § 4.1.3, § 11.1.4.g ; NFPA 1600 Ch. 4.2, Ch. 4.3, Ch. 5.7.3.2; ISF Standards of Good Practice for Information Security CB 2.5.1, CI 6.1.5 - .7; BCI Good Practice Guidelines 2.1 Process; Australia Business Continuity Management Guide Pg 52-54, Pg 57, and Pg 68-72.

You should have *more than enough* guidelines for deciding who should be involved and at what point. What you want to think through at this point is whom on the team you are going to assign what responsibilities to and how you are going to document their involvement. The best way that we know to make roles and responsibilities clear is through the use of a RACI chart where you can clearly and easily document your involvement objectives.

RACI charts: a structure for coordination

What in the world is a RACI chart? In the simplest of definitions, RACI stands for defining the roles of those **Responsible, Accountable, Consulted,** and **Informed** during an operational process. As brought to our attention by John Schnizlein, a member of the RFC committee for policies and procedures, and a distinguished reviewer, if you identify a *person* who is responsible for a task, versus identifying someone filling a *role*, you could run into problems if that person is not available to perform the task. In the real world, you have to have a backup if a person is unavailable for any number of reasons. Therefore, it is much safer to assign roles for each position and then have a clear understanding of which sets of people can fill those roles. For the world of compliance, CobiT 4[16] uses RACI charts throughout their documentation – and maybe you should too.

The RACI model is used by process management professionals the world over and is very useful to describe *what* should be done *by whom* during an operational process. A typical RACI chart is a grid with the person (or title) listed along the top and the activities listed along the left side as shown in the diagram that follows. For each activity, a person can be assigned any combination of an R, A, C, or I. The goal is to ensure that *somebody* is assigned both an "R" and an "A" for each activity (the same person can be assigned an "RA," meaning that they are both responsible and accountable).

	Role 1	Role 2	Role 3	Role 4
Activity 1	R		A	
Activity 2	A	R		C
Activity 3	A		C	R
Activity 4			A	R

RACI table

The typical steps in a RACI process are to:

1. **Identify all of the processes and activities** involved, listing them down the left side of the table.

---

16   Control Objectives for Information and Related Technology: A framework, control objectives, and audit guidelines developed as a generally applicable and accepted standard for good practices for controls over information technology.

2. **Identify all of the roles or key staff** that would be needed to accomplish the mission or objective and then list them across the top of the table.

3. **Identify who** is responsible (R), then who is being held accountable (A), who must be consulted (C), and who must be informed (I).

4. **Resolve overlaps** between the people and activities, because there should only be one "R" and one "A" per activity. If there is overlap between people, one person will think the other is taking care of the issue and it will be dropped.

5. **Resolve gaps** for each of the activities, ensuring that someone is assigned an "R" and an "A" per activity. This is just as important a step as resolving overlaps because someone has to be held responsible and accountable for each activity.

RACI versus RASCI and advanced charting

There's one addition to the RACI chart that some use, and that's the addition of the **support** function, making it a RASCI chart. The supporting role is one of helping to facilitate the execution of the task.

The other addition to the charting method is that of adding time commitments to the chart. By adding time expectations per activity, per role, the person assigned to the role and activity will have a much clearer sense of understanding about their commitment levels for the project overall, and the chart can then be easily turned into a GANTT chart or timeline of activities.

	Role 1	Role 2	Role 3	Role 4
Activity 1	R/5		A/2	
Activity 2	A/2	R/3		C/5
Activity 3	RA/2		S/5	
Activity 4			A/1	R/3

Advanced RASCI chart showing hourly time commitments

While this is nice, it's a bit much for our purposes here. We'll stick to the simpler RACI chart for now and let you make up your mind if you want to take the documentation to the next level.

RACI provides structure for policies and procedures

What this all boils down to is a methodology for the coordination of personnel when documenting policies and procedures. By coordinating the knowledge, talents, and political decision making capabilities of staff, team effort can be leveraged and divided into different key areas of policy and procedure activities.

Because policies and procedures define organizational roles, RACI charts become quite effective when documenting and communicating the assignment of those roles.

Establishing a RACI chart for creating repeatable processes

For our purposes here, we'll leave out specific titles of who should be involved and simply list the RACI chart for your first goal set showing generic titles. You should be more than capable of filling in the team members that your organization needs to have on board in order to ensure that key stakeholders aren't left out of the decision making loop.

Creating repeatable processes	CXO Level	Director Level	Manager Level	Doer Level	LOB Tech Specialist
Determining the ground rules for working together	RA	C	C	I	I
Establishing an initial process test timeline and timelines to test alternate control processes	RA	C	C	I	I
Agree on milestones and meeting dates	C	RA	C	C	I
Determine communications and documentation practices for the team	I	I	RA	C	I
Determine what the control is supposed to accomplish	A	R	C	I	I
Document if there are any controls that support this particular control and any controls that this control supports	A	R	C	I	I
Assess the control process attributes in terms of decisions, documentation, assets in use, etc.	I	I	A	R	C
Identify problems and potential mishaps with the tested control process (and what the mishap reaction steps should be)	I	I	A	R	C
Begin to test and describe control process flows (visually/textually)	I	I	A	R	C

Creating repeatable processes	CXO Level	Director Level	Manager Level	Doer Level	LOB Tech Specialist
Determine which personnel, applications, and supporting systems are involved in the control	I	A	R	C	I
Determine the roles that are required to carry out the control	I	A	R	C	I
Determine any prerequisite knowledge needed to carry out the control	I	A	R	C	I
Determine any prerequisite tools needed to carry out the control	I	A	R	C	I
Assess control process expectations for success	I	I	A	R	C
Create the success reports and edit the control process description	I	I	A	R	C
Have someone else run through the process	I	I	A	C	R
Identify short term improvements with the control process	I	I	A	R	C

RACI chart for creating repeatable processes

The policy and procedure lifecycle team

In addition to the people who are working on documenting *your* processes, you also need to establish the policy and procedure lifecycle team. The team consists of four basic roles. For our purposes here, we are going to lump processes, policies, standards, and procedures into the same generic term – *document*.

Document owner

The document owner is the creator of the document in question. The document owner has the responsibility of creating draft documents and should oversee the document's lifecycle in the publishing process from draft through its pending approval. The document owner should also be responsible for status reports while the document is under his or her control.

Document reviewer

Document reviewers read and edit documents – they do not have authority to approve them. When a document owner assigns a person to the role of reviewer, that person must do one of the following during the review stage:

- Defer the document to another reviewer

- Accept the document as it stands

- Agree in general with the document and apply non-critical changes

- Decline the document and add comments regarding the issues that must be *addressed* in the document

Document approver

This is the person ultimately responsible as the approving authority for the document. The document approver has the same action choices during the *approval* stage that the reviewer had in the review stage.

Document control administrator

The person in this role (which can also be the document reviewer, owner, or approver) ensures that the document:

- Is catalogued and indexed correctly

- Moves through all stages (draft, review, approval, pending, live, archived, deleted)

- Is distributed correctly (removing older copies and replacing with new ones, etc.)

- Manages the document library if that library is technical in nature (database, website, etc.)

Together, these four roles need to be defined and implemented in order to ensure that documents move through the proper lifecycle stages and are ultimately destroyed when appropriate. Remember that these are *roles,* and as such, in smaller organizations a single person can fulfill multiple roles.

Working together

The first thing that needs to be assured is that your group *wants* to work together. That means that they must be prepared to share their knowledge with the rest of the members of the team instead of hording that knowledge. It also means that they must be willing to *make decisions* along the way.

Because working together also means working with senior level staff as well as line of business staff, this also means that those not familiar with information technology terminology, processes, and tools be brought up to speed by the rest of the team. This doesn't mean that business managers *will* need to understand how to use the tools or which buttons to push – what it means is that they need to understand the implications *of* the tools and button pushing.

It also means that your team is going to need to expand their horizons regarding the usage of documentation techniques. How you create the initial models of what you are describing can be handled multiple ways. You'll be documenting everything from business rules, through data flow diagrams, security threat models, systems use cases, activity diagrams, and probably more. Because there are so many ways of describing your processes, we've added a special section that covers modeling and documentation techniques courtesy of Scott Ambler, author of multiple books about the Unified Modeling Language (UML).

Avoiding the meeting to get ready for the meeting syndrome

We hate meetings. Not just us authors, but most folks hate meetings. Our editor, Lynn Heiberger, once said that "meetings are the single reason that mankind is continually restricted from reaching its potential." Hear hear. The best way to make meetings simple, short, and productive is to *plan* for what will happen in the meeting (as opposed to having a rough idea and winging it like most meetings). Here are the things you *have* to consider when planning your control analysis meetings:

1. Which control is going to be discussed, and does this control have an equivalent in current organizational policies and procedures? If so, bring the written policies and procedures.

2. How much time should be allotted? Based upon the allotment needed to conduct the meeting, are there any staff that will be constrained by this timeframe?

3. What level of detail are you going to expect from this meeting? Are you there to discuss the basic topics of the control, or are you there to drill down into the process to ensure that each step is correct?

4. Based upon what you've decided in the previous step, what types of questions do you think will be asked? Will you have the correct documents and supporting material to answer their questions? Have you invited the right people to answer the questions? And are you allotting enough time for the meeting and the questions that are going to arise (if not, change point 2 and re-think).

5. What level of controversy is this topic going to create in the meeting? Will this be presented as oppositional *feelings* or oppositional *facts?* What are the objections, complaints, and complaint tactics going to be like?

6. For every oppositional complaint raised in the preceding point, how do you plan to work with the complainer to resolve the issue?

7. What is the "to do" item you *must* have coming out of the meeting? With all that's been thought through now, do you think you can finish the meeting with an action item and the "to do" you want (or at least one that you can live with)?

Bringing stakeholders into the loop to help document a process you've never performed

This topic is courtesy of Scott Ambler, author of multiple books regarding the Universal Modeling Language, and Dr. L. Murphy Smith of Texas A&M University, both of whom have let me "borrow" material from their websites[17].

There will come a time (quite quickly for some of us) when we need to document or audit a process that we 1) don't quite understand, or 2) have never performed before. How do you put into writing something you don't comprehend? How do you communicate the process so that others can identify the salient points of what needs to be accomplished?

There are five points you need to know to achieve your task:

1. find someone who knows the process (we'll call this person the expert),

2. bring note taking tools with you,

3. *listen* to them,

4. determine the best method of modeling the process, and

5. read the process back to the expert to catch errors in communication.

We'll move through all five phases, touching on some points lightly and touching heavily on the idea modeling portion heavily.

Finding your expert

The best expert in the world is someone who is a *stakeholder*. For our purposes, stakeholders are those people in the organization who may affect, be affected by, or perceive themselves to be affected by, the processes, procedures, and controls

---

17   You can find Scott's UML material at http://www.agilemodeling.com/ and Dr. Smith's material at http://acct.tamu.edu/smith/system_tools/systools.htm

in question. Stakeholders may be interested in the activities, targets, resources, or deliverables of these processes. Stakeholders may include customers, partners, employees, shareholders, owners, etc. The term stakeholder may also include other interested parties, such as upper management and even key suppliers or clients.

By reaching out to your stakeholders and asking them to help you document their key processes, you are including them "in the loop," which will go a long way in helping to inculcate these processes into formal policies and procedures.

Your note taking tools

The first thing you want to do is ensure that your note taking tools don't interrupt the flow of communication between yourself and your expert. When people describe processes, they usually do so in a "stream-of-consciousness" methodology. Interrupting that stream of consciousness interrupts the expert's ability to reconstruct the process accurately. So while pen and paper or typing on your computer might seem like a good idea, it isn't. Because it is interruptive.

The number one tool you can have at hand when working with an expert to learn a new process or one you are having a hard time comprehending is a digital tape recorder. Seriously. You can use your pen and paper or computer to record this or that key thought and then let the conversation flow because you know that you are recording it and can go back over it any time. I normally save all of these types of conversations into a "research" or "interview" directory associated with the process or procedure that I'm documenting.

If the person you are interviewing is showing you something quite complex, such as moving through the paces of using software, then you'll want a good screen capture application such as the one we use called Snagit. Snagit lets us capture everything from active menus through scrolling windows. And if the process includes something that isn't on screen, then your best bet is a *simple* digital camera. Not one of those massive, intrusive cameras, but a small, easy-to-use model like the Kodak EasyShare or others. All you need is to capture the essence of what is being shown to you, you aren't creating great art.

And finally, because many people like me can't even *talk* without waving arms and drawing something on the wall or in mid-air, you'll also want to have some form of digital whiteboard. We use the Mimio digital whiteboard because it is portable and can be connected to anything, with the information being printed directly or saved as a series of vector graphics that we can import to the computer. We've also worked extensively with the Panasonic digital Panaboard that also connects to the computer and printer and saves files digitally.

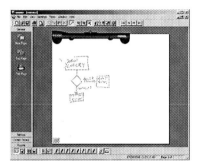 

Mimio portable digital whiteboard (left) and Panasonic Panaboard (right)

Whatever tools you use, the goal is to ensure that they are *unobtrusive* and aren't in the way of allowing your stakeholder expert to share their information.

Actively listening

Active listening is the next key point. Active listening focuses on *who* you are listening to and has absolutely nothing to do with your being interruptive. Active listening means being able to repeat back to the speaker what they are saying (which comes next under inclusive modeling). It doesn't mean that you have to *agree* with what they are saying, and it doesn't mean that you have to repetitively say "what I hear you saying is…" which drives most people crazy.

Active listening means picking up on the *key points* in what the other person is saying. Did the person inflect more when a point was made? Then that point is probably more important than others. Do you understand the point your expert is making? Then be able to summarize and communicate the point. Which brings us to inclusive modeling.

Inclusive modeling

Most stakeholders don't understand the complex diagrams preferred by many traditional modelers, nor do they want to take the time to learn them. The secret is to adopt inclusive models[18] which use simple tools and simple techniques that stakeholders can easily learn and therefore use to help capture and analyze requirements for your policies and procedures. We'll go through a number of these modeling techniques here.

The narrative outline

The narrative outline is probably the most ubiquitous form of process and procedure communication. A simple narrative outline is shown below where we've separated short sections of information and identified them with numbers and letters (or an alphanumeric combination).

1. analyze website hardware
   a. document configuration
2. analyze software
   a. document configuration
3. share configuration documentation with security team

Narratives are ever-present because they are *very* easy to follow and provide quick identification of logical groupings and the relative importance of the information being presented.

The narrative playscript or RACI chart

A slightly different concept of a narrative is called a playscript. And if you are wondering, yes, a play as in "theater." No, you don't have to dress up in tights and quote Shakespeare (if you do, send me the video, I need a laugh). Like a narrative it uses the indented, alphanumerically identifiable outline of short

---

18   http://www.agilemodeling.com/essays/inclusiveModels.htm

action items that need to be performed. And it adds an extra touch by listing the name or title of the person who is supposed to take the action.

			Analyst	Security team
1.		analyze website hardware	X	
	a.	document configuration	X	
2.		analyze software	X	
	b.	document configuration	X	
3.		share configuration documentation with security team	X	X

While a true RACI chart displays who is **Responsible, Accountable, Consulted** with, and **Informed,** the playscript will usually focus on only those responsible, consulted with, and informed.

The biggest benefit of a playscript narrative over a simple narrative is that the reader immediately knows who is supposed to be performing the activities being described. There is no question and the "who should be doing this" part of the narrative can't be accidentally missed.

Frequently Asked Questions (FAQ)

The FAQ is a question and answer format that is popular with helpdesks and support sites. It is primarily used to simulate a conversation where one person asks questions and the second responds with a great answer. These can work well if the questions posted are commonly asked (hence the "frequently" part of frequently asked questions). The best way to use FAQs is to create a question and answer bank to fend off staff who are going to be opposed to new policies and procedures. By thinking through what the skeptics might say, and then posting FAQs that correspond to new policies and procedures, you can address concerns *before* they actually arise. A sample short FAQ follows.

Q: Why do we have to come to work every day?

A: Because that's what we pay you for. We don't pay you to stay home and play Doom.

Q: Why is organizational management always cranky by noon?

A: Because we continually have to call and tell you to stop playing Doom and come in to work.

Index cards

Index cards are great, simple, and cheap by the dozens. One great use for index cards is when documenting the various sub items that your controls are calling for. When we document controls, we use index cards to write the name and ID of the control along the top of the card. Below that, we list each of the major aspects, steps, or processes that the control calls for.

> 01380 Website and intranet considerations
> –
> document the website's hardware and software configuration
>
> test the website's programming and coding to ensure that IP addresses map to domain names
>
> coordinate the continuity solutions with the appropriate security policies and security controls assigned to the website
>
> coordinate the continuity plan for the site with the incident response team and their procedures
>
> review all general support systems' and interconnected systems' documentation to ensure coordination

Simple index card method

By using something as simple as an index card, you can quickly and easily document your controls and then pass the cards around to the members of the team for their input as well. You can later transfer these cards over to some other type of documentation – but initially using the cards will ensure that your team doesn't get caught up in the formalities of writing instead of the process of analysis and understanding.

Troubleshooting tables

Troubleshooting tables are best used for documenting troubleshooting processes as they are neither a narrative nor an FAQ, and users are guaranteed to *not* read the whole document. Why won't they read it? Because if troubleshooting tables are written properly, the most likely causes will be listed first and the least likely causes will be written last. Therefore, as the reader progresses through the table, once they find and fix the problem they will cease to read the rest of the table.

Symptom	Indicator	Potential cause	Solution
Tape Library is not visible to Server	No green light on Fibre Adapter	Fibre Cable	Swap cables (LC/LC)
	Fibre Adapter isn't in device list	Fibre Card	Swap Fibre cards and setups Reboot tape library
	Green light is on fibre adapter. Fibre adapter shows up in device list.	Configuration Item Attribute not set properly	1. Refer to CMDB and check each CI to ensure that the current state matches the recommended state 2. For any CI that has changed, 2a. note the change in the discrepancy report 2b. make correction 2c. reboot affected device

Sample troubleshooting table

Troubleshooting tables are fine for easy solutions to common problems. However, with complex problems that require certain decisions to lead down one path and others to lead down another path, you have to move to flowcharts.

Flowcharts

Flowcharts are a modeling technique introduced in the 1940/50s. There are three basic symbols on this flowchart: squares which represent activities or tasks, diamonds which represent decision points, and arrows which represent flow of control. Flowcharts support other types of symbols, such as off page connectors (for when your diagrams get too big) and input/output symbols to represent printed reports and data storage options.

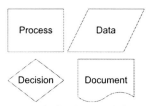

Basic flowchart symbols

In order to create a flowchart, you simply need to work through the logic of the process one step at a time. The best place to start is at the top left of the diagram and then map down and to the right.

Each time a decision is made, the diagram calls for a diamond shape. Each arrowhead leaving a decision should be labeled with the appropriate condition.

The best way to stay agile when working with flow charts is to keep things simple. Sketch them on whiteboards with your stakeholders to discuss important business logic, take a digital photo if you want to save it, or simply erase it once you're through. The value often isn't in the models that you create, but instead, it is in the act of modeling because it helps you to think things through.

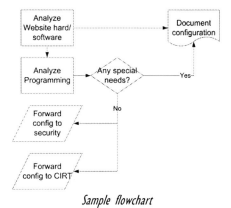

Sample flowchart

Data flow diagrams

Data flow diagrams are used to document the logical flow of data through the process. On one hand, they are very much like flow charts. On the other, their symbols and process flowers differ greatly.

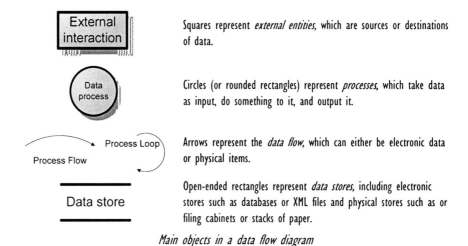

Squares represent *external entities*, which are sources or destinations of data.

Circles (or rounded rectangles) represent *processes*, which take data as input, do something to it, and output it.

Arrows represent the *data flow*, which can either be electronic data or physical items.

Open-ended rectangles represent *data stores*, including electronic stores such as databases or XML files and physical stores such as or filing cabinets or stacks of paper.

Main objects in a data flow diagram

The data flow diagram of documenting the configuration of a system would be represented by something akin to the diagram that follows.

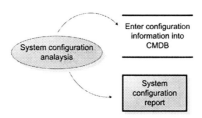

Sample data flow diagram

Universal Modeling Language (UML) activity diagrams

UML is a general-purpose modeling language that includes a standardized graphical notation that may be used to create an abstract model of a system, sometimes referred to as the UML model. UML may be considered as an extensible modeling language since it offers a profile mechanism to customize the language. UML diagrams have supplanted flowcharts as *the* tool for organizational process modeling. In many ways, UML activity diagrams are the object-oriented equivalent of flow charts and data flow diagrams (DFDs) from structured development. There are several more symbol types in a UML activity diagram than there are in a basic flowchart. We'll list the most common ones here.

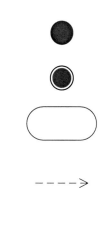

Initial node. The filled in circle is the starting point of the diagram. An initial node isn't required although it does make it significantly easier to read the diagram.

Activity final node. The filled circle with a border is the ending point. An activity diagram can have zero or more activity final nodes.

Activity. The rounded rectangles represent activities that occur. An activity may be physical, such as *inspect forms,* or electronic, such as *display create student screen.*

Flow/edge. The arrows on the diagram. Although there is a subtle difference between flows and edges I have never seen a practical purpose for the difference although I have no doubt one exists. I'll use the term flow.

Fork. A black bar with one flow going into it and several leaving it. This denotes the beginning of parallel activity. The opposite is a join.

Join. A black bar with several flows entering it and one leaving it. This denotes the end of parallel processing.

Condition. Text such as *In emergency* on a flow, defining a guard which must evaluate to true in order to traverse the node.

Decision. A diamond with one flow entering and several leaving. The flows leaving include conditions although some modelers will not indicate the conditions if it is obvious. The opposite is a merge.

Merge. A diamond with several flows entering and one leaving. The implication is that all incoming flows must reach this point until processing continues, unless otherwise noted.

Partition. Also called swim lanes, indicating who/what is performing the activities (such as the HR group, IT group, or Legal group).

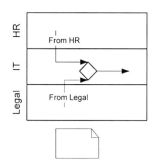

Note. Just what it sounds and looks like.

Use case. An ellipse used to indicate that an included use case is being invoked. To tell you the truth I'm not sure if this is officially allowed by the UML but clearly it should be.

Actor. A stick figured used to denote a person taking action.

Standard diagram elements of a UML activity diagram

The UML version of the flowchart that we displayed in the previous discussion would look something like this:

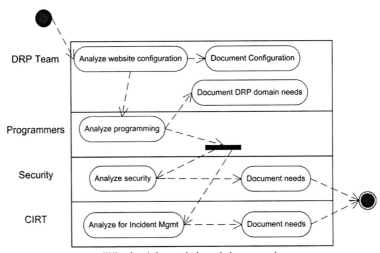

UML of website analysis and documentation

A more complete set of shapes for use with Microsoft Visio or SmartDraw can be found online at http://www.phruby.com/stencildownload.html#How

Control and process analysis – determining what the control is supposed to accomplish

Before you can write anything, you first have to analyze the control and the process that you are currently tackling. Your goal in the analysis phase is to understand all of the factors that are going to influence your actions and decisions regarding the control. **Not every control should be turned into a policy, standard, or procedure.** In our section on controls, we noted that there are over 75 different categories of controls – everything from establishing configuration items through tests, plans, audits, training, and technical controls set within software parameters.

What and why

What does this control seek to accomplish (the overall objective)? What are the intermediary goals for this control? Are you providing some type of availability? Integrity? Confidentiality? Accountability?

This first step really means that you should be going back to your authority documents and agree on what the control states. But when we say "you," that really means that the person at the highest level of authority on the team should be the one to have the final judgment call on interpreting the control, and those involved at the director and manager level should be consulted to ensure that they concur and give their harrumph to the interpretation.

If you have a good handle on the what and the why of the control, you are good to go as they say. If not, we've got you covered. We've listed as much information as we could find within the UCF website for you.

For our example, we'll use Unified Compliance Framework Control ID 01380, "Website and intranet considerations," which is one of the controls within the Systems Continuity impact zone. The question that this control asks is if the organization addresses any special considerations and contingency solutions for organizational websites (extranet, intranet, workflow). On the surface, this might sound very simple, but an examination of the control's documentation will show otherwise. Let's turn to the websites for some help.

Getting help from the UCP and UCF websites

If you have any doubt about what the control is trying to tell you to do, you can use the "note" feature built into the online spreadsheets at the ITCi Unified Compliance Project or the Unified Compliance Framework websites. Within each of the IT impact zone HTML tables you'll see small green blocks of text that say "note." These are hyperlinks that you can click which will open a window showing the meaning behind the stated control. Within the UCF site and the Excel version of the tables, the notes are replaced by UCF Control IDs.

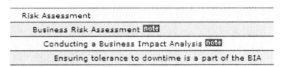

A sample of one of the IT Impact Zone HTML tables within the UCP

Once you've clicked the note hyperlink, a window will open up and will explain the control in greater detail, listing what the authority documents say about the control as well as additional commentary. Both the ITCi and UCF sites have the same information.

Detailed control note within ITCi's UCP

This should provide you with enough information to help you define the "what and why" of the control. In our example, the control analysis shows us that there are several factors that need to be taken into consideration and documented for website and intranet considerations for UCF ID 01380. The control (which you can find on the UCF website) states that *at least* the following need to be considered and documented.

• Server configuration, hardening, and security testing	Baseline documentation, technical security standards
• Server configuration imaging and offsite storage	Continuity plan
• Application serial number backups and offsite storage	Application control policy
• Decisions about spare parts/duplication/replication of components	Continuity plan
• Malicious code, patch management, anti-spyware management	Change management plan
• Server-level firewall and IDS decisions	Technical security standards
• DNS and access control considerations (are these being protected by duplicating them off site?)	Technical security policy
• Storage redundancy decisions (i.e., whether to store all data locally , within a Storage Area Network, or across the network using iSCSI)	Continuity plan
• Server-level data backup/replication and storage decisions	Continuity plan
• Server-level secondary power considerations	Continuity plan
• Server-level cooling considerations	Continuity plan

This, obviously, is a control that is somewhat complex because it involves several types of documented deliverables. Even so, you can document this *as a process* for website and intranet considerations during continuity planning. And within that process, how each bit of information would flow into the different deliverable documents mentioned above. Simply put, the control process you are documenting will need to accomplish the creating or editing of the items listed above.

Documenting all of the information requested in this control can be as simple as using index cards to list your controls and their aspects or as complex as creating a database of controls and their various aspects. We suggest that you keep it pretty simple at this point.

Documenting a complex control as a set of processes

What we just discussed deals with a one-to-one relationship of documenting a single control as a single process. But life, and control sets, can get more complicated than that. For instance, our example control set for creating continuity plan strategies has five levels to it.

	UCF Control ID	Control Title
1		
2	735	Systems Continuity Plan Strategies
3	736	Define critical business functions
4	1165	Review and prioritize each business unit and process
5	737	Define and identify critical records
6	739	Defining critical personnel
7	740	Defining critical IT Resources
8	741	SLAs include continuity planning
9	1378	Workstation protection considerations
10	1379	Server considerations
11	1380	Web site and intranet considerations
12	1383	Online and near line storage considerations
13	1382	Mainframe considerations
14	1268	Systems protection considerations
15	743	Communications systems considerations
16	1381	Local Area Network considerations
17	1294	Wide Area Network considerations
18	1396	Primary and alternate telecommunications service agreements contain priority-of-service provisions
19	1397	Alternate telecommunications services do not share a single point of failure with primary telecommunications services.
20	1399	Alternate telecommunications providers are sufficiently separated from primary service providers

Sample hierarchical control list

If you were to create a one-to-one relationship between controls and processes (which become policies), your organization could end up with around 1,500 policies, standards, and procedures. That's a *lot* of policies for *any* organization. There are going to be times it makes more sense to group sets of hierarchically organized controls together as a single policy with sub-points of grouped procedures added to it. And that's why we created the IT impact zone spreadsheets with multiple indented groupings. Instead of having 23 different processes in our example, one method of grouping would be to create 14 processes at three hierarchical levels of detail, as shown in the grouping that follows.

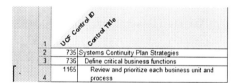

Three levels of controls (grouping one level of controls below them)

Another method would be to group more levels of controls in order to reduce the number of processes down to as few as possible, as shown in the diagram that follows.

Grouping many levels of controls in order to create fewer policies

Is there a rule for a minimum or maximum number of controls that you can group under a single process? We don't think so. If there is, we couldn't find any such rule in our research. The only thing you'll need to consider is how you are going to *document* such a complex policy and the processes that support it.

For now, we are going to stick with documenting a single process in order to keep our point clear and understandable.

What are the other controls that tie to this one?

Document if there are any controls that support this particular control and any controls that this control supports – which is easily done if you are using the Unified Compliance Framework control sets. Each set of controls is indented from the highest level to the lowest level. Therefore, the highest level controls will have supporting controls *one level* below them. And in turn, lower controls support those *one level* higher than the current level.

In other words, let's say that the level one control states that the organization must create a systems continuity plan strategy. Indented below it in the UCF tables we supply online and through download you'd find a level two control that says that a part of defining the strategy is defining critical business functions. Another control at the same level two is the consideration that must be given to websites. Therefore, the level one control would have two supporting controls. Both level two controls would support the level one control. Get it? Good.

Getting help from the IT Impact Zone tables

Each of the Impact Zone tables is already properly indented for you. This should make it relatively easy for you to determine whether or not the control has supporting controls (those one level below it) or that it supports another control (one level above it).

Audits
Internal audit programs [hold]
Audit Reporting
Assessing the quality of the audit function
Assessing the quality of audit planning and scheduling criteria
Reviewing the scope of the audit program
Reviewing and summarizing past meeting minutes
Reviewing of audit report and work papers
Reviewing past audit reports for correlation between internal and external audit groups

The UCP IT Impact Zone tables showing indents

Documenting your efforts

In our example, the control "Web site and intranet considerations," (UCF ID 1380) supports the control "Review and prioritize each business unit and process," (UCF ID 1165). There are no supporting controls for "Web site and intranet considerations.

	UCF Control ID	Control Title
1		
2	735	Systems Continuity Plan Strategies
3	736	Define critical business functions
4	1165	Review and prioritize each business unit and process
5	737	Define and identify critical records
6	739	Defining critical personnel
7	740	Defining critical IT Resources
9	1378	Workstation protection considerations
10	1379	Server considerations
11	1380	Web site and intranet considerations
12	1383	Online and near line storage considerations
13	1382	Mainframe considerations
14	1268	Systems protection considerations
15	743	Communications systems considerations
22	1254	Alternate power considerations
23	1374	Damaged site considerations

Sample hierarchy of controls

Therefore, on the back of our index cards we usually list first the controls supported (UCF ID 1165 in our case) and then a list of all supporting controls (in this case, none). You can document this however you want.

Rough cut the "flow" of the process

Assess the control process attributes in terms of decisions, documentation, assets in use, etc. List all of the necessary steps, from first to last, that it takes to accomplish this control. The best way to do this the first time is through a table-top exercise wherein the team you've assembled (all those required to carry out the control) walk through the control from beginning to end. The focus will be to determine what process steps come before others, and which are actually decisions or documentation steps. This is best done on a whiteboard or some other large format drawing table where everyone gets a chance at doodling.

Documenting your efforts

In our example, the process attributes are all spelled out:

Document the website's hardware and software configuration; thoroughly test the website's programming and coding to ensure that IP addresses map to domain names (process step) and document the results;

Coordinate (process step) the continuity solutions with the appropriate security policies and security controls assigned to the website and document any special needs;

Coordinate (process step) the continuity plan for the site with the incident response team and their procedures and document any special needs; and

Review all general support systems' and interconnected systems' documentation (process step) to ensure that the continuity plan is properly coordinated (documentation step) with these system types.

Documentation can be as simple as a flowchart like the following example.

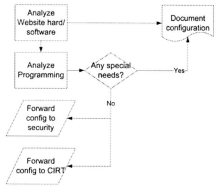

Simple flowchart of the control process

If your process involves installing hardware, you might want to think about taking snapshots of what you are installing and then tying those snapshots to the process flow step you've created in your flow chart.

The same thing holds true for working with software. As they say, "a picture is worth a thousand words." One of the tricks we've used for years is to go step-by-step through the process and take screen shots every bit of the way, tying them to each of the process steps.

Both the pictures and the screen shots can be used later in the actual documentation phase of creating policies and procedures.

Identify potential problems

Identify problems and potential mishaps, and what the mishap reaction steps should be, with the rough-cut control process. What are the actions that should be taken if something does go wrong? Should anyone be notified? Should extra precautions be taken?

In our example, there really isn't much that can go wrong other than the forms for documentation not being clear or someone not having access to configuration files. In that case, our staff would annotate what needed to be added to the forms or tests and would therefore notify the group responsible.

Documenting your efforts

The easiest way to document the potential problems you've found is to write those problems directly onto your process flow as we show in our example below. What we suggest is numbering each of the steps in the flow that have an associated problem and then annotating the found problem off to the side somewhere.

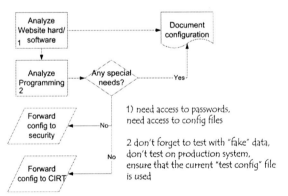

Annotating problems on the flow chart

Rough cut documentation of your process

Begin to test and describe control process flows (either visually or textually). This is where you'll do your "pre-writing" as we call it. All you are trying to pre-write here are the steps it takes you to achieve success. This can either be in a flow chart format or it can be written directions.

For our example, because the focus is on documenting systems, we chose to go with the textual version, alternating paragraphs of what to do with screen shots of what the documentation should look like when it is filled out properly as shown in the following diagram.

There is no cut-and-dried method for pre-writing. Whatever works best for your situation, your organization, and the particular control you are addressing is what you should use.

Documenting your efforts

We begin with the annotated rough cut flow chart that has the potential problems marked up on it. We combine that rough cut flow with any screen shots or pictures that we've taken and then start to write everything in a simple bullet list fashion.

If we have screen shots of software or forms (or whatever), we'll document the process by writing down what needs to happen and then following the text paragraph we'll show the screen shot or picture and annotate it if necessary.

What's the best way to write a rough cut?

Write like you are talking to your parents about technology. Unless, of course, your parents invented the Internet or something. Then write like you are talking to some CXO – simple, no padding, no complexity, no big words.

If you are wondering what "no padding" means, it means that you want to rid yourself of those extraneous, pompous, linguistically mastered words. By the way, the sentence you just read was padded. Get it? Get rid of it.

But, don't short yourself by trying to cut out words. Notice the difference between "contact the service desk" and "contact the service desk between the hours of 9 and 5"? Being frustrated at six o'clock when nobody answers the phone, that's what.

▲▼ Decisions about spare parts/duplication/replication of components should have been documented in your original philosophy and then again in your mission and vision statements. These decisions should be documented in Worksheet 5a.

Worksheet 5a

In order to ensure proper continuity between your objectives and your emergency requisition program, you'll need to compare Worksheet 5a with Worksheet CP 6 which deals with the procurement of replacement equipment. If the objectives don't match the procurement procedures (i.e., timeframes don't match, etc.), then you'll have to either adjust your objectives or your procedures.

Worksheet CP 6

▲▼ Is the most current administrator and user access information duplicated or replicated off site so that an appropriate access management server can authenticate user access to the server? You'll want to examine Worksheet 2.7c to ensure that the right listing of people and groups have been documented, along with their access level and domain of control.

Our pre-writing example

We aren't going to bombard you with any other writing tips at this point. Just get it written in a way that you *think* others can understand. You'll edit later.

Analyze scope of IT assets

Determine which personnel, applications, and supporting systems are involved in the control. This is easily accomplished by looking at your rough cut process flow and for each process or documentation step asking which system(s), network(s), application(s), and personnel does this control apply to.

 Don't forget to include those individuals who may not be employees of your organization, such as contractors, consultants, outsourced vendors, and so on. Significant security breaches have occurred because these types of folks were not considered within the scope when they should have been.

In our example this applies to all websites within the organization, whether they are extranets, intranets, or workflow sites. Therefore, as general supporting systems, this also applies to the network itself, the security servers protecting the websites, and the access control servers providing sign-on security for the sites. The applications involved, then, are all of the major applications and minor applications associated with each of these systems. And, the personnel are the managers, analysts, programmers, database administrators, security staff, incident response staff, and key line of business staff associated with the websites.

Documenting your efforts

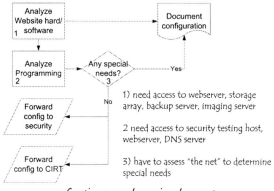

Creating a rough scoping document

We document the scope of the system the same way that we document potential problems. Given a printout of the process flow, we analyze each step and ask "what equipment and software" do we need to have access to in order to carry out the step. We then number each step that has an asset tied to it and then annotate the needed asset.

When documenting the staff you are going to need, ensure that you document the *roles* of the staff involved and not individual people's names such as Joe Schlabotnik or Veronica Clearwater. A year from now those folks might not be in their positions. And as noted above, you'll need to take special precautions to ensure that you properly document personnel that are external to your organization, but who also have to be defined within the scope of the assets you are engaging.

Analyze the *roles* of who should be involved

Determine the roles that are required to carry out the control. And, should these people's positions be listed on the RACI chart?

At this point you should have your process flow annotated with potential problems (and their resolution). You should also have a rough cut of the written process.

Now go back and examine the documentation you have so far and ask yourself "who should be involved in this process?" You've got four positions you have to fill at minimum:

- **Authorizer** – Who should authorize this process?
- **Responsible** – Who should be the person to perform this process? Should it be the same as the authorizer?
- **Supporting role (optional)** – Is there anyone who should support the person responsible for this process? How should they provide support?
- **Consulted** – Who needs to have input when this process is taking place?
- **Informed** – Who needs to be told that this process is taking place?

Documenting your efforts

You'll probably end up creating a secondary RACI chart just for this control, filling in those roles that are associated with the specific control versus the one you created for *creating* the control. Don't worry about a nice looking RACI chart just yet though. All you'll really need to do is to annotate in the documentation the steps at which people need to be involved according to their responsibility, accountability, supporting role, or being communicated with.

Determining the prerequisite tools

What tools does the person(s) carrying out this control need to have on hand in order to ensure that the control is conducted expeditiously?

In our example, when analyzing the website's hardware and software configurations, the analyst will need to have access to the configuration applications as the key tools. When analyzing the programming for the website software, the analyst will need to have access to a programming analysis tool as well as the configuration applications for DNS.

Each role will normally have their own tools that they need to apply in order to get their part of the job done. Don't worry about integrating the tools for now, that will come later.

Documenting your efforts

There really isn't much to documentation at this point, as all you are doing is annotating the tools that you'll need to have on hand. As with most other documentation of this type, our method is to annotate the process flow and then note which tools will be necessary for those steps that require them.

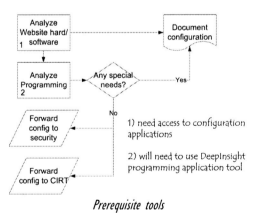

Prerequisite tools

Determine prerequisite knowledge needed

What information does the person(s) carrying out this control need to know? Is there any training or certification that the person(s) should go through before performing this control?

With regards to our example, documenting the website's configuration (and checking that of the supporting systems) means that the person should be trained and knowledgeable in systems hardening configuration and the system's setup – especially any peculiar storage and RAID arrays. In order to test the website's programming and coding, the staff should be familiar with those methods and tools. In order to test for and integrate with the security strategies, the person should be familiar with those tools and methods. The same can be said for the incident team's integration.

Documenting your efforts

Can any one person hold all of this knowledge? Probably not, which is why it usually takes a team to carry out these types of controls. Therefore, you'll be documenting the level of knowledge required for *each specific* role on the team. At this point, the best idea is to annotate the knowledge needed for each step in the process as we show in our diagram that follows.

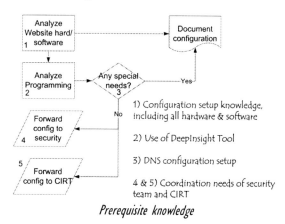

Prerequisite knowledge

Describe what "success" looks like

What should the outcome be? What should you have fixed, made more stable, made available, kept confidential, documented, or produced?

Our example revolves around documenting the website's configuration, programming, security, and incident response requirements. Therefore, "success" means that these documents have been brought accurately up-to-date and coordinated with other departments and systems.

Documenting your efforts

This is an easy one. With a blank sheet of paper, write down the answer to the question "we agree that when finished, we will have accomplished the following…"

Whatever your team writes down after analyzing the process that you've walked them through is what success looks like *to them*.

Once you've got their version of success written down, take that sheet to the person **responsible** and the person who **authorizes** this process and get *their* approval on what success should be.

Create the "success" reports

What reports (and their format) should be presented when the control is completed? To whom should the reports be presented? Don't worry too much about metrics and measurement criteria right now. You don't have enough time running this control to really know what to measure. Just create the "we're done" report and submit that.

Make sure, however, that your "we're done" report *does* include some type of after-action analysis of the policy or procedure's performance in order to make the process a better one.

In our example, the "we're done" report is an e-mail to the person responsible for the control that it has been completed and the proper documentation has been modified and is now up-to-date. The rest of the report is the actual documentation that has been either completed for the first time or updated.

Documenting your efforts

This might be a log, an e-mail (as in our case), or a formal report. It really is up to your organization and the type of process that you are working with.

Have someone else run through the process

This is where you separate hype from reality. Now is the time that you take the control process you've documented and hand it over to the line of business person or someone else on the team and ask them to follow your documentation. If you don't do this, your process could have gaps, be incomplete, or be unfeasible.

If they can repeat (roughly) what you've set out as an objective for success (and avoid the potential pitfalls you've documented), you are good to go.

Documenting your efforts

You'll not only want to give the reviewer your process, but you'll also want to give them an analysis sheet that asks several questions about the process as you've documented it so far.

Purpose

❏ Does the documentation identify why we are following this process?

Triggers

❏ Does the documentation explain when this process should be run?

❏ Does the documentation explain exceptions to the basic trigger dates and whom in the organization may trigger the process to run?

The process steps

❏ Are the process steps understandable and usable?

❏ Are all of the steps presented in their correct order?

❏ Are there any steps missing?

❏ Is the information presented sufficient to complete the process?

❏ Are there backtracking steps, and if so, are they documented clearly?

❑ Are tool usage and required knowledge detailed and assigned to the correct process steps?

❑ Did you arrive at the success point when you thought you would according to the process documentation?

❑ Did "success" look the way that the process documented it would?

❑ Were you comfortable creating the final report? Did you feel you could stand behind and endorse this report?

Identify short term improvements with the control process

Most likely, during the previous step, the person to whom you handed your rough draft of a process document will have a few substantial edits and will also have found a few more potential mishaps that you'll want to document.

Take the suggestions back to the group that originally formed to document the process and conduct a "group edit," focusing on the short term improvements. This shouldn't take too long.

Documenting your efforts

Documentation at this point involves taking your original notes, process flows, and anything else you created and then making the necessary changes.

Once you are happy with those changes, you can submit your rough process documentation for approval and incorporation into the organizational policies and procedures.

FROM REPEATABLE (2) TO DEFINED (3)

At this stage your organization is aware of the need to act and are able to communicate the basic issues.

You now have a set of informal documentation and an understanding of the procedures you need to undertake exists.

You might or might not be using automated tools yet to make the job easier.

For at least the most critical areas, minimum skill requirements have been identified and you are probably passing on-the-job training around through your more capable and attentive staff.

You are "getting a handle" on the proper roles and responsibilities, though you might be facing a bit of finger pointing when problems occur.

And at this point, metrics are binary – you are either performing the processes or you aren't.

Therefore, your overall goal is to institutionalize your processes by turning them into policies and procedures. You will need to achieve these individual goals in order to move to a level of maturity that has defined and codified your controls into groups of policies and supporting procedures:

1. Establish organizational policy documents

2. Formally document processes and procedures

3. Provide the necessary resources

4. Assign documented responsibility

5. Train the staff

6. Manage configurations

7. Monitor and control the processes

8. Objectively evaluate adherence

9. Review the status with higher level management

On writing well

Some policy book authors make a huge distinction between "professional" policy writers who only write policies and procedures for a living and "would-be" policy writers who do other things within the organization. They then go on to verbally trounce us "would-be" policy writers. To those folks, we say THHTHTHTBBBTT!

Most everyone I've ever met who has written policies, standards, and procedures for the organization actually does something else for a living. In the over twenty years I've been in this business, I haven't met a single person who only writes policies, standards, and procedures with no other responsibilities. Maybe I just haven't worked in big enough companies (and no, we didn't have them when I was CIO of the world's largest ad agency).

So for the rest of us who have other duties, with policies, standards, and procedures being a *part* of what we do, let's take a few minutes to talk about writing formats and writing well.

If you've ever read the book *The Little Prince*, you'll know the secret of the Fox was consistency. He wanted consistency in being courted. Readers want the same thing. A standard writing structure and a standard style of writing is the signature of writing well. We'll talk about the structure at another point. For now, let's focus on the written word.

Audience, clarity, logic, and brevity

Well-written policies and procedures have four points to them as the heading above shows. We'll start with the audience and work through to brevity.

Audience

All policies and procedures are directed at an organizational audience. Some policies are to be read by very technical people and others are not. When writing policies and procedures, make sure that you have the correct audience in mind. And when we say audience, we mean the *whole* audience that the policy and procedures apply to. That means going through the responsibilities matrix and looking at the various roles of people who are not only directly responsible, but who also have to be consulted with and informed about the procedures. Which means that if part of your audience consists of third party people who are outside your organization, check your jargon to ensure you aren't using terminology that is only used within your organization and would not be understood by outsiders. It also means that you need to know the cultural lingo used in the different geographic locations in which your policy will be read. Terms commonly used in one part of the world may mean something completely different in different part of the world, and may actually be inappropriate or offensive. Slang, in particular, should be avoided both because it isn't universal and because it can change meaning over a relatively short period of time.

Note that we're not saying that you have to "dumb down" your policy writing. Quite the contrary – sometimes you want to "smarten up" your policy to address the appropriate audience. If you're policy applies only to the financial senior staff members, use commonly understood financial and accounting terms. But don't expect your IT people to understand it, much less comply with it.

Clarity

Is your writing clear and easy to understand? Are you avoiding local or technical jargon and terms that aren't universal? It doesn't matter if you *think* that your audience knows those terms. Because sure enough, you'll add a term that "everyone knows" and then they'll hire someone who doesn't know the term (or worse, thinks it means something else) who will become quickly confused and then proceed to completely subvert your compliance efforts.

The best bet for idea clarity is to only have one point per paragraph. Look at all of the sentences in each of your paragraphs. Do they all support the same point? If they do, leave them in. If they don't, then start another paragraph or drop the sentences because they aren't necessary.

The best bet for reading clarity is to have sentences that don't exceed 20 or so words, because very long sentences like this one tend to confuse people and their mind starts to wander and then the thought that you were trying to impress upon them with what you are writing is totally lost. Yes, I did that on purpose. Keep it short – no more than 20 or so. That makes it easier to read.

The last point in clarity is to avoid the brain-extender approach to policies. A brain extender is the written analogy of having to drive a Porsche to compensate for certain *shortcomings*. This shortcoming in this instance is a lack of clarity. Here's a real-world version of a brain-extender policy:

> It is the organizational policy that subsequent movement into production of new system and subsystem acquisitions that all applications and hardware synergistic to the platform will leverage the organizationally-blessed security configuration STIG.

This idiot thought he looked smart when he wrote it. When I asked him what a STIG was, he couldn't respond. I looked it up. What he really meant was that:

> Before placing any new systems into production, the security configuration will be applied according to the matching Security Technical Implementation Guide, found on the intranet server in the guides and manuals section.

Clarity and pomposity *do not* go hand-in-hand. Acronyms are jargon. Avoid using them in policies and procedures, even if you include them in your glossary or definitions. You *can* strike a blow against illiteracy by ensuring that there are no buzzwords, jargon, and acronyms in *your* writing.

Finally, avoid cross-references – particularly to documents outside of the policy that's in front of you. You can virtually guarantee that nobody (except maybe the lawyers) will actually go find the document you've referenced and there goes an important part of your policy and procedure. Nobody likes too much repetition, but sometimes that's the price we have to pay for clarity. (Using hyperlinks in a web based policy document can help with the cross-referencing problem, but most people still won't click through to the next document.)

Logic

Will the reader be able to follow your train of thought? Or as one of my earlier editors used to say "is your writing linear, or does it loop around like a whirligig?" If you are wondering, linear is good, a whirligig is bad.

Most of your writing is going to be process writing, meaning that you are walking the reader step-by-step through a series of actions. The best way to check your logic is to have a flow chart of the process in front of you and then match the writing steps to the flow chart. If the paragraphs and sentences of the text follow the sequence of the flow chart, then your logic is solid. If you simply can't seem to write your policy in a linear, logical flow, perhaps the problem isn't your writing – perhaps you should revisit whether the policy itself is lacking something in the logic department.

Brevity

Is your writing short and concise? Because that's what brevity means. In terms of writing policies and procedures, it means that you are supplying details *in proportion* to their importance.

Brevity is the sign of a well-organized mind, writes William Zinsser in *Writing to Learn*. In writing, remember that short is normally better than long. Your readers need to *do* something with your policies and procedures, not just read them.

Word choices

Which words are *the most correct ones* to do the job? Which words are clear to all of your readers, versus words that only a select few will understand? Do you want to aggravate your bosses or annoy them (the answer is below)? Which words do you think your legal department **might** want to review before you commit them to paper? Believe it or not, you really do have to put a bit of thinking into your writing when creating your policies, standards, and procedures.

Using good words well makes your legal team happy

If you are wondering, you want to **annoy** your bosses because the word "annoy" means to *pester* or *irritate*. Of course once you are already annoying them, you might want to *make it worse* by **aggravating** (meaning *"to make worse or more severe"*) the situation. In other words, you can annoy your readers by creating hard to understand policies and then aggravate the problem by choosing the wrong words. Here are a few other word sets we've found misused that you'll want to think through and have someone review for word choices (also check out the difference between good and well):

All ready, already: *already* denotes something that happened in the past; while *all ready* denotes that all of something is ready. "When you pick up the backup tapes the form must already be filled out before the tapes are all ready to go off site."

All together, altogether: *altogether* denotes something is whole or complete, while *all together* means something will happen simultaneously. "Once the tape boxes have been brought altogether, they should be taken off site all together."

Alter, altar: because a person worships at an *altar* and that isn't something most IT people write about, you should know that when you *alter* something you are changing it. "Don't alter the forms once I've signed them."

Besides, beside: the difference between something being *on the side of* and something *in addition* is found within the added *"s"* in the two words – the addition of the *"s"* makes the word mean *in addition*. "Besides the tape container please take the spare cables which are beside the backup server."

Can, may: if you are trained to do something then you *can* do it – that is to say, you have the ability to do it. However, you *may* do it only if you have permission. You are also going to want to check out the difference between *will* and *may*. "You may perform this procedure if you can do it correctly."

Dual, duel: because you don't want to cause a *fight*, ensure that you are talking about *two* of something by using *dual*. "If you don't want to duel with the pickup driver, make sure that you have dual copies of the off site forms ready."

Ensure, insure: if you want to *make certain of something* then you are going to *ensure* it. If you worry about your business in a disaster, you might want to *insure* it against loss. "To ensure the DRP plan is complete be certain to insure against business downtime."

Everyday, every day: if you want to talk about something being *routine* then you will use *everyday*, because *every day* means *every single day* including weekends.

"Your procedure review process should become an everyday item in your mind so that you practice it every day at work."

Fewer, less: match *less* with single words and *fewer* with plural words. "The tape boxes hold fewer tapes. Therefore each will weigh less."

Good, well: when talking about *high quality* or a measure of *correctness* you must use *well*, because *good* is an adjective and not an adverb. "If the policies are written well, the auditor's report will be good."

In, into: when you are going from the outside *in*to the *in*side the correct word is *into*, because *in* means something is *within* something else. "Go in to the tape boxes, pull the tapes out, and put the tapes into the tape library."

Including, including but not limited to, including without limitation: if your list of items is meant to be an incomplete set of examples, but something may have been left out, the list is *including, but not limited to*, the items that follow. However, if your list is complete, but each item in the list is to be read as expansively as possible, you are *including without limitation* (a concept that is not often found in policy writing). "There are many consequences to poor policy writing, including, but not limited to, compliance deficiencies, fines, and loss of employment (yours!)."

Irregardless: just don't. The proper word is *regardless*. "Regardless of what anyone tells you, 'irregardless' is considered a non-standard or erroneous word."

Loose, lose: not being able to *find* something has nothing to do with it *not being tight* which is what *loose* means. "You will lose your job writing policies if your grammar continues to be loose."

Principal, principle: if you're talking about the primary or most important thing, then *principal* is your adjective (and it needs a noun to modify). On the other hand if you're referring to your organization's tenants, beliefs, or code of conduct, you're talking about *principles*. To round it out, *principal* the noun means that scary person whose office you avoided in grade school or the amount you owe on your mortgage before interest. "Being the principal policy writer for your organization makes you responsible for articulating the principles for behavior and compliance."

Real, really, very: if you are talking about something *in reality* or that exists then *really* is your word. If you want to denote that something is *true* or *actual* you should pick *real* as your word. However, most of the time you probably mean *very* because it is an expression of *precision*. "I'm very glad you finished the documentation because now our plan is real, and we are really ready."

Set, sit: people and animals can *sit* but objects such as backup tapes cannot, so when you want to talk about *placing something*, *putting something*, or *determining something* you'll want to use *set*. "Set the alarm code on the door and set the keys back on the key-ring before you sit down at the security desk."

Than, then: if you are *comparing* something the correct word is *than*, because *then* means *next* or *at that time*. "While tape is less expensive than disk, we will use tape. When the price falls, then we will switch to disk."

Try and, try to: none of us *try and* do anything, however we all *try to* do most things. In other words, just don't **combine** *try and* **in your meaning** at all. "Please try to find all backup tapes going off site. If you do not have a total of twelve the night shift operator will help you try and you should keep looking."

Who, which, that: both *who* and *that* are used when writing about people. "The security administrator, who wrote the procedures that we must follow, defines the anti-virus software which we must use."

Will, shall, should, and may: to *will* is to intend to do something as much as you can within your power so that something *shall* come about as a future condition. Think of the difference between the two as you *will intend* to do something that *shall mandatorily result* in an outcome. Both *will* and *shall* imply mandatory statements. *Should* implies that something is *advised* but not required, while *may* implies either the right to a person's *discretion* or uncertainty as to whether something will happen. "You will press the button that shall eject the tape from the library. You should then immediately put the tape into the tape container to protect it. For added safety, you may want to lock the container."

You're, your: *you're* most often going to see this mistake as the result of poor proofreading of *your* document.

Does you use correct grammar?

If you can spot the subject and verb disagreement in the above title, you get the idea. Chances are that you are using a word processor that will check your grammar for you. And there is an equal if not better chance that you have turned *off* the grammar checking capability. Turn it back on. And then run a grammar check on your writing. I is appalled at how many people doesn't check their grammar. That's a joke – get it? That said, the grammar checker can't always be trusted (remember, it was written by a bunch of technical programmer) and could lead you astray. It's a useful tool, particularly at the beginning of your new writing career, but don't let it run your life.

Eats, shoots, and leaves

As the title of the wildly popular book and a *very old joke* about punctuation points out, commas are important. And if you don't know the joke, here it is.

> A panda walks into a restaurant and orders a sandwich. After finishing the sandwich, the panda stands up, pulls out a gun, and shoots into the air as he is exiting. When the police arrest him, they asked him why he did that. He handed them a poorly punctuated wildlife book that had as an entry: **Panda. Large black-and-white bear-like mammal, native to China. Eats, shoots, and leaves.**

The point is – punctuation really does matter. If you have a hard time with punctuation, buy the book with the same title as this header. It's a short book and quite well written. Here are a two extra rules to get you started.

Quotation marks ""

The use of quotation marks in writing policies, standards, and procedures is to show the reader *the exact words* described by a person, a dialog box, or found in documentation. This is called a *direct quotation*. You can convey the same meaning without the use of the quotation marks by paraphrasing the original statement.

Direct: The warning label states "do not handle without gloves."

Indirect: You must wear gloves if the warning label states not to handle without them.

Guideline 1: When using quotation marks, always put the closing quotation mark *at the very end of what you are quoting*, not at the end of every sentence or paragraph you are quoting.

Guideline 2: You should put quotation marks around all jargon or other expressions outside the normal usage of your readers. *Do not* put quotation marks around all technical terms (instead, add them to your glossary or terms list).

Guideline 3: All *periods* or *commas* go inside the last quotation mark, while *colons* and *semicolons* go outside the closing quotation mark.

Apostrophes

Let me set the record straight, *apostrophes are not used to indicate the plural*. They are used in either contractions or to indicate possession.

Contractions

A contraction indicates that a letter has been omitted from a word. The contraction of *doesn't* stands for *do not*. The contraction *won't* stands for *will not*. Some common contractions are:

can't	cannot
he's	he is
isn't	is not
she'll	she will
you've	you have

Possession

Possession means that one thing belongs to another. For instance, the CIO's beer bottle denotes that the beer bottle in the sentence belongs to the CIO. There are three guidelines to help you place this apostrophe.

Guideline 1: For singular nouns the possession should be written as *'s.* "The administrator's logbook." Even if the singular noun already ends in an *s.* "Fred Jones's logbook."

Guideline 2: For plural nouns that end in *s,* the apostrophe should be added as the last character. "The administrators' logbooks."

Guideline 3: For collective nouns and plural words that do not end in *s,* the possession should be written as *'s.* "The IT staff's logbooks."

Brackets <> and [ ]

There are two types of brackets that we've seen in many policies, standards, and procedures.

The first set of brackets, the square brackets [ ] have been in use for quite some time within conventional writing. These should be used when clarifying a quote from someone or some thing. As an example, when quoting a memo about the proper method of adding tapes to a container "place the tapes [the ones you just took out of the tape library] into the container and seal it before shipping" the brackets here help define *which* tapes need to go into the container.

The newest type of brackets are the diagonal ones < > which used to simply be a math expression for lesser or greater than. However, the usage we see most often is that of enclosing a URL. Hence, in that sense it is denoting *everything which must be copied* in order for the URL to function correctly.

Tools to help

There are hundreds available that can help you with your writing – some are good, some are not. But that shouldn't stop you from looking around and finding a book or resource that works for you. In addition to a *Eats, Shoots, and Leaves* that we mentioned above, here are a few more that we like:

William Zinsser's books *On Writing Well* and *Writing to Learn*.[19] are (as you would guess) well written and easy to understand. *On Writing Well* will help your overall prose and will help you with clarity, brevity, and audience. It is a fantastic overall reference. *Writing to Learn* will help you with your logic, brevity, and how to think clearly about the subjects that you are trying to communicate. I would suggest both works be desk references for anyone who needs to communicate by typing.

A thesaurus is another vital tool to have at hand. I happen to like the *Visual Thesaurus*[20]. Available in both a desktop edition and an online edition, this thesaurus makes picking the correct word a breeze.

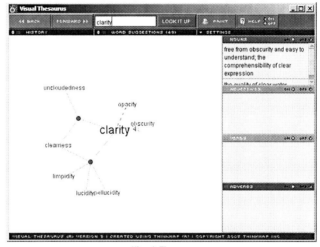

Visual Thesaurus

---

19 *On Writing Well : An Informal Guide to Writing Nonfiction*, William Zinsser (1976). *Writing to Learn*, William Zinsser (1993).

20 http://www.visualthesaurus.com

Creating policies

Policies and procedures have very much in common. Procedures extend the scope of what policies start. **Policies state who, what, and why. Procedures state how.** Here is the complete list of all of the topics that need to be covered in both policies and procedures, denoting which topics are optional and which are required.

		Policy	Procedure
	Title	Required	Required
	ID	Required	Required
	Guarantor or approver	Required	Required
1.0	Policy overview	Optional	Optional
2.0	Purpose	Required	Required
3.0	Compliance with public and organizational rules	Required	Required
3.a	Consequences of non-compliance	Optional[21]	Optional
4.0	Scope	Required	Required
4.a	Coverage	NA	Required
4.b	Assignment	NA	Required
4.c	Required knowledge	NA	Required
4.d	Required tools	NA	Required
5.0	Policy Description (policy) Extended definition (procedure)	Required	N/A
5.a	Procedure goals	NA	Optional
5.b	Supporting and supported procedures	NA	Optional

---

[21] By listing this as "optional" here, we don't mean to imply that consequences are optional. Quite the contrary – spelling out the consequences of non-compliance is extraordinarily important. We just mean that you don't necessarily need to spell out consequences within each individual policy. You can, instead, have an overriding policy that specifies the consequences and sanctions that may befall the unfortunately sole that violates the policies and procedures that you've worked so hard to create.

5.c	Procedure triggers	NA	Optional
5.d	Potential mishaps & reaction steps	NA	Optional
5.e	Successful execution	NA	Optional
5.f	Reports	NA	Optional
6.0	Procedure steps	NA	Required
7.0	Procedure checklists	NA	Optional

Optional and required sections of policies and procedures

There is no "set" look and feel of what a policy document should look like. They can be as simple as a word processing document with the required information, or they can be made to look like forms such as the one that follows[22].

Sample formatting for a policy document

---

22   We have made this version available to you at http://www.saywhatyoudo.com.

Policy identification information

The policy identification information (Title, Control ID, etc.) is used to discern one policy from the next. When working with the Unified Compliance Framework, each control statement can act as a policy title, and each control ID within the UCF can serve as the control ID for your policy documents.

The effective date of your policy should be the date that the person who is approving it signs off that it is complete.

The revision date of your policy should be automatically entered if at all possible. Most word processing applications will allow you to enter a "modified date" field into your document so that when a user makes changes to the document, the revision date is incremented to the current date.

The revision number should always start with 1.0 for the original document and then be incremented in decimals in order to keep the numbers from reaching astronomical proportions as you continually update your policies (yeah, like that's going to happen, the updating that is).

Policy Title	Control ID	UCF ID F 00001
	Effective Date	
	Revision Date	1/19/2007
	Revision Number	1
	Approved By	

Example policy title and identification information

Why we don't ask you to document revision history

Some authors will ask you to also document the revision history of your policy. That can automatically be done for you through most word processors and databases (if you are maintaining your policies and procedures in a database). Microsoft Word and Microsoft Sharepoint will both allow you to turn on version tracking and track all changes to documents as you create and edit them. Sharepoint will even go so far as to force the user to check out a document and then enter information into a field, documenting the changes when checking the document back in.

What we end up seeing if you add a manual revision history to the front of the document is that only a few cryptic notes were added that someone did this or that – nothing of substance has ever been added there. You can't recreate the older document or go back to an earlier version just by reading those notes and undoing the changes mentioned.

The better methodology is to use your software to create, and store, multiple versions of your documents that you *force* users to comment on *and that allow you to reinstate the older versions*. What follows is the version history of this section that you are reading now. Because of version tracking, we can go back to any one of the 8 earlier versions of this material and restore that that point.

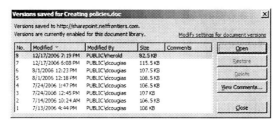

Built-in version tracking in Word

Policy overview

The policy overview is probably the most important aspect of the policy as this is the heart of the whole thing. The policy overview should reflect the tone of the organization in its direction and meaning. Remember, a policy describes your organizational management's decision to enact a control or set of controls.

The policy statement should be both easy to read and easy to understand.

Some authors will tell you that you should begin each policy statement with the words "it is the policy of *your company* that…" Malarkey. If you are writing a policy statement for your organization, it is a *given* that this is the policy of the organization. Duh. You can just as easily state "the organization will…" or "the entity will…" naming the department or business unit that the policy belongs to.

The policy overview doesn't have to be long. In fact, it is better if it is not. Short, succinct, to the point. Here's our example for a policy statement that is a one-to-one relationship between a control and a policy.

> The organization will ensure that the continuity plan addresses considerations and contingency solutions for websites (extranet, intranet, workflow) and coordinates those solutions with all relevant support groups.

When writing your policy overview for compliance, they can either be taken directly from the control statement in the regulation (if you only have to deal with one regulation) or can be taken directly from the policy statements that we supply within the Unified Compliance Framework.

Purpose

Your purpose should define the goal that you want to achieve. It, too, should be concise yet comprehensive, made up of two or three sentences at most. When finished reading this, the reader should know *why* they have to follow this policy.

> The purpose of this policy is to ensure that the websites have been properly documented for configuration changes to the hardware and the software and any configurable items have been catalogued and accounted for in the continuity plan. The coordination steps are necessary to ensure proper integration with both security plans and incident management plans.

You know you've written a solid purpose statement when you can combine the policy statement and the purpose to form a logical *what* (policy) and *why* (purpose).

Always remember to add a "why" to your purpose statement

When writing this book, we got into a wonderful dialog about what should go into a policy. In general, a policy describes **who** should do **what**. In general, a policy is a directive that obligates personnel to follow it, regardless of whether they know why. However, within most organizations, where teamwork, consensus-building, and giving promotions based upon contributions and improvements (often resulting from questioning "why's") is more of the norm, we encourage companies to incorporate the "why" into their policy statements. Even though it adds a bit to the size of a policy, and is different from conventional views on the purpose of policies, we think that is okay. We're all for changing convention, and incorporating the human factor, if the ultimate result is (in this case) more effective information security and compliance. There are five reasons for adding the "why" to the purpose statement.

1. From a psychological impact perspective, most people in non-government and non-military enterprises will not blindly follow an order unless they know why they are being told to do so, and know and understand how it impacts them personally. If they can clearly and easily see how it impacts them, they are more likely to comply with it. If you want a policy to be effective and be followed (most of us do) then folks in these organizations must understand the reasoning behind them by being provided with the "why."

2. From an awareness perspective, incorporating the "why" of the policy into the policy itself makes the policy easier to understand and justify in the reader's mind. It also draws your personnel back to the policy itself more often if they want to understand why a policy has been implemented. It is always good to have policies that are actually read, and read closely, by personnel. Those that are issued, quickly glanced over and never looked at again are not as effective as policies that are read more than once.

3. From a compliance perspective, including the "why" into the policy itself can, arguably, help support regulatory requirements for awareness and training. In many of the organizations whose information security programs I've reviewed, their information security training efforts have consisted almost entirely of the (poor) practice of just copying the policies onto PowerPoint slides and requiring personnel to read them from their desks whenever they have time. If the "why" is part of the policy, then at least some actual education about the need for the policy can be passed on to the employee/learner.

4. From a business leader's perspective, knowing the "why" of the policy demonstrates the business need for the policy and makes clear that the policy was not just created because someone in the information security area thought it was a good idea. Business leaders want to know why someone else in the

organization is putting restrictions upon them or giving them orders. If the "why" is right there within the policy then they can have this answer without spending what they will view as wasted time calling up someone in information security or, what is often the case, calling the CIO, or whatever CxO owns the information security area, and asking and complaining. If business leaders easily know "why" a policy is in place, they will more likely make sure the folks they manage are following the policy; their compliance actions example will then inspire compliance from their direct reports.

5. From an interpretation clarification perspective, it gives the user guidance when faced with gray areas at the edges of the policy – if they understand the "why," they are in a better position to make appropriate judgment calls when they come up.

Let's put this into practice. Below are two sets of purpose statements. Each in their original form and then followed by a version with the "why" added to it.

Original: *This policy provides guidelines to protect the organization Information systems from malicious Internet attacks.*

With the "why" included: *This policy specifies some technologies that must be implemented to help protect the organization from malicious attacks from outside networks, such as the Internet, as well as help protect against malicious code and attacks that could originate within the network. Preventing such unauthorized intrusions and attacks will not only keep the business processes available to allow everyone to perform their work and meet their deadlines, it will also help our organization to comply with multiple laws and regulatory requirements to safeguard our customer information.*

Original: *Systems and network logs are supplemented with additional tools that watch for signs of intrusions or intrusion attempts, as well as alert responsible parties when such events occur. The purpose is to accumulate data from network and servers, building a "fingerprint" of usage.*

With the "why" included: *This policy provides the actions personnel must take, and the technology that must be implemented, to help ensure unauthorized attempts to access network* *and systems resources are identified, prevented and appropriate personnel quickly alerted. Preventing unauthorized access will help ensure unauthorized individuals do not access our business resources, as well as ensure the network is kept available for business processing and that the data used for business is accurate. Implementing logs and intrusion detection tools will also help our organization to comply with multiple laws and regulatory requirements to establish such information security safeguards.*

The one caution we would add, however, is that the "why" not dilute the directive nature of the policy. A sophisticated end user may read the "why" statement, decide that the policy doesn't properly address the "why" in a particular situation and then take it upon him/her-self to make an exception to the policy. That would be the wrong answer. If they feel the policy should not apply because of the "why," they should follow the organizational policy for requesting exceptions. There are lots of different policies that could be used to address a particular "why" situation and the management of the company has determined to address it in the way articulated by the policy. It cannot be left up to the individual users to second-guess that decision based on their personal interpretations of the "why" statement that accompanies the policy.

Compliance

It is absolutely necessary to enter the citations for the authority documents that your policy complies with. This doesn't have to be anything fancy or complete, just a listing of the known documents and their citations. Why? Because they validate the policy. They demonstrate they are not just fluffy ideas, but necessary controls.

If you are using the Unified Compliance Framework's IT Impact Zone spreadsheets, audit guides, or policies and procedures, you'll have a full listing of all of the regulatory citations for each of the controls and you can use that list.

Consequences of non-compliance

Many policy authors add a section about the action steps that will be taken when users ignore or circumvent the policy. We feel that this is optional. However, in the absence of such information, you definitely need to ensure you have a sanctions policy; most regulations require them. See our section on "Crime and punishment: the missing policy" a little later in this chapter.

Scope

The scope always calls out *who* in the organization must abide by the policy in question. It is as simple as that.

Policy descriptions

A well written policy description will synthesize the *what* of the policy with the *who* of it as well as the *why* of it. There are two general types of policies, program-level policies and issue-specific level policies. We'll start with a simple issue-specific policy description first.

Issue specific policies need to be developed to address particular activities and sometimes particular systems. The policy revolving around documenting the website for the continuity plan is an issue-specific policy. Here's our purpose simply restated to thread the who, what, and why together.

> The systems continuity and disaster recovery team will coordinate with the website design and management team to ensure that the websites have been properly documented for configuration changes to the hardware and the software and any configurable items have been catalogued and accounted for in the continuity plan. These coordination steps are necessary to ensure proper integration with both security plans and incident management plans.

Your description for the policy can also be a "Reader's Digest" version of your procedure steps if you have already written them – which is why this part is optional. Here's our example description to give you an idea:

> While creating the documentation of the websites for the organization, the staff will ensure that the following information is being gathered and certified:
>
> • Server configuration, hardening, and security testing
> • Server configuration imaging and off site storage

- Application serial number backups and off site storage
- Program code testing to ensure that proper domain information is being supported (versus static IP addresses)
- Decisions about spare parts/duplication/replication of components
- Malicious code, patch management, anti-spyware management
- Server-level firewall and IDS decisions
- DNS and access control considerations (are these being protected by duplicating them off site?)
- Storage redundancy decisions (i.e., whether to store all data locally on RAID storage, within a Storage Area Network or across the network using iSCSI), including configuration information
- Server-level data backup/replication and storage decisions
- Server-level secondary power considerations
- Server-level cooling considerations

In addition to this documentation, the organization will ensure that proper coordination is conducted with the security team and the incident response team.

The whole point is to distill the contents of the procedure steps down into something that a manager will take the time to read and be able to understand as a policy. Which means that they should be able to read it in under 60 seconds and you shouldn't use technology words that might scare them.

Writing a program-level policy description for a grouped set of controls

Writing a program-level policy description for a grouped set of controls is slightly different, and can become much longer, than writing a statement where the policy and the control is a one-to-one relationship. The primary purpose of a program-level policy is to 1) document the organization-wide goals, 2) define the program management structure, 3) define the reporting responsibilities, and 4) clarify roles and responsibilities across a set of multiple controls.

For an example, let's look at a set of hierarchical controls from the UCF that have to do with reviewing and prioritizing each business unit's information processes (shown in the following diagram). For the sake of argument, we are going to tie all of the controls under "Communications systems considerations" (UCF ID 743) together into a single policy. And there isn't anything that we can find that says you can't do that. This means that our policy statement can't just reflect the policy for this single control. It must also state top level direction for each of the controls that fall beneath the one we chose to become our policy driver.

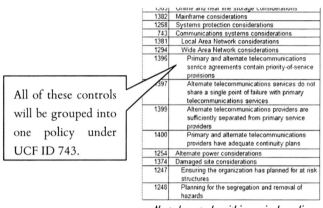

All of these controls will be grouped into one policy under UCF ID 743.

1385	Online and near line storage considerations
1382	Mainframe considerations
1268	Systems protection considerations
743	Communications systems considerations
1381	Local Area Network considerations
1294	Wide Area Network considerations
1396	Primary and alternate telecommunications service agreements contain priority-of-service provisions
1397	Alternate telecommunications services do not share a single point of failure with primary telecommunications services
1399	Alternate telecommunications providers are sufficiently separated from primary service providers
1400	Primary and alternate telecommunications providers have adequate continuity plans
1254	Alternate power considerations
1374	Damaged site considerations
1247	Ensuring the organization has planned for at risk structures
1248	Planning for the segregation and removal of hazards

Nested controls within a single policy

The grouped policy would look something like this:

Emergency procedures for critical network equipment and services will include system capacity, and cabling provider, route, and central office diversity. [UCF ID 743] This will entail additional considerations as well, including:

1. Local Area Network considerations: The organization will ensure that the continuity plan addresses considerations and contingency solutions for the local area networks that are critical to the communications infrastructure. [UCF ID 01381]

2. Wide Area Network Considerations: The organization will ensure that the continuity plan addresses considerations and contingency solutions

for the wide area networks, internet connectivity, and telecommunications services that are critical to the communications infrastructure. [UCF ID 01294]

3. Primary and alternate telecommunications service agreements contain priority-of-service provisions: The organization will ensure that both the primary and alternate telecommunications (WAN, MAN, Internet connectivity, voice) service agreements contain priority-of-service provisions in accordance with the organization's availability requirements. [UCF ID 01396]

4. etc....

The point we are trying to make here is that the policy *can* be written effectively as a one-to-one relationship between controls and policies, or just as effectively as a grouped set of controls under a single program-level policy. Of course, the grouped set of controls will have to be broken into several procedures. And we'll deal with that when we talk about procedures.

The completed policy

Web site and intranet considerations	Control ID	01380
	Effective Date	7/13/2006
	Revision Date	1/24/2007
	Revision Number	1
	Approved By	Dorian J. Cougias

1. Policy overview

The organization will ensure that the continuity plan addresses considerations and contingency solutions for websites (extranet, intranet, workflow) and coordinates those solutions with all relevant support groups.

2. Purpose

The purpose of this policy is to ensure that the websites have been properly documented for configuration changes to the hardware and the software, and any configurable items have been catalogued and accounted for in the continuity plan. The coordination steps are necessary to ensure proper integration with both security plans and incident management plans.

3. Compliance

NIST 800 34 § 5.3

Organizational SLA #187

MOU with ITCI and Schaser-Vartan Books

a. Recourse for non-compliance

Those not wishing to comply with this policy may seek employment elsewhere.

4. Scope

The organization will ensure that the continuity plan addresses considerations and contingency solutions for websites (extranet, intranet, workflow) and coordinates those solutions with all relevant support groups.

5. Policy description

During the documentation of the websites for the organization, the staff will ensure that the following information is being gathered and certified:

- Server configuration, hardening, and security testing
- Server configuration imaging and off site storage
- Application serial number backups and off site storage
- Program code testing to ensure that proper domain information is being supported (versus static IP addresses)
- Decisions about spare parts/duplication/replication of components
- Malicious code, patch management, anti-spyware management
- Server-level firewall and IDS decisions
- DNS and access control considerations (are these being protected by duplicating them off site?)
- Storage redundancy decisions (i.e., whether to store all data locally on RAIDed storage, within a Storage Area Network or across the network using iSCSI), including configuration information
- Server-level data backup/replication and storage decisions
- Server-level secondary power considerations
- Server-level cooling considerations

In addition to this documentation, the organization will ensure that proper coordination is conducted with the security team and the incident response team.

A completed policy document

Crime and punishment: the missing policy

Just as compliance requires policies, a lack of compliance requires consequences. It's basic human nature – sure the satisfaction of a job well done is a good motivator, but sometimes nothing beats a good old fashioned threat to get someone's attention. An old Army maxim that a friend of ours, General Chet Ward says, "people are motivated by head, heart, and hide – in that order." While *hide* motivation is an option, it should always be the *last* option.

It may not seem like it at first, but just as with everything else we've been discussing, the consequences to an individual of failing to comply with a policy or procedure should be spelled out in both policy terms and procedural terms.

The policy, in this case, can be pretty straightforward – failure to comply with the organization's policies and procedures will result in disciplinary action which may include demotion or dismissal. If only the implementation were so easy.

This is the point where you gather your human resources folks and lawyers together to help. Labor laws are complicated and differ greatly from state to state and country to country. There may also be unions or collective bargaining agreements in place or employment contracts that need to be considered.

In addition to knowing the possible consequences for various infractions, you'll want to document the process by which infractions are investigated, documented, evaluated and acted upon, who has the authority and responsibility for each part of the process, and how the process will be implemented. The goal is to make the process objective, repeatable and measurable. Starting to sound like your other procedures?

Of course in this case you're talking about human behavior, not changing back-up tapes, so some additional sensitivities come into play. For example, a back-up tape won't sue you if you do something wrong. Not so a disgruntled former employee. Having clearly defined expectations together with objective disciplinary processes and procedures *that are regularly followed* can help the organization fend off accusations of discrimination or worse.

Telling you what to put into a disciplinary policy is beyond the scope of this book. Besides, as with all of your other policies, it will have to be fit your organization's situation and culture. However, here are a few things to consider when talking with your HR and legal team:

- **Reporting Infractions** – Have a process for people to report infractions in some formal way. It might be a link on your intranet, an email address, a designated person (make sure there are at least two people in case one of them is the offender), or, in larger companies, a "whistle-blower hotline" (which is required by Sarbanes-Oxley and certain other regulations). Make it easy and safe for the employee - no matter what the infraction, you'd much rather hear about it from an employee than from the FBI or Attorney General's office.

- **Processing Infractions** – Someone has to take the lead in chasing down reported infractions. It could be the HR group or the legal team, but someone has to be responsible for it. Depending on the severity of the infraction, having legal involved could (if properly and carefully done) help to preserve the attorney-client with respect to any information that is uncovered in the investigation. There should be an escalation process to bring those resources to bear. Keeping the group small is also generally advisable to help prevent leaks that could either impair the investigation, compromise confidentiality or personal privacy, or simply embarrass people involved (whether guilty or not).

- **Proportionality** – In some cases, an infraction may simply be a case of someone doing his or her job poorly but the consequences to the organization are slight. The normal employee review process might be sufficient to record and handle the poor performance in the ordinary course. In other cases, the infraction could place the entire organization (or, in extreme cases, people's lives) in jeopardy and might appropriately be dealt with by summarily terminating the guilty party. Legal action or criminal prosecution could also result from extreme cases. In any case, the punishment should fit the crime and repeat offenders may certainly be subject to harsher penalties than first time offenders. It may also be appropriate to adopt a "zero-tolerance" policy for certain things – particularly those involving health and safety – but if you choose to go that route, be prepared to fire your best friend or first cousin if he's the one that crosses that particular line.

- **Documentation** – Again, talk to legal counsel about how best to document adherence with the disciplinary process, but as a general matter, you'll need to collect evidence of the infraction and demonstrate that you're following defined protocols.

⚡ **Create a Culture of Enforcement** – People need to know that enforcement and disciplinary action is taken seriously and is administered regularly. There is case law on the books that indicates that a failure to enforce a policy may make that policy unenforceable. Selective enforcement opens the door to allegations of favoritism, discrimination, harassment, or worse. The trick, however, is to make it known that enforcement is taking place without 1) making the workplace seem like a police state or 2) unduly embarrassing or violating the privacy of those that are being disciplined.

Documenting your procedures

If you are migrating from the previous maturity level, you have already done most of the work in creating a formal procedure. Because a procedure is nothing more than a formalized version of the process documentation that you've already been working on. The purpose of a procedure document is to institutionalize and formalize the processes that your staff have been using. The objective is to have everyone use the same tools and techniques and follow the same repeatable steps so that you can quantify how well the procedure is working and train future staff members who might not currently know the routine. Ensuring consistency is a critical component for ensuring security. We'll start where the policy document left off and continue from there.

Scope

The scope of the procedure covers the *who* and *what* is being affected by it. The scope is broken down into coverage, assignment, required knowledge, and required tools.

Coverage

Which system(s), network(s), application(s), and personnel does this control apply to? This should identify all of the people and IT assets that are affected by the procedure. Our example shows how to list both assets and personnel inside the organization and outside:

> This procedure covers all web servers (both hardware and software), their storage devices, interconnected systems, and in a tertiary fashion, the supporting systems for security, access control, and domain authentication. This also includes all web server administrators, any applicable database administrators, related security staff, and related incident management staff. If the web servers have interconnected systems outside of the organization, this also covers those systems and their administrators to the extent necessary for proper coordination.

Assignment

Assignment is more in-depth than just coverage. Assignment should be documented according to the RACI model. For every major step in your procedure, you'll want to include a line item in the RACI assignment chart ensuring that *one* person is designated as having the authority for the step and *one* person is designated as having the responsibility for the step. If you have more than one person who is assigned the authority or the responsibility, both will shuck their duties and finger point at each other when a problem occurs.

R = Responsible A = Accountable C = Consulted I = Informed	Server Admin	Code Mgr	DBA	IT Security	CIRT	LOB Mgr	Client Contact	DR Mgr	IT Director
Document server hardware and software configurations	R		C			C	C		A
Document configuration imaging management	C		C					R	A
Document application serial number backups	C							R	A
Document records backup procedures	C		C					R	A
Document spare part & storage redundancy decisions	C							R	A
Document system hardening configurations	C			R					A
Document system security configurations	C			R					A
Test application programming techniques for security and access control		R		C				I	A
Document access control (including domain issues) configurations	C			R				I	A
Document system cooling and secondary power configurations	R								A
Document system configurations with incident management	C				R				A

RACI assignment chart

You can have the *same* person assigned to both responsibility *and* authority. And you can have multiple people consulted and informed for each step.

Required knowledge

What information does the person(s) carrying out this control need to know? Is there any training or certification that the person(s) should go through before performing this control?

With regards to our example, documenting the website's configuration (and checking that of the supporting systems) means that the person should be trained and knowledgeable in systems hardening configuration and the system's setup – especially any peculiar storage and RAID arrays. In order to test the website's programming and coding, the staff should be familiar with those methods and tools. In order to test for and integrate with the security strategies, the person should be familiar with those tools and methods. The same can be said for the incident team's integration.

Very much like creating a RACI chart for your team's assignments, you'll want to use the same team member listing across the top of the required knowledge table and then list the skills necessary in the left column, indicating which team members need to have a proficiency of knowledge.

	Server Admin	Code Mgr	DBA	IT Security	CIRT	LOB Mgr	Client Contact	DR Mgr	IT Director
Use of organizational system documentation template	X	X	X	X	X	X		X	X
Use of imaging software								X	
Use of records backup software								X	
Database Management system			X						
Storage management hardware and software	X		X						
Knowledge of system hardening methodology	X			X					X
Application code review skills		X							
Domain Naming schema for the organization	X	X	X	X	X			X	X
System security plans	X			X	X				X
Incident management procedures	X				X				X
Systems Continuity planning and documentation	X							X	X

Team knowledge chart

Required tools

As with the knowledge table, you'll be creating a tools table. List the necessary tools down the left side of the table and then list each of the individuals or roles that will have to have access to the tools in order to complete the assigned procedure.

	Server Admin	Code Mgr	DBA	IT Security	CIRT	LOB Mgr	Client Contact	DR Mgr	IT Director
Imaging software								X	
Records backup software								X	
Configuration management software	X		X						
Application code review tools		X							

Team tools chart

Extended definition

The extended definition should provide the reader more information by providing them the goals, triggers, and other cues regarding the procedure.

Procedure goals

Think of the goals for the procedure as a cross between the policy statement and the policy description. It should be more in-depth than the policy statement and should create an overall summary of the policy description.

When you initially created the process that this procedure is documenting, you analyzed the "what and why" of the process. You can use what you documented in that step to write down your procedure goals. For our example, we wrote:

The goal of this procedure is to ensure that all aspects of the organization's websites (intranet, extranet, and workflow) have been accounted for regarding systems continuity and restoration. In order to accomplish this goal, the objectives are to document each website's hardware and software configuration fully, and to share that configuration with the computer incident response team (CIRT) and security teams. Sharing the configuration with those teams will ensure proper coordination between the continuity team, CIRT, and security. An additional objective is to analyze the website application programming to ensure that static IP addresses are *not* being used and that proper domain naming rules are adhered to in the case that the website has to be moved to a different facility and different IP range.

Supporting and supported procedures

From your earlier research you'll want to list the procedures that this one supports. You'll also want to list any procedures that support this one. For our example, because we are using the Unified Compliance Framework control IDs, that's what we listed:

This objective supports UCF Control ID 735: Systems continuity plan strategies.

Procedure triggers

Procedure triggers indicate when the procedure must be run. At minimum, most procedures should be run yearly just to test them if nothing else. During the creation of your process, you should have documented when the procedures should be triggered and if an exception to that timing can be made, who has the authority to trigger the process and why.

When documenting your process triggers, it is best to list each trigger on its own line as we've done in our example that follows:

This procedure will be conducted when:

new web servers are added to the network,

new websites are added to existing web servers,

any website undergoes a major code change,

any web server changes configurations,

or annually if no major changes take place on either the web servers or websites.

Potential mishaps & reaction steps

When documenting potential mishaps and the correct reaction steps, you'll want to use a simple three-column approach to documenting the *symptom*, any *possible causes*, and the *solution*. In the example that follows, we show two process steps and their potential mishaps and reaction steps.

Analyze website hardware & software configurations		
Symptom	Possible Cause	Solution
Can't access configuration programs	Invalid AD rights	Check with AD admin for proper rights and account information
	Are you using the right software?	Check the prior configuration documentation for the configuration application's version number and compare that to the one you are using.
		If incorrect, re-install the configuration management application from the application library.
	Have you checked the password?	If you are having password problems, call the AD admin and have the password reset.
Analyze website application programming		
Symptom	Possible Cause	Solution
The server's software is live and in production	The test load data set is not set to live	Call the DB Admin and have the test load data set brought to "on line" status for testing.

Documenting potential mishaps and reaction steps

Successful execution

During your procedure analysis your team gathered together and documented what they believed success was. You then passed that information through the person **responsible** for the procedure and the person who **authorizes** the procedure. You'll want to record that collective definition of success here. As with the procedure triggers, the best way to document this is as a list of items as we show in our example that follows:

This procedure has concluded successfully when:

the web server's hardware and software configurations have been documented, including all storage, network access, and security configurations,

each website's application code and programming has been reviewed for security and DNS violations and any violations have been documented and corrected (with the corrections also documented),

each system's backup and imaging plans have been documented as a part of the configuration documentation, and

the configurations have been coordinated with the organization's security staff and CIRT teams and all parties agree that the configurations have been accounted for completely.

Reports

The job isn't finished until the paperwork is done. Everyone knows that. Whatever method of reporting you are using to describe what "complete and successful" means should be documented here. In our example, we are using a combination of Sharepoint's notification feature and e-mail as a reporting mechanism.

When finished, all configuration documents will be checked into the Continuity Plan Sharepoint site. Notification of document updates will be sent out automatically by the site.

A final "procedure completed" e-mail will be sent to the procedure authorizer.

Procedure steps

The easiest way to document procedure steps is through a simple outline format of each of the steps and sub-steps. If the procedure has anything to do with using software, you might want to include screenshots. If using hardware, you might want to employ the use of digital pictures. Remember that a picture *is* worth a thousand words and that many people respond better when looking at a visual than when just reading text.

During the process creation phase, you more than likely created some type of flow chart to document the process. Should you use the flowchart *and* provide a textual reference? It depends upon how complicated the procedure is. In our example, most of the procedure has to do with filling out system documentation forms for hardware and software configuration. That process of filling out the forms wouldn't benefit from the flowchart, but others would.

For database, e-mail, file sharing, workflow, and any other serve type that requires specific data to be transferred back before it can be usable – have you tested the data restoration process? Is the data complete and usable? You'll want to check Worksheet 2.3a (the description of documents) to ensure that it is complete and up to date.

Dept: Department Name		System Name	
Description of Documents, Templates, & Fonts		Worksheet 2.3a	
	Name and purpose of documents, templates, & fonts	UNC directory & file path	Directory Owner
1	SOW template	Sharepoint ClientNameID ClientProjID ProjectMgmt	Heiberger
2	Plan template	Sharepoint ClientNameID ClientProjID ProjectMgmt	Heiberger
3	Project template	Sharepoint ClientNameID ClientProjID ProjectDocs	Cougias
4	Clipart library	Sharepoint Clipart	Kasten
5	Project layout, project files, project artwork	Sharepoint ClientNameID ClientProjID Layouts	Kasten
6	Project layout client final PDF	Sharepoint ClientNameID ClientProjID Finals	Kasten

Worksheet 2.3a

You'll then want to compare that to Worksheet CP 3 and ensure that you are backing up the right data, and that you have correct procedures for restoring that data.

Dept: Department Name		System Name					
Key documents and work in progress backup and restoration plan		Worksheet CP 3					
			A	B	C	D	E	F

Documenting the procedure steps

There are certain types of procedure steps that do not lend themselves well to writing in this simple format. These include procedure steps that involve *several* people that have to share responsibility for completing the procedure (wherein you should use the playscript format), and complex logic or troubleshooting steps (which should use the troubleshooting table format).

Procedure checklists

The procedure checklists are there for your use to provide your staff with clues about what should be on hand before beginning the procedure. If there are certain tools that need to be used, or people to be notified, you'll want to list those items of importance in the checklist.

❑ Ensure that you have the network names of all web servers and the LANsurveyor map of the network.

❑ Ensure that you know the proper sign-on authentication for each server.

❑ Check out the web server's system documentation workbook from the Sharepoint server.

❑ Notify security, the CIRT, the server's DBA and administrator, and programmer that you are going to be conducting this procedure.

Detailed revision history

There are myriad ways to track a procedure's documentation history. Most manual methods are greatly ignored, or the changes that are listed are meaningless in their brevity. But, all is not lost.

Microsoft Word has a nifty little feature called *version tracking* that you can turn on when you are editing your procedures. We suggest that you turn it on and allow *it* to create a very detailed listing of all changes that are being made in the document. You can even save a change report and have that attached to the document.

And most database-centric policy and procedure documentation systems provide the same type of version history and change tracking methodologies.

So don't waste your time with those all-too-short change fields that most people ignore. Let software do what it does – automatically track and report things.

The policy and procedure review and approval process

Writing policies and procedures is one thing. Reviewing, editing, and approving them is something quite different. The writing process is normally collaborative. The review and approval process is often political. There isn't an organization that we've worked with in the past that hasn't utilized multiple reviewers for the policy approval process. If handled badly this political contention can delay policy implementation by months, years, or result in no policy at all. The point that we're trying to make here is that there are two types of teams that can come together to review your policies and procedures; cross-functional teams and high-performing teams.

Cross-functional teams are organizational groups made up of team members from different functions across the organization that report to a single leader and that may or may not have to *work together* to meet the group's goals. In other words, a cross-functional team might just be a group of people who have to meet periodically to approve your policies and procedures – but who aren't integrated into a team structure.

On the other hand, while a high-performing team is also made up of members from different functions across the organization, these people have committed themselves to interacting with each other to achieve a common objective. In other words, the high-performing team *wants* to interact, share common performance goals, and a common approach to solving the problem for which they hold *themselves* collectively accountable.

The difference between a high-performance team and a cross-functional team is that a high-performance king can outperform an individual. High-performance teams don't *just happen*. Here are some tips to make the job of creating and managing high-performance teams less painful.

Policy and procedure politics and the review process

Chances are you are going to need to assign at least a couple of people to review each of your policies and procedures. Picking your team, deciding how you are going to communicate within the team, and overcoming political problems are the three biggest issues you'll face during the team review process.

Guidelines for working together

Your policy, standard, and procedure editorial review team is going to be made up of various members and a few roles. Here are the key team roles and their duties, along with rules for working together.

Team Leader	forms the team
	guides without dominating
	understands the overall process
	provides whatever support is necessary
Meeting Facilitator	schedules and conducts the team meetings
	serves as a meeting resource person
	ensures full participation of all members
Subject Matter Experts	focus their energy on their assigned tasks
	listen to, and interact, with other SMEs
	edit policies and procedures accordingly
Document Manager	manages the overall editing process
	tracks all changes and final documents
	maintains logs as necessary

When putting your teams together, you will want to have Subject Matter Experts (SMEs) for each area of policy, standard, and procedure that you are dealing with (i.e., one for disaster recovery, one for security, one for privacy, etc.) as well as an SME who focuses on *the written word* (meaning the grammar, legalese, etc.).

How do you find your team members? That isn't an easy one to answer. You will want to recruit people who can work together as your primary goal. Therefore, look for folks with common sense and basic good behavior. The next trait you'll want to look for is whether they have problem-solving and decision-making skills. There are plenty of really bright people in many organizations who couldn't make a decision to save their life. You don't want them on your team because your team will have a limited amount of time to *make decisions* about the validity of the documents they are reviewing. Therefore, you are going to want to find people who have both the content knowledge *and* feel they have a stake in making a decision that creates a positive outcome. And the last point about your recruits is that they should understand *process,* because that's what this type of team is about.

There are five basic rules for working together. In short, the list can be summed up as "compartmentalize your editing and communicate your standards."

1. **Utilize the right people in the right roles.** Subject matter experts should only be allowed to verify, validate, or correct the substantive matter. Writers, editors, and proofers should be the ones to correct the written communication style.

2. **Be specific about what each person's role is.** The best way to ensure that you are asking for detailed, constructive feedback in a specific area is to give each reviewer their own form that fits what *they* are critiquing. In other words, give the substantive reviewer a checklist form regarding process flow, diagrams, and methods. And exclude questions about jargon, punctuation, and grammar.

3. **Request the process changes to the policy or procedure be in writing.** Any process changes should be documented. If the process change is in regards to the flow chart, a hand-written change should suffice. If the process change is in-depth, then the changes should be documented electronically in the change request form that you provide the reviewer.

4. **Use the same stylesheet and glossary.** To ensure that everyone is on the same page, your organization should develop a stylesheet for writing. The same goes for a glossary of terms. Yes, I know that I said not to use jargon. But jargon and specific terms are different. If you don't have a working organizational glossary, you should start with the one that we've created23.

---

23   http://www.glossarybook.com

5. **Agree on a markup methodology for grammar, punctuation, etc.** There is nothing worse than receiving a 20 page in-depth process manual marked up by a slew of red slashes that are not differentiated. If you are going to utilize editors who want to create distinct marks, then there should be a standardized markup dictionary that everyone shares. An outstanding example of an editorial markup stylesheet follows, and many of them are online24, such as this one.

Instruction	Editing Marks (in the line only)	Proofreading Marks (in the line and in the margin)	
delete	Boulder campus events	Boulder/campus events	↗
delete and close up	Boulder campus events	Boulder campus events	ℨ
replace	~~Boulder~~ campus events (Denver)	~~Boulder~~ campus events	Denver
insert	Boulder events (campus)	Boulder events	campus
insert and close up	Bould campus events	Bould campus events	r
transpose	Boulder events campus	Boulder events campus	TR

Markup stylesheet from the University of Colorado

Pick the team decision style and your leadership style

There are four basic team decision-making styles and four basic team leader styles (that will work) for this type of team. You'll need to pick the styles that compliment each other and match your team's personality.

Leader decides with input: is the fastest method to arrive at a decision and the one *least* likely to enjoy team support. This can only be pulled off if everyone on the team believes that the leader is a better subject matter expert than they are.

Small group of experts decides: is an extension of the leader decides style, with the bulk of the trust in several key subject matter experts. This works well

---

24   http://www.colorado.edu/Publications/styleguide/symbols.html

for certain specialty policies and procedures such as disaster recovery or privacy *if* the group considers the subject matter experts truly experts in their field.

Majority decides: is the greater than 50% vote methodology that is naturally going to leave the losing voters in a distasteful state. While this is a commonly accepted decision making process, it does tend to irk off the losing group – especially the closer the vote gets to being almost 50-50.

Consensus decides: is the hardest to pull off and the one that is guaranteed to prove to have the best long-term results. No, this does *not* mean that every member will agree upon the final decision. What it does mean is that even though some members will not agree, they will agree to *live with* and *follow* the decision.

Once your team has made their decision about how to decide, you as a leader will have to adjust your leadership tactics accordingly. Remember that there are really only four leadership styles that will work with the decision making styles and team personality within a policy, standard, and procedure review and approval team.

Leader as model: sets the leader up to shape the behavior and performance of the team to reflect the leader's style and expectations. This really only works if the team has put the decision authority in the leader.

Leader as initiator: puts the leader into the role of setting in motion the processes needed for policy, standard, and procedure review as well as developing the team's performance and capabilities. This works particularly well when the team has chosen the small groups of experts as their decision makers, as the team leader can begin the process and then step aside to let the experts run the show.

Leader as coach: works with most models of decision making because the leader serves as a counselor and teacher, drawing the best out of the team members. This style of leadership *won't* work where the small group of experts believes they are better subject matter experts than anyone – they will see the leader as demeaning if this style of leadership is attempted.

Leader as negotiator: works well for both small group decision and consensus decision making groups. Undoubtedly the members of the team are going to have different viewpoints and methodologies for interacting and making decisions. Recognizing which differences are productive and which aren't, the team leader can draw out the qualities of the members and quiet as necessary the difficult ones. This, by the way, is the hardest leadership style to learn well, and coupled with decision by consensus will form *the hardest* team styles, but the most productive as well.

Planning for productivity

The first step in planning for your team's productivity is to understand the team's purpose and methodology when they gather together (even if some of the members are "gathering" virtually). Every member of the team should understand how the team will handle the "big five" questions for productivity.

1. **Which policies and procedures are going to be discussed?** You'll want to ensure that the review process *only* examines those policies and procedures that are up for critique, and doesn't bleed into an examination of everything ever written. *Prevent scope creep.*

2. **How much time should be allotted?** Based upon the allotment needed to conduct the meeting and then the walk-throughs of each policy, standard, and procedure, are there any staff that will be constrained by this timeframe? *Establish realistic timeframes.*

3. **What types of questions will be asked?** Will you have the correct documents and supporting material to answer their questions? Have you invited the right people to answer the questions? And are you allotting enough time for the meeting and the questions that are going to arise (if not, change point 2 and re-think)? *Plan thoughtful questions.*

4. **What level of controversy are these policies and procedures going to create in the meeting?** Will the controversy be presented as oppositional *feelings* or oppositional *fact?* What are the objections, complaints, and complaint tactics going to be like? *Anticipate turf wars.*

5. **For every oppositional complaint raised in the preceding point, how do you plan to work with the complainer to resolve the issue?** If you don't have

a plan to resolve the issue, don't call the meeting, because you won't get your policies and procedures approved (if there's enough controversy, they might not even be tested). *Plan to be a diplomat.*

Policy and procedure validation process

As stated above, when giving your policies and procedures to your subject matter experts to review, you'll want to be specific about what you are looking for and how they should provide the necessary feedback to make the changes in the policy or procedures. Here's a list of questions you are going to ask your subject matter experts:

1. **Does the policy or procedure link directly** to a control as *defined in* your *control* framework list? Somehow, somewhere, you should be able to find out *the* authority behind your policies and procedures. Because the organization should have already formalized the control list and framework (which can be accomplished using the UCF matrices), you should be able to link the document being reviewed to one (or several) controls in the list. If not, you'll want to know where the authority for this policy or procedure comes from, and why that authority isn't documented in the control framework.

2. **Is this a policy or a procedure? If the document states who, what, and** why it is a policy document. If the document begins *to* state *how,* it has moved into being a procedure. If your organization plans to separate your policies from your procedures, then you'll want to annotate when to cut off your policy from your procedure. If you are okay with running policies and procedures together in the same document, then that's fine too – as long as the document itself separates the policy material from the procedural material.

3. Is the policy or procedure valid – in other words, can it be accomplished? This means that the policy, standard, and procedure should be *both* understandable *and* usable. In order to answer both of these questions, you are asking the reviewer to validate whether the reader can follow the steps in sequence to the conclusion of the procedure. A second question you might want to ask is whether or not the reader can take immediate action, or if further reading (manuals, tech notes, etc.) might be necessary. If further reading is necessary, that should be noted and the material that is referenced should be added to the procedure.

4. **Does the final policy and/or procedure compare equally to the original draft and annotated change notes?** You know that the process documents (flow charts, tables, notes) are correct or have been annotated for changes. Does the final written policy, standard, and procedure accurately reflect these original source documents? If anything additional was added or material was subtracted in the final document, this should be noted.

5. **Does the math work?** Run through any numbers, calculations, formulas, and other statistical data and ensure their correctness.

6. **Are there any additional mishaps that should be considered?** Often when conducting a final procedure review, the subject matter expert will come across several more potential mishaps that should be noted. The reviewer should not only note the potential mishaps, but also their solutions.

7. **Does the procedure come to a different conclusion or "success" point than documented?** There have been times when we've checked procedures only to have them conclude at a different point than originally documented. If this is the case, the final step should be documented and the two versions of "success" should be investigated.

8. **Does the procedure require the reader to exercise discretion or good judgment?** If so, what information and resources does the reader need to have in order to implement that judgment? Does the reader have the education and experience necessary to understand the issues when exerting judgment? Can you, as the editor, discern the standards upon which the judgments are to be made? What are the limits and boundaries set for the judgment, and does the reader know that he or she will be held accountable for the judgment and actions taken?

Editorial validation process

When critiquing the policies and procedures in an editorial context, there are seven points to look out for. You should pay special attention to item three — assessing the format for correct usage.

1. **Graphics usage** should be appropriate and not misleading. If the graphics are too large or too small, or don't support the documentation, they should be changed or removed.

2. **Consistency** should be checked for the writing style, numbering, list usage, terminology, use of formats across multiple procedures, etc.

3. **Use of formats** (narrative, outline, flowchart, FAQ, etc.) should be checked to ensure that they are being properly used.

Narrative	Is the procedure written in short groupings of information?
Outline	Is the numbering system consistent?
	Can you identify the main categories?
	Are there too many levels?
	Is the flow and sequence ordered correctly?
Playscript/RACI chart	Does the procedure involve at least two sets of readers?
	Does each step contain an action to be carried out?
	Are the assignments according to title versus named individuals?
Flow chart	Are non-standard symbols defined somewhere?
	Are the symbol uses consistent?
	Can the type in the symbols be read easily?
	Are long flowcharts broken down into several smaller ones?
FAQ	Are the questions relevant?
	Do the answers fit the questions?
	Are the answers accurate and concise?
Symptom, cause, solution	Do the symptoms relate to the causes?
	Do the causes relate to the solutions?
	Are all of the pertinent pieces of information included?

4. **Language and grammar usage** need to be checked for subject and verb agreement, phrases and clauses, and tense (i.e., not using past tense).

5. **Vocabulary** needs to be checked for sexist language, clichés, regional colloquialisms, and an abnormal use of technical terms.

6. **Punctuation** needs to be reviewed for the use of hyphens, commas, colons, and semicolons.

7. **Reading level** needs to be checked. There are about nine different ways to calculate reading levels, so the best thing to do is either to utilize a reading level calculating tool or to use the simple calculator provided here.

A. Count the number of steps in the whole procedure.

⚡ Count the number of action verbs in the whole procedure.

⚡ Divide the action verbs by the steps.

⚡ If the result is 2.0 or greater, then there are too many actions per step, and the steps should be broken down further.

Change review forms

The best way to document your validity checks and your editorial checks is through a form format as shown in the diagrams that follow. These forms, and all others in this book, are available online at the unifiedcompliance.com website.

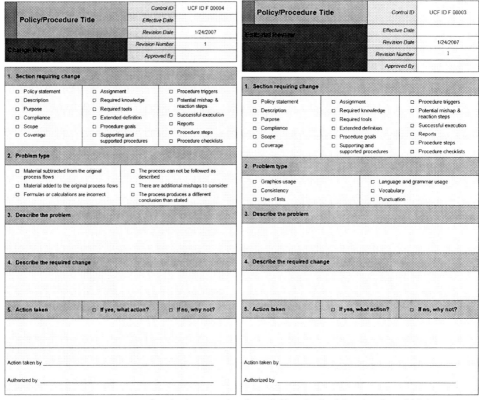

Sample change review form (left) and editorial review form (right)

Providing the necessary resources

You've created your policy statement.

You've documented your procedures.

You've edited your policies and procedures.

Now is the time to provide the necessary resources for your staff to do their job. That means that you need to not only provide them the tools that were identified in the procedures but also the *time* to get the job done.

The realities of tool selection and budgeting

Just because your procedures call for certain tools doesn't mean that the tool fairy is going to drop them off to you. In reality there's this thing called a budget and some person who is responsible for this budget. The person's type who gets selected to be the budget director is the type to say "not a chance in Hades" to most every request. Even for a paperclip.

Welcome to cost-benefit analysis 101. Here's a spreadsheet that works *some* of the time. The concept is to correlate the cost of non-compliance with the cost of manually running the procedure and the cost of using the tool to run it.

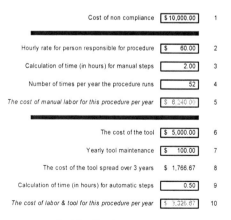

Tool justification spreadsheet

1. The first cost is the cost of non-compliance. This can be provided by your auditors, your budget person, or your bookie as far as we are concerned. They will often give you a range. Choose the upper range number. *Always* display this number in red in hopes of getting a rise out of the reader.

2. The second line is the hourly rate for the person or a generalized rate for the people that must run the procedure. We aren't going to get into a "loaded vs. non-loaded" number[25] here.

3. The third line is the calculation in hours that it takes to run the procedure using manual steps.

4. It will be important to note how many times per year the procedure is actually run. We used the calculation for running the procedure once a week.

5. This is a calculation that equals (line 2 ★ line 3)★ line 4. Notice that the line is green. We used the Excel conditional formatting to denote any number *less* than the cost of non-compliance. This shows that even though the procedure costs the company a good deal of money, it is cheaper to run the procedure than to be fined.

6. The cost of the tool should be added here.

7. The tool's yearly maintenance costs should be added here.

8. This is a calculation of spreading the tool's cost over three years and then adding the yearly maintenance fees to give you the cost of the tool *for one year*.

9. This should be the estimated time it will take to run the procedure when using the tool you want to purchase. Note here folks – if you can't show a time savings, your argument is lost.

10. The cost of the tool for one year, plus the labor cost for that year is calculated here (the same as line five, but with the addition of the tool's cost). Again, as with the earlier calculation, we used Excel's conditional formatting to show green if the cost of the tool is less expensive than the cost of the manual operation.

---

25   This means adding their overhead, insurance, taxes, etc. Not necessary for this argument.

Don't think that just because you submit a spreadsheet that shows a reduction in cost that the budget wonks are going to approve doing the right thing. They just might come back and say that they are cash poor and people heavy. And that as long as the cost of manually running the procedure is less than the cost of non-compliance, often the budget wonks are happy.

At least you will have made your documented argument and begun a method of quantification for your procedures.

Assigning responsibility and training the staff

Its one thing to have a person's role or name on a RACI chart and something completely different to ensure that their responsibilities are denoted in their job description.

You'll need to update the job descriptions for every role and every person who has been denoted in the procedures responsibilities matrix. Will there be gnashing of teeth and requests for raises when this happens? You betcha. Will raises be forthcoming? About as soon as Bill Gates becomes a Mac user. Therefore, let's turn to training the staff.

I'm not going to pull any punches – initial training at this point is going to be more ad hoc than formalized. Think about it – you *just* finished formalizing the policies and procedures that you were working on. There's no way that you can formalize training too.

Given your new policies and procedures, training at this point is going to look more like "show, coach, repeat, reinforce." Don't worry, you'll have plenty of time to build up the training curriculum.

Monitoring and controlling the process

How you plan to monitor adherence and disobedience? That is the point at which most organizations fail very quickly.

Too often we see "policy prognostications emanating from on high," our BS term for the BS that is coming out of some executive's office. It makes us cranky because we *know* that the leadership of the organization is only rattling sabers and making noise with absolutely no intention of following-through – because we see no indication of monitoring and control. If you don't intend to monitor and control your policies and procedures, then you might as well not bother to create them in the first place.

Monitoring your efforts

Each policy and each procedure will require different monitoring techniques.

In our example that we've been alluding to throughout this work, the website's configuration information needs to be assessed every time a configuration item is changed or at least yearly. Because the procedure calls for the review of the system's configuration documentation, the documentation can be placed on a Sharepoint server and configured so that when the documentation was checked out and then checked back in, both the check-out and the check-in will be logged (as well as any changes to the document). Updates of the log can then be passed along to all concerned.

The best practice technique for monitoring is to include a "success report" at the end of each procedure. By creating a procedure-ending report, monitoring can be built into every written procedure.

Controlling your efforts

Controlling your procedures is a management and director level effort. At this point it involves the review of each procedure's success report. As your organization matures in procedure management, it will involve a deeper level of analysis.

FROM DEFINED (3) TO MANAGED (4)

At this step existing practices have been formalized into policies that have been documented and communicated. Procedures that carry out these policies have been standardized, documented, communicated, and key staff trained.

Management is formal and structured in its communication of their understanding of the need to act.

The policies, procedures, and processes are defined and documented for all key activities. Usage of good practices has emerged.

A plan has been defined for the use and standardization of process automating tools. However, they may not be integrated with each other.

Skill requirements are defined and documented for all areas. A formal training plan has been developed, but the actual training that takes place is based upon individual initiative.

Process owners have been identified with process accountability and responsibility defined and documented. However, process owners are unlikely to have full authority to exercise their initiatives.

Tolerances of change for metrics are being established. However, more than likely there is no continuous monitoring and measurement that the processes are being followed according to procedure.

Therefore, your goals are fivefold:

1. Ensure the *full* dissemination of defined policies and procedures

2. Begin the standardization process

3. Begin the configuration management process

4. Add change management to your processes

5. Collect procedure improvement information for better metrics

Ensuring full dissemination of defined policies and procedures

Before we talk about *how* you should disseminate your training plan, we want to stop for a minute and fill you with dread by telling you *why* you *must* disseminate your policies, standards, and procedures and train your staff accordingly – not just once, but on a regular and ongoing basis. While the rules that we are going to cite are United States centric, the rules have similar counterparts in most every country we've done research on (space won't permit a full comparison here).

The *why*

Plain and simple, the communication of policies, standards, and procedures has a significant impact on legal case decisions. References to training and communications in past judgments seem to have been significant in determining fines and penalties.[26] Especially when it is now included as a consideration within the U.S. Federal Sentencing Guidelines[27], which we'll cite here.

Page 102

(1) The organization must have established compliance standards and procedures to be followed by its employees and other agents that are reasonably capable of reducing the prospect of criminal conduct.

---

[26] There is also substantial case law indicating that failure to enforce a policy is as bad, and possibly worse, than having no policy at all. The argument seems self-evident: the existence of the policy demonstrates that you know what "should" be done, while the failure to enforce it demonstrates that you willfully did the wrong thing anyway. Tell that to a jury and see how much sympathy you get!

[27] http://www.ussc.gov/2006guid/APPC2006.pdf

(2) Specific individual(s) within high-level personnel of the organization must have been assigned overall responsibility to oversee compliance with such standards and procedures.

(3) The organization must have used due care not to delegate substantial discretionary authority to individuals whom the organization knew, or should have known through the exercise of due diligence, had a propensity to engage in illegal activities.

(4) The organization must have taken steps to communicate effectively its standards and procedures to all employees and other agents, e.g., by requiring participation in training programs or by disseminating publications that explain in a practical manner what is required.

(5) The organization must have taken reasonable steps to achieve compliance with its standards, e.g., by utilizing monitoring and auditing systems reasonably designed to detect criminal conduct by its employees and other agents and by having in place and publicizing a reporting system whereby employees and other agents could report criminal conduct by others within the organization without fear of retribution.

(6) The standards must have been consistently enforced through appropriate disciplinary mechanisms, including, as appropriate, discipline of individuals responsible for the failure to detect an offense. Adequate discipline of individuals responsible for an offense is a necessary component of enforcement; however, the form of discipline that will be appropriate will be case specific.

(7) After an offense has been detected, the organization must have taken all reasonable steps to respond appropriately to the offense and to prevent further similar offenses -- including any necessary modifications to its program to prevent and detect violations of law.

Page 105

(4) (A) The organization shall take reasonable steps to communicate periodically and in a practical manner its standards and procedures, and other aspects of the compliance and ethics program, to the individuals referred to in subdivision (B)

[below] by conducting effective training programs and otherwise disseminating information appropriate to such individuals' respective roles and responsibilities.

(B) The individuals referred to in subdivision (A) are the members of the governing authority, high-level personnel, substantial authority personnel, the organization's employees, and, as appropriate, the organization's agents.

Page 107

Examples of the informality and use of fewer resources with which a small organization may meet the requirements of this guideline include the following: (I) the governing authority's discharge of its responsibility for oversight of the compliance and ethics program by directly managing the organization's compliance and ethics efforts; (II) training employees through informal staff meetings, and monitoring through regular 'walk-arounds' or continuous observation while managing the organization; (III) using available personnel, rather than employing separate staff, to carry out the compliance and ethics program; and (IV) modeling its own compliance and ethics program on existing, well-regarded compliance and ethics programs and best practices of other similar organizations.

Page 116

Fourth, § 8B2.1(b)(4) makes compliance and ethics training a requirement, and specifically extends the training requirement to the upper levels of an organization, including the governing authority and high-level personnel, in addition to all of the organization's employees and agents, as appropriate. Furthermore, subsection (b)(4) establishes that this communication and training obligation is ongoing, requiring "periodic" updates.

The *how*

There are many methods for distributing and disseminating your policies and procedures – the list we set forth below is not exhaustive. Because the culture and practices of each organization are different, there is no one "best" method of dissemination – the "best" method is the one that works for you. Often a combination of methods is the most effective choice for a given organization. It is also important to note that one of the first two methods described below – the printed book or the policy and procedure website – is almost required as a method for maintaining a complete set of policies for reference and, in both cases, changes to policies should be systematically archived to show the evolution of the policies and to make it possible to determine what version of a policy was in effect at any given time.

Delivery method		Best practice usage
Policy and procedure printed book	*Usage*	For day-to-day, hands on usage by the staff that must perform the procedures associated with the policies. The "book" should be a binder for policies and procedures so that when either a policy or procedure changes, the changed document can be swapped for the older version.
	Strengths	Printed documents are easy to read and can be annotated by staff.
	Weaknesses	Older versions of policies and procedures can be intermingled with newer versions. Updating the binder can be time consuming and expensive. Relying on individual employees to update their own binder can lead to errors. Difficult to customize for different groups of employees that may be subject to different policies.
Policy and procedure website	*Usage*	For day-to-day hands on usage and reference for all staff.
	Strengths	As changes to documents take place, replacement of older documents is automatic. If posting changes on a document server, updates (or notifications of update) can be sent through e-mail to anyone affected by the change. Documents can be indexed and searched, turning them into reference material as well as procedures.
	Weaknesses	If not printed out, the documents are not portable, and therefore a secondary posting site or other method should be considered for continuity planning and for ready reference if access to the website is not available.
Organizational newsletters, BBS or e-mail lists, and brochures	*Usage*	Announcing new policies and procedures and creating executive summaries.

Delivery method		Best practice usage
	Strengths	Covers anyone who reads the organizational newsletter, communicates on the bulletin board, or reads the brochures and might bring to light the need to include others in the dissemination of the policies and procedures who might not have been on the list. Regular dissemination of policy and procedure information reinforces the need to follow policies and may promote a "culture of compliance" within the organization.
	Weaknesses	Doesn't guarantee that people reading the summary of the policies and procedures will read the actual policies and procedures and important nuances in the policies may be missed.
Team meetings in person, through conference calls, and web casting	*Usage*	Teams can be brought together and the policies and procedures communicated to the team en mass.
	Strengths	For all delivery methods except conference calls, visuals can be presented along with the audio delivery of the information, making the presentation of the policies and procedures much stronger.
		When presenting the information in a team surrounding, support from the team that created the policies and procedures can be voiced, giving them more strength than if communicated in writing.
		Questions about the policies and procedures can be asked and answered.
		The meeting, if a webcast with video and audio, can be recorded for those in the team that could not attend.
	Weaknesses	Difficult to enforce attendance by all team members. If you aren't planning on recording the event, bringing a large team together can be a painstaking task of hit and miss coordination. Even if recorded, it can be difficult to ensure that team members that missed the event actually review the recorded proceedings. In person meetings can also be costly, particularly in geographically diverse organizations.
CD, DVD, or Flash-ROM distribution	*Usage*	Policies and procedures are collected together, along with any self-paced training, and distributed to members of the organization.
	Strengths	Multimedia presentations are always the strongest method of delivery.
		A great many policies and procedures can be distributed easily.
		Policies are made portable for easy reference.
		Learning Management Systems (LMS) can log and track each individual who has taken training for specific policies, providing documentation for regulators and auditors.

Delivery method		Best practice usage
	Weaknesses	Either a single media will need to be managed, thus delivering policies and procedures to staff that aren't affected by them. Or multiple media need to be managed, breaking the distribution of policies and procedures media into groups that affect certain staff. This latter process could become complicated quickly in a large organization.
Training Classes	*Usage*	Training classes for affected staff are set up and the policies and procedures are explained and trained. Copies of the policies and procedures can be disseminated to attendees.
	Strengths	The only stronger method of delivery than a multimedia presentation is an in-person presentation using multiple media formats.
	Weaknesses	Getting people to the class. In person meetings can also be costly, particularly in geographically diverse organizations.
Mentoring	*Usage*	Mentoring is the oldest training methodology known to man. Before we could read and write, those who "knew how" were teaching those who didn't through personal mentoring.
	Strengths	A strong mentoring program helps not only disseminate the policies and procedures *as written*, but also *as intended* because some teaching points cannot be communicated through writing.
	Weaknesses	If you don't have a strong mentoring program, this won't work.. Inconsistent training among staff as some mentors are better than others. Could also lead to inconsistent interpretations of policies as different mentors approach things differently and may or may not keep current on policy changes (*e.g.*, reinforces the attitude of "this is the way we've always done it, so it must be right").
One on one executive briefings	*Usage*	When communicating new or changed policies and procedures, many organizational leaders want to have individual briefings on the subject at hand.
	Strengths	You can use this time to build more of a bond with the leadership of the organization.
		If you are smart, you'll give the leaders a "talking points" card for each new policy and procedure. This "talking points" card is an executive summary coupled with why the policies and procedures are important to the leader and those within the leader's purview.
		Can help to promote a "culture of compliance" within the organization by increasing leadership buy-in.

Delivery method		Best practice usage
	Weaknesses	It takes time and knowledge of the leadership in order to get this one right. Doesn't guarantee that the leadership will read the actual policies and procedures and important nuances in the policies may be missed.
Direct e-mail messages with attachments	*Usage*	The policies and procedures are summarized in an e-mail, and the e-mail is sent to those affected by the policies and procedures.
	Strengths	You can force people to show you they read the e-mail through the use of return receipts.
		You can use the e-mail message to open a line of communication with the recipient to ensure that they understand how the policy or procedure affects them.
	Weaknesses	The "delete" key — just because a message is opened, doesn't mean it's been read. Doesn't guarantee that people reading the summary of the policies and procedures will read the actual policies and procedures and important nuances in the policies may be missed.
		This should not be used as a substitute for training or a method to avoid a team meeting — and all too many times it is used that way.

Policy and procedure dissemination methods

These is just a sampling of available tactics. You'll need a strategy to decide which to use and when.

Establishing a communications strategy

Once you understand all of the communication and dissemination tactics, you'll want to create a strategy for when to use them and in which order. Communication of information is *a political process*. Why? Knowledge is power. And if you subvert the power of certain people in the organization by communicating policies and procedures for *their* group but without *their* blessing, you are creating a political embarrassment for them (in their eyes). Therefore, you'll need to develop a strategy that meets your organization's and staff's needs. If you don't, then you'll face stern resistance to change.

Before you can understand the best strategy for communicating your policies and procedures, you should understand a bit about how people accept technological change and how your relationship to these people affects your ability to communicate with them. The point is to understand that communication is not about what is *said*, but about what is *heard*. And what is *heard* is derived from the listener's background and the prejudices and opinions that the listener brings to the conversation. In order to be successful in the world of high tech, you have to understand that there are those who adopt technology readily and those that do not wish to adopt it at all.

Very much like a football coach, you have to create a strategy that says in effect "this person might block our project, so let's get them out of the way. That person might try this, so let's counter with that." A few years ago there were two wonderful books written, that when combined, create the basis for such a strategy in the technology world. Geoffrey Moore taught us about technology adoption and Seth Godin has taught us about our relationship to others and how that affects communication with them.

Geoffrey Moore's analysis of the technology adaptation market

What defines a market? A market is any set of **actual or potential customers** for either a **product or service** who have **common needs and wants**, and who **reference each other** when making a business decision. Since this is a guide for technologists within the business world, then the members of your company who use (or should be using, or need to use) your policies and procedures, are your market.

What further defines a market is that within any given market there are those who adapt to changes and "new" things more readily than others. Within an adaptation scale, in this case a *new policy and procedure* adaptation scale, there are five major divisions within the whole market, split between the folks who are most likely to adapt something new on the left and those who'd rather never have to adapt *anything* new on the right. The graph below shows the relative size of the five markets, and also shows that the movement from one market to the next is *not* automatic, that there is a break between each. The break between market two and three has been defined as a **chasm** by Geoffrey Moore.

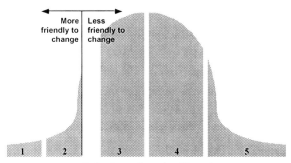

Technology adaptation life cycle

1. **Technology Enthusiasts** make up the membership of the first market subgroup. They are the first on the block to try anything new, simply because of the product or service's coolness factor. Their marketshare (the number of people within the subgroup versus the number of people in the total market) is relatively small.

2. **Visionaries** make up the membership of the second market subgroup. They are also people who want to try something new very quickly, but usually wait until they can figure out how trying something new gives them some personal or professional leverage. The marketshare of the visionaries is greater than that of the enthusiasts, but not by a whole lot.

3. **Pragmatists** are the third sub-grouping within the market. Once they know that a product or service will work, they will jump on the bandwagon. This is the first of the two largest marketshares within the whole market.

4. **Conservatives** are the fourth sub-grouping within the market. They usually don't adopt something until they are forced to, until it is more painful for them to stay where they are than make the switch. This is the second of the largest marketshares within the whole market.

5. **Laggards** are the final sub-grouping within the market. They'd rather die with the dinosaurs than move forward. These guys have a larger marketshare than do the enthusiasts, but is it really worth focusing upon?

The reason that you have to know all of this stuff is that as you develop policies and procedures, you are still going to need to do a bit of convincing many folks that they should adapt to the new changes you are proposing. You have to use your knowledge of the folks within your organization, and where they fall within this spectrum of technology adaptation, to form relationships with them so that you can convince them they need to adopt these new policies and procedures, and even, if possible, to promote your initiatives to the others on the right side of the chasm. Knowing about where they fall in line within this adaptation continuum, you'll know when to approach them about making changes and when *not* to approach them about making changes.

The technology market (friendly to "new" things)

Taken together, technology enthusiasts and visionaries make up the early market. Although their personal motives are quite different, they are united by their drive to be the first, the techies desiring to explore and the visionaries desiring to exploit the new capability. No one else in the Technology Adoption Life Cycle has any interest in being first, as you will see from the profiles that follow.

Innovators = Technology Enthusiasts

Technology enthusiasts are those who appreciate the technology for the technology's sake. They are the Eric Hoffer True Believers. They are the nerds. The gear heads. These are people who are fundamentally committed to new technology on the grounds that, sooner or later, it is bound to improve our lives. Moreover, they take pleasure in mastering its intricacies, just in fiddling with it, and they love to get their hands on the latest and greatest innovation. And thus they are typically the first customers for anything that is truly brand-new.

They appreciate the architecture of a product. They will spend hours trying to get it to work properly, even if you are shipping a product that isn't quite ready for the real world. They will quickly forgive ghastly errors in programming, will almost never read the documentation, and will critique your product devastatingly – all because they love it and want it to be better.

The technology enthusiast is the gatekeeper for any new technology. As such, they are the first key to entering any high-tech product market.

As key influencers for buying decisions, they pose fewer requirements than any other group in the adoption profile. However, this does not mean that you can ignore their issues.

When they have a technical problem, they want access to the **most** technological person on your team to answer that problem.

Early Adopters = Visionaries

These are the true revolutionaries in business and government who want to use the discontinuity of any innovation to make a break with the past and start an entirely new future. They have that rare insight to match an emerging technology to a strategic opportunity, the temperament to translate that insight into a high-visibility project, and the charisma to get the rest of their organization to buy into that project. Their expectation is that by being first to exploit the new capability, they can achieve a dramatic and insurmountable competitive advantage over the old order.

Their business goal is to launch their organization forward with a quantum leap thus giving them a high degree of personal recognition and reward. And herein lies the key point: *Visionaries are looking for revolutionary breakthroughs, not evolutionary change. Policies and procedures represent evolutionary change.*

The economic market (generally opposed to anything "new")

Mainstream markets are dominated by the early majority, the pragmatists. Funny enough, these folks are usually seen as almost visionary leaders to the conservatives and skeptics.

Early Majority = Pragmatists

They do not love technology for its own sake, so are different from the techies, whom they are careful, nonetheless, to employ. Moreover, they believe in evolution not revolution, so they are not visionaries, either. Instead, they are interested in making their companies' systems work effectively. So they are neutral about technology and look to adopt innovations only after a proven track record of useful productivity improvement, including strong references from people they trust.

Pragmatists are the people most likely to be in charge of a company's mission-critical systems. They know this infrastructure is only marginally stable, and they are careful to protect it from novel intrusions. Therefore, policies and procedures are right up their alley.

The biggest thing you need to understand about the difference between the pragmatist and the visionary is that the visionary is into "revolutionary" products, services and advancement, while the pragmatist is into "evolutionary" advances. The goal of the pragmatist is to make measurable, predictable progress. So if you use terms about "new" versus "improved" you'll get nowhere with this group.

Late Majority = Conservatives

These customers are pessimistic about their ability to gain any value from technology investments and undertake them only under duress – typically because the remaining alternative is to let the rest of the world pass them by. However, they can't be ignored because there are as many of them as there are pragmatists. They are very price-sensitive, highly skeptical, and very demanding. Rarely do their demands get met, in part because they are unwilling to pay for any extra services, all of which only reconfirms their sour views of high tech.

The conservatives will be in favor of any policies and procedures that "rein in" technological change and quick adaptation to new systems. They will be adverse to any new technology used to automate the new procedures.

The Blocking Market (foes of anything "new")

There is one last segment that we have to understand, and that is the one that will attempt to actively **block** any new technological innovation.

Laggards = Skeptics

These are the gadflies of high tech, the ones who delight in challenging the hype and puffery of high-tech language and the desire for "new." They are not so much potential customers as ever-present critics. As such, your goal is not to sell *to* them but rather to sell *around* them, and ensure that they don't have a chance to block forward movement.

In all fairness to the skeptics, their arguments are normally based upon some vague (and usually BS-ridden) over-promising and under-delivering of both projects and products. While most systems do deliver value, most cannot live up to the hype that surrounds them. And this is the perfect tool for the skeptic.

You cannot communicate to a skeptic the belief that the value of a policy and its associated procedures will be discovered rather than known at the time of acceptance. You'll have "quantified" the value long before you can communicate to a skeptic.

The best thing to remember in communicating with a skeptic is to not attempt to steam roll them, or even defend against their arguments. It is to listen and learn. If you want to know what *could* go wrong, listen to the skeptic.

Seth Godin's analysis of customer acceptance level

Have you ever had some idiot send you a direct mail marketing piece that *assumes* you are good friends - even if you've never heard of the person? Since my first name is Dorian, I often get mass mail directed to "Ms" Dorian Cougias (even though I'm a 6'1", mustachioed former paratrooper!). Don't you hate that? Well, guess what – you aren't the Lone Ranger.

Your ability to communicate with those around you stems, in part, with understanding what types of acceptance level they are willing to grant you. You have to format a piece of information one way for a good friend, and a wholly different way for a complete stranger. This is because people grant a certain level of acceptance to those that they don't know, and a greater level of acceptance to those that they do know. Another way of saying this, is that people give you different levels of *permission* when you communicate with them. The more they accept you, the more permission you have to ask things of them and communicate in a closer personal style.

This type of customer acceptance level has been defined as a part of Seth Godin's consumer growth cycle outlined in his book Permission Marketing. It is broken down into five distinct categories, all measured by how accepting each of the categories would be to being approached by the person or company in question.

Strangers

These are people that you will have to interrupt in order to gain their attention. They are not used to hearing from you, and will tend to either ignore your initial requests or hold them in disdain because they are interruptive in nature. Your initial chance of success with a stranger is about 2 - 6%.

Friends

A friend is someone who you have a passing acquaintance with. You may feel free to contact this person with an interruptive type of message, as long as the message is brief, to the point, and trades something for the person's time.

Customers

A customer is someone with whom you have already had regular business relations. They welcome your call and are not interrupted by an e-mail or other offering from you. While not as fully integrated or "on board" with anything you'd cook up as a loyal customer would be, you have served them well and have been courting them for some time.

Loyal Customers

These are folks that you've "been around the block with" so-to-speak. The loyal customer can and should act as a lead bowling pin to help knock over others in any new market niche strategy. You have earned their respect and earned the privilege of asking for their assistance in new ventures.

Former Customers (an Alumnus)

If you do it right, your former customers will remember how you helped them, and will be just as loyal (if not more so because time tempers memories for the good) as your loyal customers.

Keep them in the loop with what you are doing, and they will more than likely become customers again when the need arises and you have products that match those needs. Asking their advice will keep you close to them.

How to use this information when rolling out policies and procedures

Now it comes time to introduce your new policies and procedures to your organization. What you'll want to do is to take a strategic approach to which folks you'll be introducing them through.

When introducing an update to your compliance plan with new policies and procedures within the organization, you'll be able to go directly after the pragmatist market. Remember, pragmatists want improved processes. So by starting with an evolutionary improvement to your compliance plan, you'll be selling to their comfort factor.

The steps that you'll want to run through can be divided into three different communications stages as shown in the diagram that follows. The basic strategy is to lead with the pragmatists and get their blessing first. Then, you'll extend communications of the policies and procedures out to the conservatives in the organization. With each group's blessing in hand, you'll extend the communications one more time to the skeptics, hoping to sway them by sheer force of having the rest of the groups approve the policies and procedures first.

The Whole Market	Technology-based decisions		Chasm	Economic-based decisions		
	Enthusiast	Visionary		Pragmatist	Conservative	Skeptic
Alumnus						
Loyal Customer				1.1	2.1	3.1
Customer				1.2	2.1	3.2
Friend				1.3	3.1	3.2
Stranger						

The strategy for communicating policies and procedures

1.1 Communicating with your *loyal* pragmatist customers

The first stage is to sell the benefits of the addition of new policies and procedures to the compliance framework to the loyal customers that you have. Most, if not all, of the members of this group should have been involved from an early point and will have had a hand in the creation, or at least editing, of these policies and procedures. Therefore, it should be clear sailing for approval and acceptance of your polices and procedures.

Because this is to the leadership, and this is the first group you are communicating with, you'll want to deliver the information in person with an "executive briefing." Be sure to have the talking points cards on hand so that you can give them to the executives and have them start passing the word for you.

They will tell you the best way to communicate with the rest of their group.

1.2 Communicating with pragmatist customers

The second stage is to communicate the new policies and procedures to the pragmatists that you've been working with. Because they are customers of your policies and procedures, you should have been keeping them in the loop about the progress of the policies and procedures. So this shouldn't be new to them and there should be no acceptance issues.

Your communications tactics should include an informal meeting with the leaders and then request a team meeting with their teams to communicate the policies and procedures with the entire team. This will be your first in person training event and you should have someone record the questions that are being asked when you present the policies and procedures. You'll be able to use those questions in the next step when communicating outside of your comfort zone. You may also want to incorporate these questions into your Frequently Asked Questions (FAQ) documents.

1.3 Communicating with pragmatist friends

Your third stage of communication will be with people who are not customers of your policies and procedures, but who also have to be consulted or informed of them. Because this is the first time you are communicating with staff that you haven't been actively working with, you'll want to ensure that you *only* communicate with the pragmatists and *not* conservatives or skeptics.

Why? Because these policies and procedures will be more "new" to them than to others and they will have more reservations about them than the people you've been working with so far. Because you are on friendly terms with them, you'll be able to leverage the answers you've developed to earlier questions during your other two briefings. If the answers you have fit the questions they bring up, you know you are on the right track. If the answers don't fit, at least you'll have a friendly audience to work through the issues with.

Therefore, your communication tactics with this group should also be an in-person briefing for any leaders first, followed by a team meeting. If you can't answer the questions of the leader, you aren't ready for the team.

Because these are people who have been outside of the communications loop until now, you will more than likely have a lot more questions and issues than before. Again, have someone record all of the issues and their answers as you'll need those answers to help your case with the conservatives.

2.1 Communicating with conservative customers and loyal customers

Remember that the conservatives are all about control and reining in technology. When you present to them, you'll want to be up front with all of the questions and answers to this point, not only briefing them on the policies and procedures at hand, but also the issues that have been raised and addressed.

The best method I've found when addressing conservative customers is to bring up the matter of new policies and procedures as an "update" to the current compliance books or manuals. Bringing along a printed copy of the policies and procedures, along with the FAQs you've been developing will make your presentation to this group much more powerful.

Because they are going to be reluctant to allowing you a team meeting or access to their groups at all, you'll have to give them a choice of delivery. My suggestion is to have your earlier briefings turned into a mini training plan that can be delivered through a recorded PowerPoint presentation or recorded webcast that their staff can view at their leisure. After a couple of weeks of them ignoring even watching something recorded, you can come back and be more forceful about formal training.

If there are questions or issues that arise from this group (other than snoring), you'll want to add them to your FAQs.

3.1 Communicating with conservative friends and loyal customer skeptics

Before you communicate with these groups, wait for at least one or two members of the previous group to move through the presentation or watch the recorded webcast. Once you know which format the previous group has taken to, you can offer that as the primary means of communicating the policies and procedures with these two groups.

By now, your policies and procedures will also be posted to your intranet site and should also be inculcated into your newsletters and discussion boards. Therefore, you can communicate the "obvious acceptance" the rest of the group has taken to the new policies and procedures.

3.2 Blocking the two remaining skeptic segments

The last two groups' focus will be on blocking their complaints. You'll need to rely heavily on your FAQs and the inculcation of the message for these new policies and procedures. If a great gnashing of teeth happens with these groups, you might want to call for a meeting of the most vocal people and work through the issues with them in person.

3.3 Everyone else

My suggestion is to send out an e-mail to everyone else affected *after* you've dealt with the previous group. By now, every issue that can come to the surface should already be there, and you won't be blind-sided by anything that comes back through the e-mail channel. Consider also sending a hardcopy memo so those technology-adverse folks will at least get comfort from holding an old-fashioned paper communication in their hands.

Creating organizational standards

As defined in <u>The Language of Compliance</u>, organizational standards are used to define the uniform use of specific measurable technologies, parameters, or procedures when such uniform use will benefit the organization. A standard can be: 1) an object or measure of comparison that defines or represents the magnitude of an item; 2) a characterization that establishes allowable tolerances or constraints for categories of items; 3) a degree or level of required excellence or attainment. Standards are definitional in nature and established either to further understanding and interaction, or to acknowledge observed (or desired norms) of exhibited characteristics or behavior. Thus, standards may function to specify minimum performance levels or describe best practice. Standards can be put in place to support a policy or a process, or as a response to an operational need. Like policies, standards must include a description of the manner in which noncompliance will be detected. ITIL states that standards are mandated, but that is not always the case.

Let's delve further into this by defining *what* an organizational standard seeks to achieve and *why* we have organizational standards. An organizational standard falls in between a policy and a procedure and supports both. Where policy is the 10,000 foot leader's view of the direction the organization should head, the procedure is the 10 foot view of how to specifically get there, and the standard is part of the "there" we're trying to reach.[28]

---

28   Note also that there is no standard way to define these terms and many well-intentioned rules, regulations, articles and authors further muddy the waters with concepts like "standard procedures" and "standard policies" or using the terms "standard," "policy," "procedure," and "guideline" more or less interchangeably. The important thing, however, is not the precision with which you use each of these terms, but the fact that all of these concepts, by whatever name, are essential ingredients in the formulation of an effective compliance program.

Consider driving and maintaining a car. Many people learn how to drive basically any type of car and what the rules of the road are by taking driver's education classes. These are like the policies for how to drive a car. There is also a driver's manual for each make and model of a car that documents how to operate that model of the car, which is like the car's procedures. Each make and model of a car also comes with a maintenance manual that documents the proper amount of pressure for the tires on the car, the grade of oil to use in the car, and so on. This maintenance manual is like a like a set of standards. The standards indicate the target to be achieved (tires inflated to 28 PSI), but not necessarily how to do it (hand pump, electric pump, gas station compressor, etc.).

These concepts parallel information security policies, procedures and standards. Procedures can, and do (and *should*), vary from one department and office location to the next. Some differences in procedures may be required by local conditions or regulations – for example fire codes in different cities may require different evacuation procedures. Other variations may be based on differences in technology – for example, the procedure for setting up a Cisco router will not be the same for the procedure for setting up a SonicWALL router (although security policies implemented by such procedures may be the same in both cases). With that said, in order to maintain commonality of products the organization might create a purchasing *standard* for routers to ensure that they are compatible with routers that are already deployed. In simple terms the *why* is focused on normalization.

Typically within a corporate environment, a standard provides the specific technical requirements for implementing corresponding policies. For example, a corporate policy may require that strong encryption be used when sending confidential information within or attached to e-mail messages. The corresponding standard might name the specific encryption solution and algorithm that must be used to satisfy the policy.

Generally, standards only need to be communicated to the personnel charged with implementing them, not to all corporate personnel. Another difference between standards and policies is that well-written policies will rarely change, but standards will change in response to changing technical environments, which may happen comparatively often.

The generally accepted use of the word *standard* implies that it is a universally agreed upon set of rules for interoperability. Fat chance, that. In reality, you should look upon standardization as a *process* for establishing various kinds of efficiencies, implementations, and syntaxes within a set of approved possibilities. Think of organizational standards as unifications or homogenizations of products, implementations, and procedures. Therefore, let's define the *what* of the *standard setting process* as **the continuous development, implementation, and adjusting of products, designs, implementations, syntaxes, and procedures to achieve and maintain required levels of compliance while maintaining compatibility, interchangeability, and commonality within the organization**. The "standard" itself is the output of this process.

A closer definition of the *why* can be found in the words "compliance, compatibility, interchangeability, and commonality." We need to focus on that word *compliance* for a second before we move on, because it is important to the methodology your organization will use when creating standards. Standards within most organizations either arise organically as *de facto* standards (meaning that they develop over time as personnel gravitate toward them and are followed for the convenience of the organization), or they are foisted upon the organization as *de jure* standards (meaning that they are externally created and must be followed in order to meet regulatory or contractual compliance).

Note first, that our use of the terms *de facto* and *de jure* differ somewhat from typical usage in the technical world where a *de facto* standard is generally considered something that is so widespread that virtually everyone uses it even though nobody ever mandated it. A good example of a *de facto* standard in this sense of the term is the use of Adobe's PDF format for document exchange – it's use has become so widespread that virtually everyone now uses and writes to that format even though PDF has never been adopted by any industry or standards body as a documented standard. However, from the policy perspective, PDF looks more like an externally imposed *de jure* standard that the organization is compelled to support.

Some *de facto* standards are so widely accepted and used that they eventually become required, or *de jure*, standards. For example, Hewlett-Packard created the interface bus (HP-IB) but it quickly became so popular and widely used within the computer industry, that the Institute of Electrical and Electronics Engineers (IEEE) committee adopted it and renamed it the General Purpose Interface Bus (GPIB) as defined within their IEEE-488, thus turning it into a *de jure* standard.

Why and how *de facto* standards are developed

Let's say that a typical organization has three departments; sales, production, and billing. The policy for the organization is that all departments will back up their computers every day. The sales department consists of a bunch of people with notebooks. Therefore, the sales department develops a procedure to back up over the Internet to an ASP-based backup provider so that the sales folks can run backups from whatever hotel room or internet cafe they happen to be working from at the moment. The billing department, on the other hand, has a series of desktops with a procedure to back them up to tape on a daily basis. Because production consists of devices that have a short backup window, their procedure is to back up to disk and then run that backup to tape at a later time. These three procedures are neither common nor interchangeable as each uses different hardware and software. There is no clear backup standard.

The first step is achieving compatibility. By selecting a software product that could run Internet, disk, and tape based backups, the organization could normalize three different applications to a single instance.

The next step is examining interchangeability. Interchangeability is looked at more of as a process than a product. Because the sales group is mobile, they would *not* be able to interchange their backup locations with disks or tape – they are stuck with Internet-based backups. However, both production and billing could back up initially to a local disk-based backup because the disk-based solution is equivalent in both performance and durability. Therefore, the organization could achieve interchangeability with a single exception (sales). Note that the exception is a *compatibility*-based exception. The sales department's traveling is not compatible with being backed up locally. Using the Internet-based backup method is a compensating solution to the exception.

For both billing and production, the question now comes down to commonality. Can the backup product be selected and procedures written in such a way for each group's backups to be operated and maintained by personnel from *either* department without any additional training? If so, the organization can achieve commonality at least for these two groups.

Notice what we are doing in this story. We are attacking the problem of creating a standard *from the ground up*. We are taking the policy (from on high) and then examining each procedure (from the bottom) to see which procedure could be brought to a higher level of normalization in order to work better across the entire organization. That's because de facto standards are created to make your life easier — you are following your own internal rules and methods that have evolved organically to solve specific problems.

De facto standards seek normalization and homogenization. Not so with de jure standards.

Why and how *de jure* standards are developed

De jure standards are foisted upon organizations by external rule makers. We write organizational standards because our organizations have to follow public rules (such as PCI-DSS that applies to everyone accepting credit card information, or HIPAA that applies to all who need to protect patient health information), as well as specific external rules (contracts and Service Level Agreements with clients or suppliers), and even internal rules (organizational policies).

Many of these rules define specific controls that must be followed. The job of the rule maker seems to be to say "do this" or "do that." But rule makers aren't always blind to reality. There's often the clause that says "we anticipate exceptions, just tell us why and where." Therefore the *why* of de jure standards is compliance.

The *how* of de jure standards is attempting to marry a set of externally written controls with existing conditions by creating rules for commonality and determining when exceptions to the standard are acceptable (and the degree of deviation that is acceptable). The first step in the process is to establish commonality between any competing compliance authority requirements. Once a common framework has been created, exceptions should be based, in order, upon compatibility and then interchangeability.

Compliance and commonality or harmonization

The first question when looking at whether to apply a de jure standard as written is to define the area of commonality, also known as harmonization. Most of us are under multiple external regulations. A typical large university, for example, must follow the Health Insurance Portability and Accountability Act (HIPAA) in connection with its medical program, the Gramm-Leach-Bliley Act (GLBA) in connection with student loan programs, PCI-DSS regulations in connection with it's acceptance of credit card payments for tuition and fees, and a great many other acts and regulations. HIPAA calls for the protection of patient records. GLBA calls for the protection of non-public personal information. PCI-DSS calls for the protection of credit cardholder data. What is common among all three of these is that the regulation deals with people's information. Therefore, instead of having three separate standards (one for a person's medical information, one for personal information, and one for credit card information), why not create a standard that defines how to protect confidential information in general? The standard could have a section defining what constitutes fields to be kept confidential, records to be kept confidential, reports to be kept confidential, and media to be kept confidential.

By focusing on the commonality of the compliance requirements, anything outside of the scope of commonality can be considered an exception. As another example, HIPAA, GLBA and PCI-DSS each require awareness and training.

The HIPAA requirement is found within § 164.306 as follows:

> (5)(i) *Standard: Security awareness and training*. Implement a security awareness and training program for all members

The GLBA requirement is found within § 314.4 as follows:

> (b) Identify reasonably foreseeable internal and external risks to the security, confidentiality, and integrity of customer information that could result in the unauthorized disclosure, misuse, alteration, destruction or other compromise of such information, and assess the sufficiency of any safeguards in place to control these risks. At a

minimum, such a risk assessment should include consideration of risks in each relevant area of your operations, including:

(1) Employee training and management;

The PCI-DSS requirement is found within Requirement 12 as follows:

12.6 Implement a formal security awareness program to make all employees aware of the importance of cardholder data security.

12.6.1 Educate employees upon hire and at least annually (for example, by letters, posters, memos, meetings, and promotions)

12.6.2 Require employees to acknowledge in writing that they have read and understood the company's security policy and procedures.

Okay, so from the University's perspective, we see we need to provide information security and training to our employees, and a policy stating this provision would need to meet the general requirements of HIPAA, GLBA, and PCI-DSS for this type of education. The standard for delivering the education will need to be documented to support this policy. When harmonizing standards, check for all commonalities between your authority documents (in our example, HIPAA, GLBA, and PCI-DSS) as well as the differences, as we've done in the table below.

Control	HIPAA	GLBA	PCI-DSS
All members of the organization will be trained on information security awareness.	§164.306(5)(i)		12.6
The new hire process will require training			12.6.1
Training will take place annually			12.6.1
All employees will acknowledge in writing that they have read and understood the organizational policies and procedures			12.6.2
The effectiveness of information security awareness training will be measured for future risk management audits		§314.4(b)	

The three authority documents harmonized

This, then, becomes your harmonized standard for what *must* be included within a training program to meet your compliance requirements. And if you are noticing, *yes*, this is the entire foundation upon which the Unified Compliance

Framework has been built. You can find unified control standards in abundance at our unifiedcompliance.com website.

De jure standards don't always play nicely with *de facto* standards – enter *operational* standards

Recall that de facto standards evolve over time out of a combination of necessity, convenience, and inertia – the "this is the way we've always done it" syndrome. De jure standards may or may not be met by organizational de facto standards. In order to implement an effective compliance program, you must operationalize the de jure standards and reconcile them with the de facto standards. Only then can you determine if the de facto standard can remain, must be changed, or must be completely discarded in favor of a new *operational standard*.

Many organizations get confused when trying to create their own operational standards to meet compliance with the externally mandated de jure standards. A common mistake is to try and take the de jure standard verbatim and make it an operational standard. Sometimes this can work, but more often than not, it will create some problems for you.

The typical lack of specificity within the de jure standards often do not harmonize well with organizational de facto standards. For example, consider the HIPAA standard from § 164.312 Technical safeguards:

"A covered entity must, in accordance with § 164.306:

(a)(1) *Standard: Access control.*

Implement technical policies and procedures for electronic information systems that maintain electronic protected health information to allow access only to those persons or software programs that have been granted access rights as specified in § 164.308(a)(4)."

Do you see any problem with trying to use this exact statement as a standard? Would your IT folks know what this means? Would this type of standard lead to consistent implementation of access controls within your organization, or would it open the door to inconsistent use of technology and inconsistent access control implementations? If you tried to include the referenced text from § 164.308(a)(4) you would end up including all the following:

"(4)(i) Standard: Information access management.

Implement policies and procedures for authorizing access to electronic protected health information that are consistent with the applicable requirements of subpart E of this part.

(ii) Implementation specifications:

(A) Isolating health care clearinghouse functions

(Required). If a health care clearinghouse is part of a larger organization, the clearinghouse must implement policies and procedures that protect the electronic protected health information of the clearinghouse from unauthorized access by the larger organization.

(B) Access authorization (Addressable)

Implement policies and procedures for granting access to electronic protected health information, for example, through access to a workstation, transaction, program, process, or other mechanism.

(C) Access establishment and modification

(Addressable). Implement policies and procedures that, based upon the entity's access authorization policies, establish, document, review, and modify a user's right of access to a workstation, transaction, program, or process."

Huh? Did this help? More likely all this verbiage just muddied the waters. And, since it references yet another part of the regulatory text, there are still more passages from this regulation that would need to be included if we continued to follow this logic. We have seen organizations actually try to do this, though, and they ended up with the following:

A✔ The de jure standard that was dropped-in covers more topics than applies to the organization, confusing those who must follow them. For example, if the organization is not a clearinghouse, those reading this standard will wonder how they are supposed to comply with the "required" clearinghouse statement.

⚠ Documenting a statement as "addressable" usually gets incorrectly interpreted as meaning "optional." If the people who must follow the standard think an action is optional, nine times out of ten they will choose not to follow it.

⚠ De jure standards typically read more like policies, not standards. There are no specific solutions provided in de jure standards (such as this one from HIPAA), leading to multiple solutions being implemented throughout an organization that all do basically the same thing. This not only wastes your organization's money, it leads to a maintenance and compatibility nightmare – it completely undermines our goal of commonality.

⚠ The writing style does not match the other standards within the organization, making them seem strangely out of place to the readers who must follow them.

⚠ Your organization's standards can not be harmonized for multiple de jure standards if you take the statements verbatim from each of the regulations. You thus leave it to the individual readers to attempt to interpret and harmonize these standards in a way that they believe makes sense for their own jobs without knowing the impact of their interpretations on other parts of the business. As discussed in the previous section, this harmonization is important for making organizational standards as succinct and understandable as possible while complying with multiple regulatory requirements.

When using de jure standards as the basis of your organization's operational standards, boil them down to the concepts that apply to your organization and then write them consistently with the way your other standards are written, sticking with the language with which your readers are familiar.

An example to use for this HIPAA standard for an organization that is a covered entity but not a clearinghouse might look like the following:

Access to confidential information must be given only to groups and individuals who:

- *Have a documented need to access the information to perform their job responsibilities, and*
- *Have been authorized to access the information in accordance with the organization's change control procedures.*

Notice – we set two **parameters** for the policy (need to know, need to access). Operational standards define **common parameters** for policies and procedures.

Compliance and compatibility

Let's consider the common control statement inferred by many public regulations that mandates organizational firewalls must be set up as a default "deny all" access policy. If an organization were to deny all traffic from entering their network, there would be no reason to have the network – web traffic, e-mail traffic, and other business related traffic would be stopped by the firewall. This type of extreme compliance, implemented to meet the letter of the law, would be incompatible with doing business.[29] Therefore, the organization must create a process to ensure that both compatibility and compliance are balanced. They have to define and document compatibility exceptions.

In the case of our firewall scenario, the compatibility exceptions are based upon the addresses, ports, and protocols needed to carry traffic between the organization's computers, its clients, and suppliers (or even the general public).

A simple exceptions table could list all of the open ports, what runs on those ports, the reason for the port to be open, where the traffic should be routed, and which group the exception came from.

Port/Address	What	Why	Where	Group
80	HTTP	Web traffic	DMZ web	Sales
25/110	SMTP/POP	Mail sending	DMZ e-mail	All
1596	EDI	Supply Ordering	Production Server	Production
ALL Internal Addresses	Use of private IP range	NAT will be used	All non-DMZ devices	All

---

29   Of course there are certain situations where this type of extreme isolation is perfectly appropriate. We've worked with companies in the defense industry where the policy for certain highly secure environments simply states that they may not be connected to the internet at all, directly or indirectly. As always, it's all about context.

Again, the standard here is addressing **parameters** (in this case ports) that should be normalized unless an exception is made.

Another way to look at compliance and compatibility is technical compatibility. Walking through the Center for Internet Security's various systems hardening guidelines (which are now mandated by PCI-DSS), we determined that many of the hardening guidelines simply aren't compatible across *all* operating systems (and neither does the Center for Internet Security claim them to be). What follows is a small segment of system configuration standards and which operating systems they apply to.

	Windows NT	Windows 2003 Server	VSE-ESA	Unisys	Sun Solaris	Novell Netware	Linux	HP-UX	AIX
Install patches	X	X	X	X	X	X	X	X	X
Install Service Packs	X	X							
Convert to Trusted System								X	X
Install Login warning banner			X	X	X	X	X	X	X
Login parameters	X	X			X	X	X	X	X
Single-user login mode							X		
Convert File System	X	X							
Remove un-needed software							X		

When it comes to technical compatibility, any system which is simply not capable of meeting the standard either must be wholly eliminated from the organization's use, or must *automatically* be excepted from the standard.

In addition, rules for deciding upon general compatibility exceptions, and the exception request, review, and approval process can (and should) be documented.

Compliance and interchangeability

Another reason for exceptions to a de jure compliance rule is based upon interchangeability, or what is being called *compensating controls*. For the most part, organizations that are unable to follow external rules due to technical or business limitations can employ compensating controls *as long as they have undertaken a risk analysis and can show documented decisions* to do so, and as long as the compensating controls are interchangeable with the controls the rule calls for. By interchangeable here, we mean that the compensating controls put into place by the organization are equivalent in performance and durability, or provide greater protection than those stated by the rule maker.

When creating the rules for analyzing a compensating control's interchangeability with a control published by the rule in question, the compensating control in question must:

1. meet the intent and rigor of the external requirement;

2. mitigate the threat with similar (or greater) effect; and

3. be commensurate with the additional risk imposed by not adhering to the external requirement as stated.

As an example, let's take another widely defined rule – that of "separation of duties." Many regulations call for the complete separation of duties between positions such as the database administrator and the security patch manager. This means that there should be two physical people, one to administrate the database and another to ensure its continued security. But what about offices with a single administrator? Other than hiring someone with a split-personality (which carries a whole different set of security risks!), the small office might not have the salary budget for two people. That's when a compensating control can be decided upon. Because the intention of the rule is to ensure that no single person can take action without oversight, a compensating control would be one that provides the necessary oversight the original rule called for. Here's a model for documenting interchangeability.

Original	Interchangeability parameter
Intent: separate security change-related tasks from normal admin tasks by assigning them to different people	Submit all changes for approval from home office before making them, and then allow the home office to review changes once they've been made. Each server should have individual accounts for security and DBA and DBA should only log on as security admin when performing changes.
Threat mitigation: Threat is that DBA will have access to security measures	By forcing DBA to log in using a separate security admin account when making changes, and tracking *all* access, the home office can ensure that DBA isn't making unapproved changes or continually logging in as security vs. DBA. By reviewing changes, home office ensures only approved changes are made.
Commensurate equality: Ensure that DBA actions and entitlements do not cross with Security actions, and that there is change oversight	By enforcing a strict change management approval and review process, entitlements will be managed appropriately and commensurately. By establishing a strict logging and log review process, actions will be managed appropriately and commensurately.

Types of standards parameters

Now that you know what a standard is, you need to think about the acceptable parameter values to use within standards. Organizations should not write standards if the standards cannot be measured or evaluated in some objective way. Think about it. How would you ever know if the standards were effective, reasonable or needed to be changed without being able to measure or evaluate them? How could you ensure security was applied consistently throughout the organization without establishing acceptable parameters? Security controls containing organization-defined parameters give organizations the flexibility to define specific values and characteristics of controls to support organizational requirements or objectives consistently.

We have boiled it down to ten categories of parameters. Let's look at each category in more detail and consider some examples. As you read through these notice how, in each category, you would be able to evaluate or measure whether or not the standard has compliance based upon the stated parameter.

1. Informational parameters

Informational parameters describe such things as roles, responsibilities, actions or characteristics. For example, a security program roles and responsibilities standard would describe the responsibilities for each formally identified role. For example, such a standard could look like:

The Director of Information Security is an employee that is assigned the leadership role for the organization's security program. The responsibilities include:

- *Managing implementation of the organization's security program,*

- *Creating and maintaining the information security policies and standards,*

- *Managing the selection and implementation of security tools, and*

- *Managing the security staff and providing direction to security representatives.*

The four bullets provide the descriptions for the Director of Information Security's specific job responsibilities.

When documenting system configuration informational parameters, you are usually describing the information that would be a part of a sign-on or warning banner. Or the information parameter could contain what should be included in the privacy policy or license agreement presented to a user prior to allowing access to an application.

A sign-in banner will be created for all systems that hold company confidential information and the banner will be displayed during the login process.

2. Variable preference parameters

Variable preference parameters provide those individuals with security implementation responsibilities a choice of specific options for how to establish security based upon the circumstances. For example, such a standard could look like:

The organization's information systems contingency plan must be tested at least annually and as soon as possible following major changes to systems and applications.

The variables are annually *and as* soon as possible following major changes.

When documenting system configuration standards, the variable preferences normally define string lengths, addresses, ports, protocols, which fields should be reported in a log, etc.

> *The password length for all devices will be 8 characters in length, with a mix of upper and lower case characters.*

3. Capacity parameters

Capacity parameters define values for security related information related to storage and size. For example, such a standard could look like:

> *The organization's information systems must be configured to provide a warning when allocated storage volume reaches 90% of the maximum audit record storage capacity.*

The specified capacity in this example is *90% of the maximum audit record storage capacity*.

4. Boolean parameters

Defining settings that have only two possible values, such as "yes/no;" "on/off;" or "connect/disconnect." For example, such a standard could look like:

> *The information systems must terminate a network connection at the end of a session.*

In this example, either an active session has a network connection *or* a terminated session has no connection.

5. Retention parameters

Retention parameters specify the time periods for which certain types of information is retained. For example, such a standard could look like:

> *The organization's information systems must be configured to automatically disable inactive accounts after three months of inactivity.*

This retention period for keeping active accounts in this example is *three months of inactivity,* after which the account is disabled.

6. Named access parameters

Named access parameters list the types of access and related security controls that must be implemented for certain information assets or resources. For example, such a standard could look like:

The information systems must limit each defined user to one concurrent session.

The requirement for one concurrent session is the named access parameter in this example.

When writing this type of parameter into a configuration standard, the parameter normally defines specific users and groups that should be enabled or disabled.

The Remote Administrator account must only be enabled if the Remote Administration application and other settings have been enabled.

7. Data list parameters

Data list parameters provide a list of values that must be implemented. For example, such a standard could look like:

All the organization's information systems must generate audit records for the following events:
- *Login time*
- *Login user ID*
- *Login date*
- *And so on…*

In this example each of the bulleted items represents each of the data list parameters.

8. Named path parameters

Named path parameters indicate what roles, positions or individuals are authorized to perform specified information security related activities. For example, such a standard could look like:

The organization must document and use an identified custodian at all times to transport information systems backup media outside corporate facilities. No other individual is authorized to take backup media outside facilities.

The *identified custodian* in this example is the named path parameter who must be the only individual to transport backup media.

Named path parameters for configuration standards are very explicit and are either defined as URLs or Windows file paths.

http://sharepoint.netfrontiers.com/compliance/Shared%20Documents/The%20UCF%20Book/3%20to%204/

\\sharepoint\compliance\Shared Documents\The UCF Book\3 to 4

9. Permissions parameters

Permissions parameters define what specified roles, positions or individuals can or cannot do. For example, such a standard could look like:

The organization must develop and keep current a list of personnel with authorized access to the facility where the information system resides (except for those areas within the facility officially designated as publicly accessible) and must issue appropriate authorization credentials. The Information Security Officer must review and, if applicable, approve the access list and authorization credentials at least annually.

In this example the requirement to keep current a list of personnel with authorized access is the permissions parameter.

10. Patches parameters

Patches parameters define the values associated with each type of security-related systems and applications patches that must be used when security and software patching occur. For example, such a standard could look like:

> *Before systems and applications patches are put into production, all security controls must be tested to determine what impact they have on system security, functionality, and usability, and to take appropriate steps to address any issues identified.*

The requirement that all security controls must be tested is the patches parameter in this example.

When describing patches within a configuration standard, you'll usually want to specifically list the **oldest** patch level that you'll allow.

> *All Windows XP systems must have Service Pack 2 installed*

Some parameters belong to multiple categories

Don't get frustrated if you have a standards parameter that seems as though belongs in more than one category – some of them will! Consider the example we used earlier in this chapter,

> *Access to confidential information must be made to only those groups and individuals who:*
> - *Have a documented need to access the information to perform their job responsibilities, and*
> - *Have been authorized to access the information in accordance with the organization's change control procedures.*

Both of the above standards parameters can be considered as both a *named access* parameter setting (because of the requirement to have a *documented need to access*) and a *permissions* parameter setting (because of the requirement to *have been authorized*).

Using standards parameter categories is not bureaucratic busy-work meant to bog you down with trying to figure out where a specific category goes.

Established parameter values help you ensure your standards are measurable, realistic, and will be implemented throughout your organization in the most consistent manner possible.

Sometimes more restrictive values are needed

All areas throughout the organization need to follow the established minimum and maximum values for organization-defined standard parameters with one notable exception: if applicable laws, Executive Orders, or regulations require *more* restrictive values, or when risk assessments indicate *more* restrictive values are necessary in order to adequately mitigate risk for certain situations.

Consider the example discussed earlier to disable user accounts after three months of inactivity. If you created an administrative user account for an outside regulator to use while performing a compliance audit you may wisely decide to disable that regulator's user account immediately upon the conclusion of the audit instead of waiting until the account has not been used for three months.

Keep the characteristics of organizational standards in mind

Standards and their defined parameter values have a huge impact on how the information risk within your organization is mitigated, and they must be constructed in a thoughtful manner with your own organization's unique environment and compliance requirements in mind. So as you create your own organizational standards, keep the pointers we've discussed in mind. From a mile high view they include:

1. An organization's de facto standards point the way for operational standards that provide the specific technical requirements for implementing corresponding policies.

2. De facto standards seek normalization and homogenization throughout the organization.

3. You will usually not be able to use de jure standards verbatim as your organization's operational standards; more often than not the typical lack of specificity within de jure standards will not work as operational standards.

4. You must create a process to ensure that both compatibility and compliance are balanced, defining and documenting compatibility exceptions for the standards.

5. Compensating controls for exceptions need to meet the intent of the standards as written, and also *equally* mitigate the threat and any additional risk created by not having the stated control.

6. Standards must specify measurable parameter values.

Parameter categories

Again, here are the list of parameter categories.

Category	Policy descriptions	Configuration descriptions
Informational	Descriptions for such requirements as roles and classifications	Banner text or policy statements that should be included as warnings
Variable preference	Specified options for how to establish security based upon the circumstances or the choice of the responsible individual	String (think password here) length, addresses, ports, protocols, which fields should be reported or in a log, etc.
Capacity	Values for security related information related to storage and size	
Boolean	Settings that have only two possible values, such as "yes" or "no;" "on" or "off;" or "connect" or "disconnect"	For enabling or disabling services, accounts, applications, etc.
Retention	Time periods for which certain types of security-related information or resources are retained	
Named access	Types of access and related security controls that must be implemented	The users and groups that should be enabled or disabled
Data list	List of values that must be implemented	These are lists of parameters or other items not otherwise covered
Named path	Roles, positions or individuals authorized to perform specified activities	These are the directory and share names that are included or excluded from access
Permissions	What specified roles, positions or individuals can or cannot do	This covers access rights to named paths and applications for users or groups
Patches	Values associated with each type of security-related systems and applications patches that must be used when security and software patching occur	

Managing your configurations

One of the first things that you are going to learn when creating standardized policies and procedures is that your computing equipment (both hardware and software) is *anything but* standardized. Configuration management, as the regulatory authorities describe it, has not yet become a reality in your world.

If you are to move from initial to defined processes, you will also have to have a defined configuration set. Which also means that you are going to have to have some form of defined configuration management database, even if that database is an over-extended Excel spreadsheet. You can't have a defined set of processes, policies, and procedures without the *process* of identifying, controlling, tracking, and reporting all versions of hardware, software, and documentation. That process is configuration management.

Defining our terms

Because configuration management as defined by the regulatory folks might be new to you, we'll start out with defining the language that we are going to use[30].

Configuration Management Database (CMDB)

A database used to manage configuration records throughout their lifecycle. The CMDB records the attributes of each Configuration Item (CI) and relationships with other CIs. A CMDB may also contain other information linked to CIs, for example, incident, problem, or change records. The CMDB is maintained by configuration management and is used by all IT service management processes.

---

[30] All terms are taken from Dorian J. Cougias & Marcelo Halpern, <u>The Language of Compliance</u>, Schaser-Vartan Books, 2006. http://www.glossarybook.com

Configuration Item (CI)

Component of an infrastructure (or an item, such as a request for change, associated with an infrastructure) which is (or is to be) under the control of configuration management. CIs may vary widely in complexity, size, and type, from an entire system (including all hardware, software and documentation) to a single module or a minor hardware component. Information about each CI is recorded in a configuration record within the CMDB and is maintained throughout its lifecycle by configuration management. CIs are under the control of change management. CIs typically include hardware, software, buildings, people, and formal documentation such as process documentation and SLAs.

A computer system *is* a CI.   A helpdesk ticket is *not* a CI.

A building *is* a CI.   An off-the-shelf software package is *not* a CI.

A business service *is* a CI.   A contract is *not* a CI.

Configuration attribute or parameter

A piece of information about a configuration item. Examples are name, location, version number, and cost. Attributes of CIs are recorded in the Configuration Management Database (CMDB).

Configuration baseline

A configuration of a product or system established at a specific point in time, which captures both the structure and details of that product or system and enables that product or system to be rebuilt at a later date.

Configuration control

The activity responsible for ensuring that adding, modifying or removing a CI is properly managed, for example, by submitting a request for change or service request.

Which configuration items are important?

In all truth, we can't answer that for you. Because the items that are important for one organization aren't the items that are important for another organization. With that said, though, we want to walk you through some of the basic configuration items that you should be tracking in *any* organization. To do this, we have to take a quick look at a typical network *as a system of configurable items*. The following diagram shows a small network that extends out to third parties and mobile users and then internally covers the DMZ, secure database subnet, and the users' wired and wireless subnets. For discussion purposes, we'll say that this network is used to create forms that IT managers can use, and then sell those forms from the organizational website.

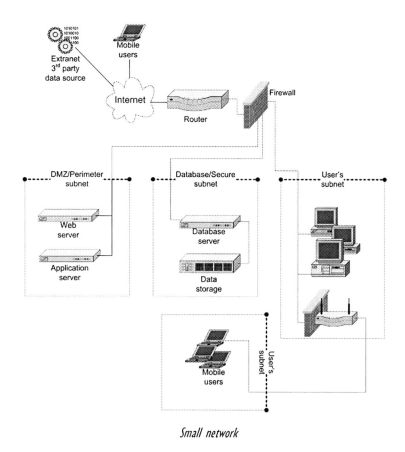

Small network

In order to determine the scope of configurable items that we're going to have to track, we will need to refer back to our original scoping process where we examined our IT assets from documents through facilities. Each asset will have its own unique configurable items that should be tracked in your configuration management documentation system. We'll start with the documents in the system and then proceed all the way through facilities.

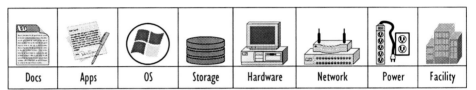

| Docs | Apps | OS | Storage | Hardware | Network | Power | Facility |

IT assets

The list of configurable items below is *not* a complete list. It is merely a *suggestion list* of all of the configurable items we've come up with to date.

Documents

Because the system is used to **create forms**, the configurable items that keep the system running at the document level will be the templates and the fonts used to create those forms. While the templates and fonts *per se* aren't configurable items, the **list** of which fonts and templates need to be tracked, where they are stored, and who owns them is. Therefore, the CI list for documents will be:

- List of templates and fonts
- UNC file path
- Directory owner & user/group rights

Another document type that will need to be tracked are the database tables for the database connected to the document tracking system and to the commerce system. Again, the tables themselves aren't being tracked as configurable items *per se.* however, the directory path, ownership, and directory rights are all configurable items. The CI list for the database should then at least include:

- List of key database files
- UNC file path

❧ Directory owner & user/group rights

Applications

You probably won't want to track all of the applications on your network, as nobody really cares what version of Freecell and Hearts you have on your laptop. However, you *will* need to track your major, minor, and support applications.

❧ Application & Publisher

❧ Type of application (Major, Minor, Support)

❧ Device ID where the application is located

❧ Revision level

❧ Serial Number

Operating systems

You'll want to know which operating systems you have running, on which devices. Therefore, you'll want to track the following configurable items:

❧ Operating System

❧ Device ID for each OS

❧ Revision level or Service Pack/Patch Level

❧ Serial Number

Storage volumes

Notice that we didn't say storage *devices* here, because we are only interested in the logical volumes at this point. The configurable items for each storage volume should contain at least the following:

❧ Volume/Partition Name

❧ File System

❧ Capacity

❧ RAID Level

✓ Drive or Cluster Info

✓ Device ID

Computing devices

Each computing device should also be tracked for the configurable items within it. Computing devices, because they are complex, have a couple of sub sets of information that need to be tracked; the device per se, its connectivity interfaces, the installed cards, and the installed peripherals.

The device

The main configurable items for computing devices are as follows:

✓ Device ID

✓ Manufacturer

✓ # CPUs & MHz Memory

✓ # Power Supplies & Consumption

✓ Cluster Info

Connectivity interfaces

How a device connects to the network is also a set of configurable items.

✓ Network Interface

✓ MAC Address

✓ IP Address

✓ DNS Name

✓ Logon Domain

The installed cards

Each of the installed cards also needs to be tracked as a configurable item *of the computing device*. You should track *at least* the following:

✓ Card Name/Manuf./Type

A✞ Card Slot

A✞ Supporting Programs/drivers

Installed peripherals

The same holds true for the installed peripherals.

A✞ Peripheral Name/Manuf/Type

A✞ Connection method

A✞ Supporting Programs/drivers

Network

The configurable items in your network are legion. Here is a listing of some of the most important items you should be tracking.

Subnets

For each and every subnet that your system belongs to (some systems can span multiple subnets), you need to map out your beginning and ending subnet range addresses, whether or not those addresses are static, dynamic, or mixed, and the subnet mask, default gateway, and name server information that you will need.

A✞ Subnet start is the beginning number in your subnet range, and subnet end is the ending number in your subnet range

A✞ Obtain address should either be static, dynamic, or both

A✞ Subnet mask is the subnet mask assigned to the subnet range

A✞ Default gateway is the default router addressed to the subnet range

A✞ Name server 1 and name server 2 are the primary and secondary authoritative DNS or AD servers for the subnet range

Static addresses

If you do have devices that are statically addressed, you should maintain a static address table. That means that you will need to map your addresses, net masks, gateways, the type of device that is using the address (server, workstation, printer, etc.), and the DNS node name.

⚡ Device ID is the network visible name for the device or the DNSed name

⚡ IP address is the IP address that you've assigned the device, and net mask is the network mask that you've assigned the device

⚡ Default gateway is the default router address that you've assigned the device

⚡ Name server 1 and name server 2 are the addresses of the two DNS servers you've assigned to the device (if you've assigned them any DNS servers)

⚡ Proxy server is the organizational proxy server (if assigned) that the device must traverse

Managed hubs and switches

Many times organizations will statically control the ports of their managed hubs and switches, or create filtered settings for them. If this is the case, and those settings are important for security (integrity) and continuity/disaster recovery (availability), then you'll want to ensure that the information is being tracked properly.

⚡ Device ID is the same thing as node name in other fields and is the name that the administrator created for the device or the default name that the manufacturer set up for the device

⚡ IP address is simply the IP address for that port of the switch. On switches that are not running any special VLAN software, this port address will be the same (or at least *should* be the same) on all ports. VLAN devices could have different IP addresses on different ports, depending upon how the VLAN is configured

Port Index is the port number that is being reported on

⚡ Ethernet address will be the physical network address (00.40.10.16.cb.b7), also known as the NIC, or MAC address of the network card driving the interface

⚡ Mapped IP address will only have an IP address if a *single* computing device is listed on that port. If multiple computing devices are connected to the port, more than likely nothing will be reported for this field

✦ Mapped node name will be the Device ID of the device as found in Active Directory or DNS if there is *a single device* found on the port. If there is more than one device attached to the port, this will more than likely be blank

Basic routing and firewall information

You will want to gather basic information about your routers and firewalls. Without these devices in place and running, you will not have connectivity to the outside world or other subnets within the organization.

✦ Device ID is the name that the administrator created for the device or the default name that the manufacturer set up for the device

✦ You will want the SNMP description of the device as well – just in case the administrator called the router "Homer Simpson" (like you haven't seen that one out there)

✦ The SNMP ID is used to track the device using network management software

✦ If the device is set up properly, you will have the e-mail address or phone number of the appropriate contact person for this router or firewall

✦ Location information for the device which will tell you which wiring closet that the device is located in

Router and firewall ports

You will want to know each interface type as well as each interface address. Here are the fields you'll want to fill out:

✦ Device ID is the name that the administrator created for the device or the default name that the manufacturer set up for the device

✦ Interface type will either list Ethernet, software loopback, RS-232, or whatever other format the interface is running

✦ Interface address will be the physical network address (00.40.10.16.cb.b7), also known as the NIC or MAC address of the network card driving the interface

MAN and WAN basic info

It is just as important to document the configurable items of your metropolitan area network and wide area network as it is to document the configurable items of your local area network.

- The segment information (what *you've* named your MAN or WAN segment)
- The connection type (T1, DS3, Cable, DSL, etc.) and speed
- Whether or not the connection is a primary (up and running) connection
- You'll need to follow the basics with two more configurable items; the first containing information about the carrier and your contract, and the second for getting ahold of your point of contact at the carrier should you have problems

You'll also want to ensure that you've documented how and where the connections are made from the local exchange carrier into your building and your network.

- The Main Distribution Frame (MDF) location the carrier's biscuit or input feed
- The connecting device and port on your outbound router which should the information you entered into the configurable items for your routers
- The interface address for the connecting device

The list of interconnected systems

In the diagram of our small network (can you remember back that far?) we showed an external 3rd party interconnection outside the firewall, a web & application system in the DMZ, and a database & storage system in the secure subnet. These three systems interconnect with each other. What needs to be tracked as a CI for interconnected systems are the systems themselves, their security category, and their certification and accreditation status. If any of the following items changes (other than the name which is just an identifier), your organization should be informed and take the appropriate action.

- System Name
- Organization the system belongs to
- Connection Type (or DNS name)

- Connection agreement
- FIPS 199 Category
- C&A Status

As you can see, there are a *lot* of configurable items you have to think about, and track, for each and every system. How do you know which configurable items are important? Here's the benchmark we use. In our scenario the item in question is changed without your knowing it. If the system failed, could you rebuild the system properly without knowing about the changed item? To make the example more concrete, let's say that your staff changed the DNS address on the server. Your documentation shows an older DNS address. Your system them fails and you need to rebuild it back to working order. You bring it back and assign it the older DNS address. Would it work? Of course not, because the computers would be looking for the newer DNS address and not the older one. The configurable item is important if it changes the way the system operates. It is also important if it affects other configurable items.

The configurable items in each of your systems and your IT assets are going to affect your organizational standards and your organizational procedures. It is going to be very important for you to ensure that each time you change a configurable item in your systems, that you check your standards and your procedures to ensure that they are updated to reflect the changes. The same thing for your standards and procedures. When you change your standards (for which PCI cards you might purchase, or how much RAM should be in a computer, or your security settings), you'll want to ensure that your configurable items are updated as well. The same goes for changing your procedures.

Why use a configuration database?

Because the knee bone is connected to the shin bone, and the shin bone… Most of the IT assets that you use to get your job done are connected together and leverage each other, that's why. Configuration Items are related to other Configuration Items. The writing process for this book, just the checking in and out and editing of the Microsoft Word documents, has a multipart relationship of dependencies between Microsoft Word, Sharepoint, my workstation, the Sharepoint server, and the disk drives holding all of the data in both the server and my workstation.

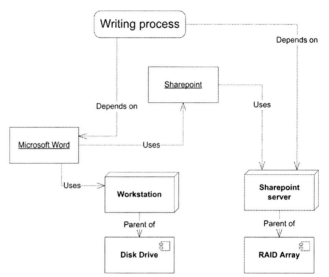

My writing process as a relationship example

A general process flow for configuration management

Without trying to write a book on configuration management, the basic process flow comes down to four steps.

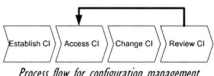

Process flow for configuration management

1. **Establishing the CIs** involves deciding the appropriate level of detail that you need to control and track. Items are then added to and managed by the database.

    Before you can establish your CIs in the database, you have to agree on the boundaries of management. This doesn't mean which computing equipment or geographical zone you are going to manage. This means agreeing on the *purpose* and *level of tracking* that you want to establish. You can track every attribute of your computer (motherboard, CPU speed, number of buses, etc.), or you can track user or IT staff changeable items such as memory, registry settings, applications installed, disk space. The best practices that we suggest are to set your boundaries only to manage those configuration attributes that

- are necessary for *effective* operations of your systems, meaning that they can alter the assurance of availability, integrity, or confidentiality of the system or its components, or
- can be impacted by *changes* to other CIs within the system.

How do you know if a configuration item meets either of these criteria? When analyzing your processes and procedures, you'll want to examine each process step to determine if it involves a configurable item. If it does, the best practice is to ensure that the process or procedure notifies any group that could be affected by any changes in the CI. In the example of examining organizational websites for systems continuity considerations, process step 1 and 2 involve documenting the configuration of the system (1) and a more in-depth documentation of the configuration of the server's critical applications (2).

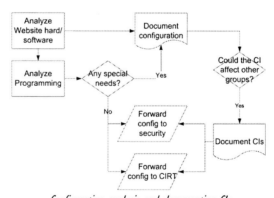

Configuration analysis and documenting CIs

When documenting the configuration of the system and the critical applications, the team has to ask if those configurable items could affect other groups within the organization. Any item that is necessary for effective operations of security or incident response would fall into this classification. In this case, if the CIs could affect the security group or the incident response team, the CIs need to be documented and not only does the configuration need to be forwarded to both groups, but also the groups also need to be notified of the CIs themselves. Items in this case would be IP setup, ports in use, registry settings, user accounts, etc.

For this reason, one of the policies and procedures that the organization employs should be to establish standards for configuration management and the definitions of CIs and their inter-relationships with other CIs. But that's for another time.

The last point to establishing the CIs in the organization is to *discover* the CI components and then document them. We have an entire book on that methodology[31].

2. **Accessing the CIs** becomes a day-to-day procedure for such groups as security, help desk, and incident management. The CMDB becomes a basic resource to help identify which CIs have changed, need to change, or need to revert back to an earlier state because the current state is causing a problem.

3. **Changing the CIs** is a process and procedure unto itself, and should be automated in the database whenever the CIs of any asset are modified. It is *imperative* that an automatic link between asset configurations and their CI entries in the CMDB database are directly linked and reported.

4. **Reviewing the CIs** becomes critical for such processes as continuity management, incident management, and security management. A review process that matches the current configuration of a system with the CI contents in the CMDB ensures database accuracy. Again, this is its own policy and procedure.

---

[31] Dorian J. Cougias and Marcelo Halpern, <u>Compliant Systems Documentation</u>. Schaser-Vartan Books, 2006. http://www.systemsdocumentation.com

In order to manage change, you will need a change model

A change model is a repeatable way of dealing with change. A change model defines specific steps that will be followed for any given change. Change models can be very simple with limited requirements for pre-approval before a change and post review after a change, or they can be quite complex, with many steps that require both approval and review.

Most change models follow the Plan Do Check Act (PDCA) four stage cycle for process management that was originally devised by W. Edwards Deming. In case you missed reading about it, here's a quick overview of PDCA.

Plan: design or revise processes that support the IT services. Plan establishes policy, objectives, processes, and procedures relevant to managing risk and improving information security to deliver results in accordance with an organization's overall policies and objectives. In relationship to change management, Plan focuses on planning for changes by communicating with others on the team about the proposed changes, reviewing the proposed changes, and not allowing changes to happen ad hoc, willy-nilly, or surreptitiously.

Do: implement the plan and manage the processes. Do implements and operate the policy, controls, processes, and procedures. In relationship to change management, Do focuses on conducting the approved changes in a timely manner and communicating with anyone necessary about the changes as they are about to take place, taking place, and have taken place.

Check: measure the processes and IT services, compare with objectives and produce reports. Check assesses and, where applicable, measure process performance against ISMS policy, objectives and practical experience and report the results to management for review. In relationship to change management, Check focuses on testing and communicating the approved and implemented changes to ensure that they've met their definition of success.

Act: plan and implement changes to improve the processes. Act takes corrective and preventive actions, based on the results of the internal ISMS audit and management review or other relevant information, to achieve continual improvement. In relationship to change management, Act focuses on post implementation reviews to identify opportunities for improvement in the overall change model in the future.

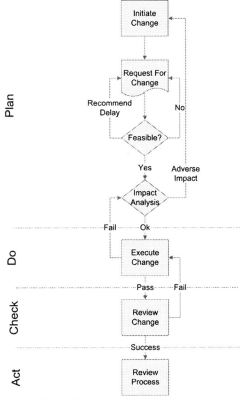

The basic change management process

If you didn't notice, threaded throughout the four point process above is the message that the various team members have to communicate with each other. In terms of change management, there are four roles that *must* take part in the RACI process; the change requester, change owner, change advisors, and change manager.

The change requester: is the person who initiates the request for change – whether the person is within a business unit, the IT group, or a vendor.

☩ **The change owner**: is the person responsible for planning and implement the approved change.

☩ **The change advisors**: (or Change Advisory Board) is a cross-functional group that evaluates change requests and either approves the changes, denies them, or modifies them.

☩ **The configuration manager**: is the person responsible for maintaining the configuration management database (which can even be a Word or Excel file) for the system in question. This person will also be responsible for scheduling the proposed changes.

☩ **The change manager**: is the overall authority for the change management process and assigns the responsibility to a change owner once a change has been approved.

Adding these roles to the mix, looking at the following diagram you can see how the change management process moves through the various staff members and how it has picked up a few steps.

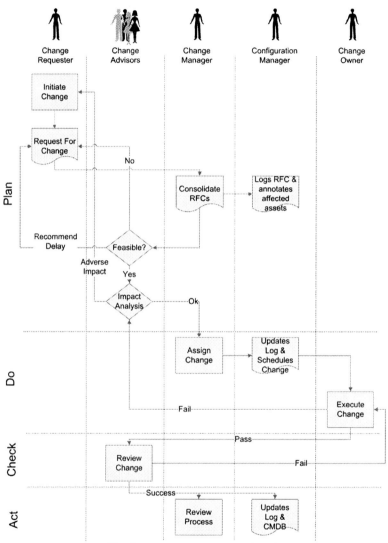

The change management process by role

However, information technologists aren't particularly adept at team communication. Therefore, in order to aid the PDCA process and ensure that your team are communicating with each other properly, you'll want to turn to another four-letter acronym called "RACI" to make your life easier, which we've discussed in depth earlier in the book.

Below is the RACI chart for our initial change management model. Notice which personnel are consulted and which are informed at the various steps. Remember that consulted means that the conversation is two-way, with the person being consulted having input. Informing someone means to simply update them on the progress without asking for their input into the process step.

	Step	Change Requester	Change Advisors	Change Manager	Configuration Manager	Change Owner
Plan	Initiate a change	RA				
	Create an RFC using the appropriate forms and submit the RFC to the Change Manager	RA		I		
	Collect and consolidate RFCs by system and ensure initial documentation is complete	I		RA		
	Determine if the proposed changes are feasible	I	R	A		C
	Determine the impact of each of the changes on any potentially affected IT assets	I	R	A		C
	Approve or deny the change request	I	R	A		C
	Log the RFC and annotate affected assets				RA	
Do	Assign the change requests to a change owner			RA		C
	Prepare for, schedule, and execute the change	I		A		R
Check	Review the changes to ensure they have succeeded	I	R	A		C
Act	Update the RFC Log and the Configuration Database			I	RA	I
	Review the overall change management process	C	C	RA		C

The RACI table for our change model

The Request For Change (RFC)

A Request For Change is based upon the need to modify a standard set by the organization – for any number of reasons. Some of the reasons include:

- Changing the system in response to an incident, SLA issue, or problem
- Changing the system in order to keep up with business unit changes
- Regular patch, upgrade, and security management
- Compliance and regulatory changes that mandate system changes

No matter what the reason for initiating the need for change, all proper change management models begin with someone filling out the organization's Request For Change (RFC) documentation. The RFC will either be a Word form or online form that contains all of the relevant information about the proposed change. Because the change advisors who will be reviewing the RFC are going to ask a great deal of "who, what, when, how, and what if" questions about the proposed change, the RFC must be able to describe those issues as much as possible in an effort to make the process as simple as possible. The reason that the RFC has to be in a "form" format is so that the information recorded in the RFC is standardized and can be consolidated with other "like" requests for change.

Here is the basic information that the form has to have *filled out* before it can be submitted for review. There is additional information that the review group will fill out later, but this will suffice for getting the ball rolling.

Basic information

- **Control ID**: is the unique ID assigned to the request so that it can be tracked.
- **Request Date/Revision Date**: is the initial date that the request was made so that the date can be taken into account for priority and scheduling purposes. The revision date should also be added in case (and many times this happens) the RFC has to be changed before it can be submitted.
- **Status**: reflects the lifecycle status of the change, which should be any of these:
  o   has been accepted,
  o   is in committee for review,

- o should be revised,
- o is declined or approved,
- o is scheduled,
- o requested change is in progress,
- o requested change has been released, or
- o requested change has been documented and completed.

⚡ **Schedule Date**: is filled out once the RFC's proposed change has been scheduled. This should correspond with a name being filled out in the **Approved By** field.

⚡ **Approved By**: is the name of the Change Manager or Advisory Team member who has authorized and approves of the change taking place.

Change initiator information

This information provides detail about the person requesting the change, the system or asset in question, the reasons for the change, and what might happen if the change doesn't take place.

⚡ **Requester's name and contact info**: should reflect the person's name, desk or cell phone, and e-mail address for later contact and clarification if necessary.

⚡ **System or Asset affected**: reflects whatever identification methodology your organization uses for their systems and assets. The reason for an ID and not a name is for definitive reference, as we know that some of you name your computers "Homer Simpson" and other silly things.

⚡ **RFC Title**: refers to the RFC by something other than its ID.

⚡ **Reason for change**: states whether this change is for regular patches, updates, the business might have changed, or that this is the result of a problem or incident. Whatever the reason, state it plain and simple.

⚡ **Implication of ignoring the change**: presents your case for what will happen to the system or asset in question (or the organization for that matter) if the change is not approved.

What you want to change and what it will affect

⚡ **Proposed change description & implications of the change**: lists what, precisely, you intend to change. If you are adding a patch, what is it patching? What will happen once the patch has been applied? If you are replacing a card, adding software, whatever, you'll want to state the change being made. *And*, you'll also want to state the implications of the change. If you are upgrading your software, the implications will more than likely be that you will lose some type of backward compatibility, or that others might have to upgrade with you. You will also want to state any *legal* or *compliance* implications of the change.

⚡ **All configurable items and staff that will be affected by the change**: lists the asset(s) being changed as well as any other asset on the device or within the system[32]. This means that you'll need to communicate with the system's configuration manager if you don't know which assets there are for the system. Also, if any staff members are going to be affected, you'll want to list them.

⚡ **All other devices on the network or external users that you think the changes might affect**: considers *anyone* or *anything* that will be affected by the change. For instance, if you are changing the DNS address, anyone attempting to find the device at the old address will be left out in the cold if they aren't informed of the change.

Your proposed change plan

⚡ **Proposed change plan**: covers *how* you propose that the changes be made to the system of the IT asset using a step-by-step method. The change plan should also include an estimated amount of time that it should take to make the change. What we've found very useful is that if there are standard changes (such as patch plans, software and hardware upgrades, etc.), these have their own procedures so that the procedure can be reference here.

---

[32]   The term *system* here refers to all devices and IT assets that must work together to support the business unit's goal.

- **Resources needed to make the change**: covers all of the resources (including people) that are needed in order to effect the change. *This should also cover the proposed cost* of the change to ensure that you have the appropriate budget.

- **Proposed roll-back plan**: covers the course of action you'll plan to take if the change can not be implemented properly. Most patches can be rolled back. Some upgrades (especially Windows XP Service Pack 2) *cannot* be rolled back.

- **Suggested change priority and category**: covers the priority that this change should have, and the category that the change should fall into. The priorities are:

  o **Low**: the change is not pressing.

  o **Medium**: to gain the benefit of other changes, this change should be made.

  o **High**: the change is important for the organization and should be implemented at the earliest convenience.

  o **Emergency**: should only be used when the organization is being put at great risk if the change is not implemented immediately.

The categories are:

  o **Standard**: is a change that has been performed many times (and has a procedure attached to it) and has therefore become a part of the operational methodologies of the organization.

  o **Minor**: is a change that is more involved than a standard procedural change and that has consequences that would affect a small number of people. This number should be pre-defined by your organization.

  o **Significant**: is a wide-spread change that would affect an entire business unit or operational department. This type of change has almost nothing to do with standard procedures and therefore will incur more resources to enact the change (as well as affect more resources adversely if it fails).

  o **Major**: is a change that would ensure your next position is that of a fry cook at McDonald's if it fails. This type of change, should it fail or the change take much longer to enact, could affect the organization materially (another definition you should have in place before you begin to put change management into action).

Request For Change (RFC)	Control ID	UCF ID F 00001
	Request/Revised Date	
	Status	Requested
	Schedule Date	
	Approved By	

1. Change Initiator information

Requestor's Name/E-Mail	
System or asset affected	
RFC title	
Reason for change	
Implication of ignoring the change	

2. Proposed change description & implications of the change

3. List all configurable items and staff that are affected by this change (including the assets being changed)

1	
2	
3	
4	
5	
6	
7	
8	
9	
10	

4. List other devices on the network or external users that you think this change might affect

1	
2	
3	
4	
5	

5. Proposed change plan (including estimated time to make the change)

6. Resources needed for the change to take place (include people as well as hardware and software)

7. Proposed roll-back plan if change fails

8. Suggested change priority and category

Change Priority: Low	Change Category: Standard

There, that's the information that the person(s) filling out the change form need to know and state in order to get the form approved and into the hands of the change manager.

Establishing the change management team

There are five key roles in change management, and those roles are;

1. The change requester or initiator

2. The change manager

3. The change advisors

4. The configuration manager

5. The change owner

We'll go over the roles and responsibilities of each of these key members, minus the change requester or initiator because that role can fall to any member of the organization.

The change manager

The change manager is responsible for the day to day activities of the change management process for the Information Management team. This person must necessarily be a process-driven person as the change manager is responsible for:

- logging and consolidating the RFCs,
- ensuring that the RFCs are filled out correctly,
- assigning the change requests to a change owner, and
- constantly reviewing the overall change process.

The change manager also approves:

- the change advisor's determination whether the proposed changes are feasible,
- the change advisor's determination of the level of impact of each proposed change on any IT asset,
- or denies change requests for all but major and emergency changes,
- the change owner's preparations and change execution plan, and
- all completed changes to ensure success.

In essence, the change manager is involved in most every step of the change management process.

The change advisors

The change advisors are decision makers with the responsibility for approving or rejecting certain RFCs based upon feasibility and risk. Therefore, the change advisors should be folks who have a stake or interest in the business end of the information management technologies being effected. This means that the change advisors will be drawn from different parts of the organization based upon each of the systems and RFCs in question. This doesn't mean that a core group of people can't or shouldn't be drawn from as "change advisor regulars" or a Change Advisory Board.

The change advisors have the responsibility for:

- determining the feasibility of each proposed change (including the necessary budget allocation),
- determining the level of impact of each proposed change on any IT asset, and
- recommending the approval or denial of change requests, and
- reviewing the changes to ensure that they have succeeded.

The configuration manager

The configuration manager is almost tangential to the change management process in that the configuration manager has no approval authority in the process. However, the configuration manager is **key** to the process in that the configuration manager must log and annotate all *proposed* changes for all affected assets, and then log the *completed* changes for all affected assets once the project has been completed. These actions will ensure that the configuration management database is kept up to date at all times.

The change owner

The change owner is the person assigned to actually prepare and then make the approved changes to the system. The change owner is consulted about:

- whether the proposed changes are feasible,
- the suggested impact of each of the proposed changes,
- whether or not the change request should be approved or denied,
- the scheduling of the change, and
- the overall change management process.

In addition, the change manager has the responsibility for preparing and then executing the approved changes.

Therefore, the change owner should be picked by the change manager early in the process, so that he or she can work with the person requesting the change as well as the change advisors who will review the change.

Change logging and managing the change process

There are two ways to handle changes to systems. The first method allows anyone to make a change at any time, once the change has been approved. This is an okay (but not great) method for small organizations with very little change to happening to their systems. However, larger organizations with multiple requests for changes to the *same* system cannot operate this way. Once multiple change requests to the same system become the norm, change requests must be consolidated and reviewed together in order to avoid confusion and prolonged downtime, as well as to allow a consolidated impact analysis.

Logging, analyzing, reviewing, approving, and scheduling changes isn't really as hard as it might seem. We've boiled the entire process down into a three page spreadsheet and associated calculations that we'll go over here in some detail. We only show the spreadsheet and our calculations here to make our point about the information that you need to track and some of the variables that you'll want to use when making your decisions. We *highly* suggest that larger organizations use change management tracking software.

Consolidating the RFCs

Once the change requester documents all of the information in the proposed RFC, the RFC is submitted to the change manager.

 Note, at this point, some authors who write about change management state that if the change requester doesn't have the RFC filled out correctly, that it should go through a screening process, and be returned for changes before it is accepted. That's just a lot of bureaucratic hogwash. Seriously. If the change requester and the change manager can't work together to ensure that the RFC process is understood, the RFC is detailed enough, and it is completed properly, then the two of them should be replaced with more competent staff. End of story.

As the change manager begins gathering the RFCs, they must be logged into an impact assessment worksheet. The sample that we provide was created in Excel, and we are sure that better ones exist. If they do, please contact us and let us know and we'll make them available to our readers. Our sample has six key fields that need to be included in the first page of the RFC impact worksheet.

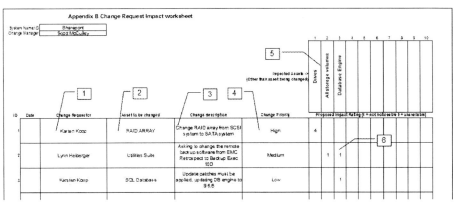

Page 1 of the RFC impact worksheet

1. The first item that needs to be tracked is the change requester's name, and possibly contact information such as e-mail or phone number.

2. The second item to be tracked is the asset that is being changed. By asset, we mean the application, cards, drives, etc.

3. The third item to be tracked is a short description of the change being proposed. This doesn't have to be lengthy as the original RFC will have the full detail.

4. The fourth item is the change priority, which we've discussed previously. This should fall from low through high, with emergency changes only happening if the system in question *failed*, or the building failed.

5. Within each RFC, the change requester listed up to ten configurable items or staff that could be impacted by the proposed change to the system in question. If you'll notice on our example form there are only ten columns for assets. Theoretically, the first RFC could fill all ten of those asset columns. In that scenario a second RFC for the same system could request a change that impacts an eleventh asset. If that can be the case, why did we limit our form to ten columns? Simple. Our rule is this – once ten assets in a system are being impacted by a proposed change, that is a significant enough change to warrant holding off any further changes until that one has been completed. For us, our rule is that once ten assets are being affected – whether that is through a single change or

multiple changes – no more RFCs can be added to the system for that change period.

6. A conversation between the change requester and the change manager should create a proposed failure rating for each asset between 1 (not noticeable) and 5 (rendering the system unavailable). This number represents a first attempt at classifying the risk of failing to properly make the change, and how that failure would impact the asset in question.

What happens if there are ten change requests before ten assets are impacted? What we've found is that the "rule of ten" as we call it seems to be working okay. All further changes to the system are frozen once *either* ten assets are affected or ten changes are being made. The complexity of troubleshooting the system once either of those numbers grows larger is too much to bear. There are very few change releases that are fault free, so keeping your changes to a manageable set will become very important to your success rate remaining high.

Reviewing the RFCs

Once the RFCs have been consolidated, they should be reviewed and the reviews consolidated as well. The change advisors shouldn't have to meet face to face, as that can be a time wasting effort. We've found that the best method is to keep the whole process simple and either route the RFCs as PDFs to each of the change advisors, or route them through a Sharepoint server as "tracked" Word documents so that all of the changes and annotations can be consolidated and reviewed in one place.

This doesn't mean that a quarterly or bi-annually meeting of the change advisors shouldn't be scheduled to review their progress and overall change management. Or that a wide spread or high classification change shouldn't call for a meeting to discuss the ramifications of the project. What we're saying is that for day-to-day routine business, change authorization should be kept at as low a level as possible.

When consolidating the change impact reviews, four points of information should be tracked and annotated in the logging system, within additional fields (the asset(s) to be changed and the affected assets) being carried over from the previous page.

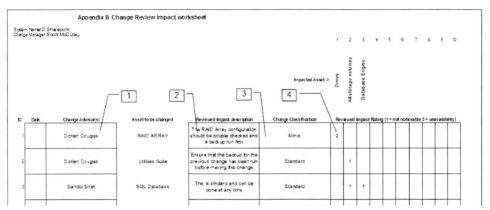

Page 2 of the RFC impact worksheet

1. The change advisor(s) for each proposed RFC should be listed by name.

2. When the change advisors reviewed each RFC, they made notes regarding the impact of the changes. The *highlights* of these notes should be added here for clarity in the decision making process.

3. The RFC's change classification (from standard through major), *as restated by the change advisors*, should be listed here. It should be noted that if all of the changes are classified as standard, then the change review process should be halted and the changes automatically approved. There is no sense in wasting anyone's time if all of the proposed changes are ones that have been happening as a matter of course and business as usual.

4. The final bit of information that needs to get added to the change review impact worksheet is the *reviewer's* take on the failure impact rating. This is important, because it is used in a calculation for the final page. The math behind this bit of input basically states that if the change requester and the change reviewer agree on the impact, there is no issue. Or if the reviewer thinks that the impact is lower than the requester does, there is no issue. However, if the reviewer thinks that the impact is *higher* than what the requester thinks, there **is** an issue that needs to be addressed.

Approving the RFCs

Once the reviews have taken place, there should be two deciding factors – do the reviewers and change requester agree on the failure impact of the proposed changes, and is any special authorization needed based upon the change classification?

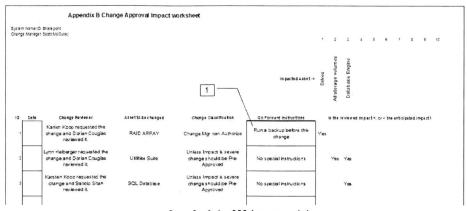

Page 3 of the RFC impact worksheet

The change classification decision making process is simple. If the change request is an emergency change, then the change advisors *must* authorize the change. If the change requests are all standard, unless the impact assessment is severe the changes should be automatically approved. All other changes can be authorized by the change manager.

Once the changes have been approved, any *go forward* instructions should be duly noted on the worksheet and the approval process ended by scheduling the change appropriately.

Collecting improvement information through a control plan

Policies and procedures are like kids – once they are born, they have to be nurtured into adulthood. Therefore, you'll have to have a control plan for scheduling and monitoring their changes and further development. The *only* way to monitor their improvement is through a structured plan which also includes ongoing communication and training.

Creating a review timetable

When should policies and procedures be reviewed? As the surrounding environment changes and as the users mature in their use of the procedures. Which means that every organization's control plan will be different. Here are some general suggestions for control points.

As the regulatory bodies change

If you are a member of the ITCi Unified Compliance Project's website[33], or you've purchased the IT Impact Zone spreadsheets with the updates[34], you'll be able to track the changes to any of the 400+ regulations and standards that we track. You'll know if something changed and if that change affects your policies and procedures because each control in the Unified Compliance Frame (which the UCP follows) has its own ID. If you've been following the steps we've recommended, you'll have a one-to-one relationship between your controls and ours and you'll be able to track updates.

---

[33] http://www.itcinstitute.com/ucp or through the unifiedcompliance.com website.

[34] Same place.

As your agreements change

Someone in your group will need to monitor organizational contracts, MOUs (Memorandums of Understanding), letters of agreement, and SLAs (Service Level Agreements).

If you are smart, you are mapping these documents to your IT Impact Zone control matrix so that you can monitor which agreements affect which controls. By doing this, you can treat local agreements just like regulatory bodies.

As the threats and vulnerabilities change

Your organization should be managing its own threat database through the CIRT team and help desk logs and reviews. This can be augmented by the Threat Explorer that Symantec publishes[35]. The US has its own National Vulnerability Database[36]. When any of the published threats and vulnerabilities target assets in your Configuration Management Database and affect your policies and procedures, those assets, policies, and procedures should be reviewed.

As your business processes change status

All assets that support business processes carry the same status as the business process. If you have a policy and procedures for managing an asset that moves from an initial stage to a strategic stage, or from a strategic stage to a factory-production stage, you'll want to change the policies and procedures accordingly.

How do you know which stage the business process is currently in, and where it is moving? How about ongoing communications with the manager of the business process? Keeping in monthly communication with these managers will give you update cues for controlling the corresponding policies and procedures.

---

35   http://www.symantec.com/enterprise/security_response/threatexplorer/threats.jsp

36   http://nvd.nist.gov/nvd.cfm?cvename=CVE-2006-3223

As your systems, assets, and configurable items change

Systems undergo constant upgrades. A hard drive dies and a new drive is put into place. Software gets updated. Whole systems get updated. Any time that a system or any of its tracked subcomponents change, this should create at least a cursory review of the policies and procedures surrounding that system and those assets.

If the environment has remained static, the annual review

If nothing in the organization has changed and there are no new laws, regulations, standards, etc., then you'll want to review your policies and procedures at least once a year. The document's last modification date will give you the yearly review date of the policy or procedure and you'll be able to enter this into a schedule.

Constant communication

You write your policies and procedures. You edit them. You introduce them and make any initial changes. Other than the review timetable just mentioned, you're done, right? Heck no!

Communicating the procedure schedule

Each procedure should be on a set schedule (even if that schedule is a "do this once a year if nothing else"). Therefore, you should have a manual or automated schedule sent out to all intended parties informing them that the procedures should be run at certain times and places.

Ongoing education

Training and awareness should be moving into a continual mode by this time. There is always something to brush up on or new technique to share. Therefore, everyone involved in procedures should either be learning or sharing their knowledge, or both. How you communicate that will be up to you.

Formal reports to higher management

Monthly and quarterly reports of all policy and procedure adherence or disobedience should be reported to higher level management. Management likes reports, and while a detailed metric plan probably isn't in place yet (that comes in the next level of maturity), you'll need to begin *some* type of regular and formal reporting.

A simple control plan that we've used in the past is shown below.

Policy and Procedure review plan			Organizational Entity		
Review dates *do not include* monthly regulation checks or daily threat and vulnerability checks			Page 1 of 1		

ID	Policy or procedure name	Last review date	Next review date	LOB contact date	Next training date
1					
2					
3					
4					
5					

Sample control plan for policies and procedures

FROM MANAGED (4) TO OPTIMIZING (5)

By now, management is able to maturely use techniques and tools to communicate their understanding of the full requirements of compliance, controls, policies, and procedures.

All aspects of processes are documented and repeatable. Policies are approved by management and documented. Standards for developing policies and procedures are adopted and followed.

Tools are implemented according to a standardized plan and some have been integrated with other related tools. Tools are being used in main areas to automate the management of processes and procedures, as well as monitor critical activities and controls.

Skill requirements are routinely updated for all areas with proficiency being ensured for all critical areas. Mature training and awareness techniques are applied according to an education plan with knowledge sharing being encouraged. Internal domain experts are involved in training and awareness development and delivery. Effectiveness of the education plan is routinely assessed.

Process owners have full authority to exercise their initiatives with accountability and responsibility fully accepted by management.

Metrics are now statistically valid with an increase in their breadth and interconnectedness.

Effectiveness and efficiency are linked to business goals and the overall IT strategy.

Therefore the goals are twofold – to establish and standardize root cause analysis of process and procedure problems through establishing quantitative objectives for policies and procedures and stabilizing sub-performance processes and procedures.

This will allow process management and measurement to take place. Through the monitoring and measurement of compliance with organizational policies and procedures, the organization will be able to intervene and take actions where processes are not effective.

Establishing quantitative objectives for the measurement of procedures and processes

Writing policies and procedures is one thing. Figuring out if they are effective, and how effective they are, is something quite different. It is now time to begin applying quantitative measurement analysis. How do you measure the effectiveness of policies and procedures?

1. The first step is to separate the measurable parts of the procedures from the un-measurable parts. Or put differently, separating the procedure into qualitative and quantitative segments.

    In our example, our procedure is to analyze the organizational websites' hardware and software configuration, document the configuration, and then coordinate with two other groups. We've broken this down into types of activities (the process, or documentation), identified whether they are quantitative or qualitative, and how they would be measured.

Type	What?	Quantitative?	How?
Process	Analyze hardware configuration for CIs	Yes	Time, accuracy
Document	Document hardware CIs	Yes	Completeness of report
Process	Analyze software configuration for CIs	Yes	Time, accuracy
Document	Document software CIs	Yes	Completeness report
Process	Coordination with security team	No	Ability to communicate
Process	Coordination with CIRT	No	Ability to communicate
Document	Update of CMDB	Yes	Completeness of report as matched to DB
Document	Update of system continuity plan (CIRT & DR team)	Yes	Time to coordinate CI attributes & system continuity plan

Dividing the procedure into qualitative and quantitative areas

2. Determine *how* it is being measured.

This isn't a qualitative analysis guide. I wouldn't know one if it bit me. But with that said, there are a few ways that we've used in the past to quantify how well procedures have been working. One method evaluates the number of errors produced by the person working with the procedure and a second method evaluates the time it takes to run the procedures as measured against a specified "goal" time. Let's discuss both.

Measuring accuracy

The first set of measurements asks if, and how well, the written procedures help the users perform the process. The best way to gather that data is to allow the users an after-action report for the procedure. This should be defined as a part of the "success" reports that are sent back to management when writing the procedure. Standard questions that we usually include are.

- Did you feel there was wasted time during the process?
- Was the procedure documentation confusing at any part?
- Were you missing any tools that were required to follow the procedure?
- What did the procedure leave out that you could have been trained on?
- Did the procedure lead you to gather inaccurate data?
- Did the procedure lead you to document information incorrectly?
- Were you prevented from integrating any of the data into other documentation?

While these questions might look like "short answer" questions, the answers can also be tallied into 1s and 0s representing problems/not problems.

What	Problems
Time wasted	2
Documentation confusing	3
Missing tools	1
More knowledge needed	1
Inaccurate gathering of information	2
Inaccurate presentation of information	1
Inability to integrate into CMDB	1

The table of problems

Seeing the information as a table is mediocre at best. Turning the information into something visually usable is what you want to do. By tallying this information as 1s and 0s and tracking those 1s and 0s over time, you can turn this type of report into a simple *Pareto* chart that can be used to present the relative frequency and importance of the problems that you are having.

The following graph has two scales, the errors (bar) which lead to a cumulative total (line). Looking at this visual you know that if you can solve three problems (time wasted, confusing documentation, inaccurate gathering of information) you'll have the bulk of the work done. Not to mention having something that an executive can grasp.

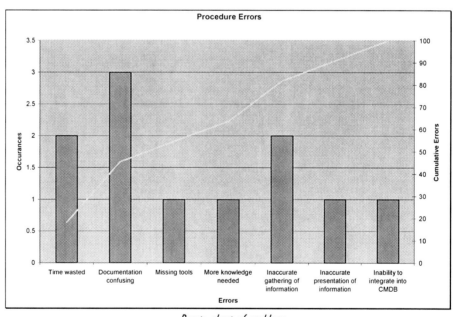

Pareto chart of problems

You'll also want to be able to measure the time it takes to run a process versus the time that the procedure states *should* be allowed. This is a pretty easy measurement and again something that you can ask the users to report on in their "success" report at the end of the procedure. And by breaking down the allotted time for each of the phases, the report should show the total time as well as the time for each of the phases within the procedure as documented in the following table.

	Actual (hrs)	Goal (hrs)
Hours to gather information	2	1
Hours to integrate information into DB	1	0.25
Time to correct configuration errors	1	0.25

Documenting actual time versus goal time

As with the previous table, turning this into a stacked bar chart tells a *much* better story.

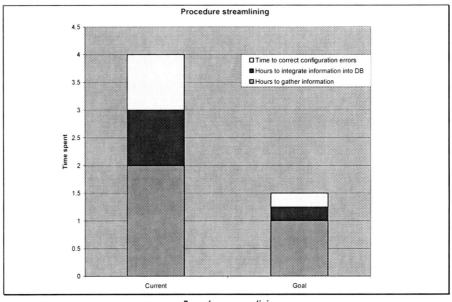

Procedure streamlining

What we are left with is two equations – one that shows we have errors and complaints about the written procedures, and a second that shows we aren't running the procedures as well as we think we could be running them. The problem is that these two charts don't show a correlation between them. What you want to do is somehow tie one set of issues (known problems) with the second set of issues (poor performance). This can be done through the magic of a bubble chart and a starting theory of where the correlation might be found.

To cut to the chase, in our example we used the hypothesis that if we could correct the confusing writing in the procedure, this would solve some of the major problems. Using the input from five people, we found that the various problems were spread across the board, but a total of 4 of them had complained about confusing documentation. So we pulled that question out of the general answers and correlated it with the other problems. When we did this, we found that 3 of the people who said the documentation was confusing also thought they wasted time. While two people felt they gathered inaccurate data, only one of them also felt the documentation was confusing. And one person who couldn't integrate the collected data into the CMDB also found the documentation confusing.

Input from 4 people	Various problems	Documentation confusing
Time wasted	2	3
Inaccurate gathering of information	2	1
Inability to integrate into CMDB	1	1

Correlation of various problems with confusing documentation

Here's the same data as a bubble chart.

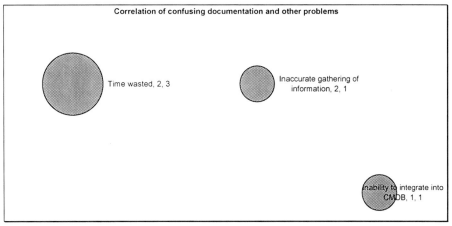

Bubble chart

There are a ton of other charts and types that you can use. The best place to start is at the Microsoft website where they teach you about the different chart types, emphasizing when to use them and how to build them[37]. And no matter how you choose to display your information, there are a few goals you'll want to accomplish when establishing your quantitative objectives. You'll want to:

1. Clearly define what should and should not be measured quantitatively

2. Define how you are going to gather, track, and display that quantitative measurement

3. Meet with higher level managers to ensure that the statistics you are gathering are correct, understandable, and useful *to them* as well as to your team

---

37   http://office.microsoft.com/en-us/assistance/CH010003731033.aspx

Stabilizing sub-performance procedures

There are four general categories for why procedures fail.

1. The procedure is wrong. It doesn't address the issue, it addresses the wrong issue, the issue has changed, or the policy wasn't a good policy to begin with.

2. The procedure was written and communicated poorly. The organization might be bad, the writing unclear, the tools or system targets may have changed, or the level of knowledge needed was not communicated correctly. Or, the procedure was written well, and yet, the front line staff could make improvements.

3. The users need more training on the procedures because subtle nuances of the procedures just can't be put into writing.

4. The users don't care because their management doesn't care because nobody is making anyone care.

Let's start with number four and work towards number one.

Stabilizing sub-performance due to lack of care

The first step is to understand what motivates people. All of us, every last one of us, is motivated through our head, our heart, or our hide. We are motivated by something because it makes sense. We are motivated by something because we intrinsically care. We are motivated by fear. One, two, or all three in combination. And yes, some are not motivated at all and should be fired.

And not everyone on the team or in the organization is going to be motivated by the same thing. For a while, we had a woman who would tell our leadership that she was motivated by "the heart," only to find out that all of our motivation tactics aimed that way didn't work. Only motivation through "skinning her hide" worked – but that got tiring for management very quickly.

If the problem really is due to motivation, you'll have to find new and interesting ways of motivating your staff and inculcate those methods into metrics management and your reward (or punishment) system.

The only thing we really have to say about motivation through "hide" is that you *do* have to indicate what will happen to your staff if they choose not to follow your policies, standards, and procedures. While this might not work for your organization, what we've found works for ours (used sparingly) is a simple statement at the end of our most important procedures that says, "we regretfully accept your resignation if you fail to follow these key procedures."

Before you attempt anything like that, clear it with HR and your organizational legal team.

Stabilizing sub-performance through additional training

There is a form of Japanese bread that the making of cannot be put into writing. There are things you need to understand with other people in a process, and how to work with them during the process, that cannot be put into writing. And there are undoubtedly many other bits and pieces of information that make processes flow much smoother than can be written down into procedural form.

For these instances, there is additional person-to-person training. But how do you know what to train on? The best way is to have people tell you what they need to know. Trust me, nobody in IT that we've ever met goes on and reads through procedures they think are goofy *without* having something to say about it. So leverage that and provide user feedback forms that generate the response you are looking for. We show an example after the next heading of a form that we use in the field that allows the front line people to add their two cents to what they think is missing. One of the checkbox items is a lack of training. And that's where your training should focus for remediation of the problems found.

Stabilizing sub-performance due to poor documentation

Just because you edited your policies, standards, and procedures doesn't mean that the writing is sufficient for the purpose. It only means that the editors were happy with it – not the people in the field who have to use the procedures on a day-to-day basis. And trust me when I say that no matter how much you edit up front, when you get out into the real world and something else is breaking that the original writers didn't think about – the game changes and the documentation has to change too.

The best way to find out what is wrong with the documentation is to follow the same example we stated with training – ask the people on the front lines. And yes, we have a form for that. It is very much like the original editing from you provided to your content editors but puts more of a focus on "the field knows best" in order to get their input.

Policy or procedure name		Control ID	
		Effective Date	
		Revision Date	
		Revision Number	
		Approved By	

1. Where you'd like to add knowledge

☐ Policy statement	☐ Assignment	☐ Procedure triggers
☐ Description	☐ Required knowledge	☐ Potential mishaps & reaction steps
☐ Purpose	☐ Required tools	☐ Successful execution
☐ Compliance	☐ Extended definition	☐ Reports
☐ Scope	☐ Procedure goals	☐ Procedure steps
☐ Coverage	☐ Supporting and supported procedures	☐ Procedure checklists

2. Problem type

☐ There are additional mishaps to consider	☐ We need more training
☐ Subtle changes have occurred	☐ This is much faster, more accurate, etc
☐ We've learned something on the front lines	☐ _____

3. What the issue you've found?

4. What would you do different?

Action taken	☐ If yes, what action?	☐ If no, why not?

Submitted by _____

Action taken by _____

Authorized by _____

Front line feedback form

Once you can gather information from the field about what they find lacking, you can begin making your changes. And then training your staff on the changes. And then measuring those changes for indications of a better process.

Stabilizing sub-performance when the issue is wrong or the target has changed

Fortunately this one is pretty easy to spot. If your users are out there expecting to analyze the documentation for your attached storage RAID array, and it doesn't exist because it's been removed in favor of an iSCSI centralized storage system, then you know that the issues have changed.

A SELF-AUDIT GUIDE FOR ANALYZING YOUR COMPLIANCE FRAMEWORK OF POLICIES AND PROCEDURES

You've come a long way toward understanding your compliance framework and the level of maturity that you need to have if you are to say that you have optimized your policies and procedures.

This chapter offers a very simple methodology for auditing your compliance framework and the level of maturity you have achieved for your policies and procedures.

Analyzing the acceptance of framework controls

The first step in your analysis will be to determine if you have defined your framework correctly. We'll walk through each of the phases, beginning with scoping and ending with the selection of controls (and the documentation thereof).

Gathering of the documents

❏ Has the organization collected a full list of all regulations, standards, guidelines, MOUs, SLAs, letters of agreement, and contracts that could influence the compliance framework control list?

If you are not sure whether you have all of the correct documents, you'll need to gather them together in one spot. Which also means that you'll need to *find* them – meaning that you'll need to be talking to the people in your organization who will know where they are. Be sure to gather documents from all countries where you do business, have customers, or outsource your data processing and customer service activities.

Contact your legal representative, HR representative, Disaster Recovery representative, your CIO, compliance staff (if you have them), and most importantly **the business group owners** who will know where those elusive MOUs, SLAs, contracts, and letters of agreement are.

Creating your control list matrix

❏ Has the organization listed all of these controls in a hierarchical manner and cross referenced them for clarity of understanding? A great example of this is the spreadsheet that follows which is taken from the IT impact zone tables available from the IT Compliance Institute's Unified Compliance Project and the Unified Compliance Framework[38] websites.

---

38 http://www.itcinstitute.com/ucp or http://www.unifiedcompliance.com

UNIFIED COMPLIANCE PROJECT

IT IMPACT ZONE: AUDIT AND RISK MANAGEMENT

Harmonized Control Title	Control Id	Sarbanes Oxley Calculation	Banking and Finance Calculation	NASD NSYE Calculation	Healthcare and Life Science Calculation	Energy Calculation	Credit Card Calculation	Federal Security Calculation	IRS Calculation	Records Management Calculation	NIST Calculation	ISO Calculation	ITIL Calculation	General Guidance Calculation	US Federal Privacy Calculation	US State Laws Calculation	EU Guidance Calculation	UK Canadian Guidance Calculation	Latin American Guidance Calculation	Other Europe Guidance Calculation	Asia and Pacific Rim Guidance Calculation	Internal Guidance
Defining critical business functions	00736	X						X			X			X								X
Review and prioritize each business unit and process	01165	X		X				X			X			X								X
Critical records identification	00737																					
Defining critical personnel	00739	X	X	X				X			X			X								X
Defining critical IT Resources	00740	X	X	X	X			X			X			X				X				X
SLAs include continuity planning	00741													X				X				X
Workstation protection considerations	01378										X											
Server considerations	01379										X											
Web site and intranet considerations	01380										X											
Online and near line storage considerations	01383										X											
Mainframe considerations	01382										X											
Systems protection considerations	01268	X	X		X			X		X	X	X		X								X
Communications systems considerations	00743	X	X								X			X								X
Local Area Network considerations	01361										X											
Wide Area Network considerations	01294										X					X						

Sample list of controls

Each of the regulatory groups can be expanded to show each guideline document with the relevant paragraph or section citation.

Harmonized Control Title	Control Id	FFIEC Business Continuity Planning
Defining critical business functions	00736	
Review and prioritize each business unit and process	01165	Exam Q 1.3, Q 3.5, Q 7.
Critical records identification	00737	
Defining critical personnel	00739	Pg E1
Defining critical IT Resources	00740	Pg E1, D2
SLAs include continuity planning	00741	
Workstation protection considerations	01378	
Server considerations	01379	
Web site and intranet considerations	01380	
Online and near line storage considerations	01383	
Mainframe considerations	01382	
Systems protection considerations	01268	Pg E4-5, Pg E6-7
Communications systems considerations	00743	Pg D1-3

Individual citation expanded from overall list

If you want to know more about any of the controls, each of the Control IDs is an active link to the Unified Compliance Framework's website where that control is spelled out in great detail, along with any pertinent commentary from our vast field editor audience.

00739

Defining critical personnel

Just as we mentioned in the last section, defining what's critical means a great deal to an organization's survival. Here, the critical asset we are identifying is people. Some people need to be around to help with recovery. Other people would just be in the way.

The organization will critical personnel necessary to carry out the continuity plan. [UCF ID 00739]

Here's some great guidance on how to identify critical personnel as well as other tips relating to communication in a disaster.

Supporting and supported controls

This control directly supports: 00735: Systems Continuity Plan Strategies

This control has the following supporting controls: There are no supporting controls.

Guidelines complied with:

AICPA Suitable Trust ¶ 24 (3.18), ¶ 20 (3.2); FFIEC Business Continuity Planning handbook Pg E1; NASD Rules R 3520; NYSE Rules R 446(g); FISCAM SC-1.2; NIST 800-14 § 3.6.2; NIST 800-53 CP-2; NFPA 1600 Ch. 5.4.3(11), Ch. 5.5.2, Ch. 4.1.3, Ch. 5.7.2.2; ISF Standards of Good Practice for Information Security SM4.5.3; Australia Business Continuity Management Guide Pg 40-41.

Sarbanes Oxley Guidance

AICPA Suitable Trust Services Criteria ¶ 24 (3.18) and ¶ 20 (3.2) calls for the business continuity plan to define roles and responsibilities for critical personnel.

Banking and Finance Guidance

FFIEC Business Continuity Planning Handbook Pg E1, requires that the business continuity plan define roles and assign responsibilities for critical personnel involved in the response and recovery process. It calls for the formation of BCP teams to cover all areas of business restoration, as well as primary contact personnel for vendors, suppliers, and third-party service providers. Personnel should also be assigned to oversee information and physical security. In addition, the standard requires the plan to include contingencies in the event that critical personnel are unavailable.

Sample control commentary found at the UCF website

You can use any of the starter sets of controls available through the Unified Compliance Framework's website online – as a way to document the publicly available authority documents that *we* track. However, we *can't* list the MOUs, SLAs, contracts, etc. that are applicable to *your* organization. Therefore, you'll want to list all of your internal authority documents on the spreadsheet as well – ensuring that you synchronize each of your authority documents with the starter matrix that we've provided for you.

Once you've listed all of your documents along with the publicly available documents, you are ready to begin scoping which controls are right for *your* organization.

❑ Have you gone through the list of controls to determine if processes, policies, standards, and procedures are in place that match the controls being called for?

The next step is to gather all of your IT documentation and determine what you have already accomplished – and have documented – that you can say "yes, this assurance activity we are currently doing fits the criteria of the control listed in the control matrix." If the first step is to ensure that your internal authority documents align with the control matrix, this second step is to ensure that your internal control documents align with what the controls are asking for.

❑ Are there whole impact zones that you can ignore? The Unified Compliance Framework is broken down into twelve impact zones, listed below. If your authority documents don't call for controls in any of the impact zones listed, you can ignore that impact zone. In addition, even if the authority documents call for controls in a specific impact zone, such as Design and implementation, and you *aren't creating your own software or hardware*, then you can ignore the impact zone as it doesn't apply to you. Otherwise, you'll want to ensure that you are covering each of the impact zones that you are called upon to support.

⚡ Leadership and high level objectives

⚡ Audit and risk management

⚡ Monitoring, measurement, and reporting

⚡ Technical security

⚡ Physical security

⚡ Systems continuity

⚡ IT human resources management

⚡ Operational management

⚡ Records management

⚡ Design and implementation

⚡ Acquisition of technology and services

⚡ Privacy protection for information and data

You can obtain matrices for each of the impact zones (or an über matrix of all of them) from both websites we've already mentioned.

❑ Has the organizational leadership formalized its scoping authority document to ensure that you can defend your position regarding whether or not you wish to accept certain controls and ignore others? If not, go back and reference *A guideline for scoping controls*. If you don't have an internal scoping document, you can use the one that we've provided as a sample in the book called **Authority Guidance criteria**.

❑ Has the organization stepped through the process of accepting (or not) each control in the master control list? There are five choices for each of the controls:

1. Accept the risk and ignore the control

2. Decide the control is not applicable

3. Decide the listed control is a duplicate of a pre-existing control

4. Decide to implement an alternate control

5. Implement the control as stated

This decision should be documented along with your complete control list. The documentation can be as simple as filling out the completed CMMI checklist in the control matrices as shown below.

Harmonized Control Title	Control Id	Acceptance	Accept risk	Not applicable	Duplicate control	Implementing alternate	Implement as stated
Does the organization develop, disseminate, and review: 1) a formal change control policy that addresses purpose, scope, RASCI info, and compliance; and 2) formal procedures to facilitate implementing the policy?	00886	Yes					X
Does the organization document and control changes to the information system, with appropriate organizational officials approving information system changes in accordance with organizational policies and procedures?	00887	Yes					X
Does the organization monitor changes to the information system and conduct security impact analyses to determine the effects of the changes?	00888	Yes				X	
Does the organization ensure that management and all appropriate parties sign off on each planned and implemented change, and that the system detects and protects against unauthorized changes?	00889	Yes				X	
Does the organization develop, disseminate, and review: 1) a formal emergency change policy that addresses purpose, scope, RASCI info, and compliance; and 2) formal procedures to facilitate implementing the policy?	00890	Yes				X	
Does the organization ensure that new or modified hosts prepared according to documented procedures for secure configuration or replication, and does vulnerability testing takes place prior to deployment?	00891	Yes					X
Does the organization ensure that there is a full software release policy that also includes changes, upgrades, and patch management as well as back-out procedures for each planned and implemented change?	00893	No	X				
Does the organization develop, disseminate, and review: 1) a formal patch management policy that addresses purpose, scope, RASCI info, and compliance; and 2) formal procedures to facilitate implementing the policy?	00896	Yes					X
Does the organization have patch management standards with patch identification, evaluation, request and approval, testing, rollback, implementation, and documentation procedures?	00897	Yes					X
Does the organization ensure that all security and update patches are tested for new vulnerabilities as well as operational functionality before they are deployed?	00898	Yes					X

Documenting the control framework

Determining your various levels of maturity

Beyond accepting your controls, you'll need to audit the level of maturity each of your controls is at. This means that for each and every control, you are going to move through a series of six question categories: Awareness, Policies and Procedures, Tools and Automation, Skills and Expertise, Responsibility and Accountability, and Measurement.

Within each of these categories, you are going to need to determine the level of maturity that you are currently performing that control (1 through 5). Here are the categories with each of their questions.

Awareness

1. Recognition of the need for the process is emerging

2. Management are firmly aware of the need to act

3. Formal communication from management exists

4. Management are leveraging communication tools and techniques

5. Management are proactively communicating

Policies and Procedures

1. The approach to processes and practices are ad hoc

2. Informal processes exist

3. Policies and procedures are defined

4. Policies and procedures are fully disseminated

5. Policies and procedures are becoming automated

Tools and Automation

1. No planned approach to tool usage

2. Some users are leveraging tools

3. A plan has been created for tool usage

4. Tools are being related and implemented according to plan

5. Tools are fully integrated and related

Skills and Expertise

1. Required skills are not identified

2. Minimum skill sets are identified for key areas

3. All skill requirements are defined and a training plan has been developed

4. Mature training techniques are being applied

5. Continuous improvement training is underway

Responsibility and Accountability

1. Ownership is based upon personal pride

2. Informal responsibility has been assigned

3. RACI charts have been defined

4. Process owners have full authority to exercise initiative

5. Process owners are taking charge and making their own decisions

Measurement

1. No trusted metrics

2. Metrics are binary

3. Tolerances of change for metrics are defined

4. Metrics are now statistically valid

5. Metrics are being used adaptively

Documenting your efforts

We aren't going to tell you the type of evidence that you need to provide to support your decision about which level you are at for each control. We believe that is up to you. However, we also aren't your auditor. Your auditor will have a formal method of documentation for each decision. What we will give to you to make your life easier is a sample template for scoring your level of maturity. The IT Compliance Institute can provide you with IT Impact Zones wherein each of the tables has the list of all of the regulations and also a method to record whether or not you've accepted the control, and the level of maturity you are at within each of the categories.

UCF Control ID	Control Title	Acceptance	Awareness	Policies and Procedures	Tools and Automation	Skills and Expertise	Responsibility and Accountability	Measurement
735	Systems Continuity Plan Strategies							
736	Defining critical business functions							
1165	Review and prioritize each business unit and process							
737	Critical records identification							
739	Defining critical personnel							
740	Defining critical IT Resources							
741	SLAs include continuity planning							
1378	Workstation protection considerations							
1379	Server considerations							
1380	Web site and intranet considerations							
1363	Online and near line storage considerations							
1382	Mainframe considerations							
1268	Systems protection considerations							
743	Communications systems considerations							
1381	Local Area Network considerations							
1294	Wide Area Network considerations							
1396	Primary and alternate telecommunications service agreements contain priority-of-service provisions							
1397	Alternate telecommunications services do not share a single point of failure with primary telecommunications services.							
1399	Alternate telecommunications providers are sufficiently separated from primary service providers							
1400	Primary and alternate telecommunications providers have adequate continuity plans							
1264	Alternate power considerations							
1374	Damaged site considerations							
1247	Ensuring the organization has planned for at risk structures							
1248	Planning for the segregation and removal of hazards							

Maturity level documentation

Each of the categories can be expanded to show the individual questions.

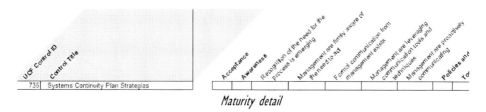

Maturity detail

Say what you Do

GUIDANCE FROM THE AUTHORITIES

The material in this chapter is directly derived from the Unified Compliance Framework and directly matches the control lists found within the tables of the Unified Compliance Project on the IT Compliance Institute's website.

The idea behind this chapter is to provide the list of tasks as presented by the authors of the compliance documents themselves so that you can have the information "from the horses' mouths" and use that to understand why these steps are important. Or, if the authorities we cite don't apply to your organization, why you can skip those steps in the process.

Defining the scope of the organizational compliance framework and controls for your organization

Organizations should have a process in place that ensures all requirements that are necessary for information and IT processes and infrastructure. Requirements include compliance, legal, contractual and policy issues.

> The organization will ensure that it can define the scope of the framework used to assure information processes and systems maintain proper confidentiality, integrity, availability, and accountability controls. [UCF ID 01241]

This section covers what to include in a compliance framework in terms of requirements and controls.

Guidelines complied with:

AICPA Suitable Trust ¶ .09a; The Institute of Internal Auditors GTAG § 2.2, § 7.0, § 9.1; HIPAA § 164.306(c) and (d); NIST 800-66 HIPAA Security § 4.7; DIRKS Step A, Pg 11; NIST 800 34 § 3.1; ISO 17799:2000 § 4.1, § 4.2.1, § 11.1.4; CobiT Version 4 ME3.1, ME3.2; CERT OCTAVE App A: Contingency Planning/Disaster Recovery (SP6.4) Pg A-10; BCI Good Practice Guidelines 1.1 Process.

Sarbanes Oxley Guidelines

The AICPA/CICA Suitable Trust Services Criteria calls for the organization to set its policies in order (¶ .09a) relevant to any particular security principle within the audit document they provide. In other words, this document, much like the AICPA/CICA Privacy Framework by the same authors, implicitly relies on the organizational framework to set the tone for all policies regarding information management.

The **IIA Global Technology Audit Guide**, § 2.2 states that each organization should use the applicable components of existing IT control frameworks to categorize and assess IT controls, and to provide and document the organizational framework in terms of:

⚡ Compliance with applicable regulations and legislation.

⚡ Consistency with the organization's goals and objectives.

⚡ Reasonable assurance that activities comply with management's governance policies and are consistent with the organization's risk appetite.

Section 7.0 goes on to state that there is no universally applicable means of defining an organization structure or framework for IT control. Instead, the organization needs to identify where IT control responsibilities lie and assess their appropriateness within regard to an overall framework.

Section 9.1 delves into choosing a control framework. The document defines a framework as a structured way of categorizing controls to ensure that the whole spectrum of control is adequately covered. The framework can be informal or formal, with a formal framework satisfying regulatory and statutory requirements. Choosing a framework is accomplished by examining existing frameworks to determine which of them (or which of their parts) most closely fits the organizational needs.

Healthcare and Life Sciences Guidelines

Section 4.7 of **NIST 800-66** calls for the organizational establishing of a framework for contingency planning, and refers back to HIPAA § 164.308(a)(7) in so doing.

HIPAA, § 164.306(c) covers the formation of a standards framework for the organization, pointing out that some of the controls are required while others are addressable. § 164.308(d) then goes on to specify how to decide which addressable controls the organization should follow, which it should not, and how to document the difference. The methodology it mentions is that the organization should 1) assess whether each implementation specification is a reasonable and appropriate safeguard in its environment, when analyzed with reference to the likely contribution to protecting the organizations confidential information; and 2) as applicable to the organization — a) adopt the implementation specification if reasonable and appropriate; or b) If adopting the implementation specification is not reasonable and appropriate documenting why it would not be reasonable and appropriate to adopt the implementation specification; and then Implement an equivalent alternative measure if reasonable and appropriate.

Records Management Guidelines

DIRKS Step A, Pg 11 suggests that as a part of scoping the project, a general canvas of all issues, options, and recommendations are reported.

NIST 800 Series Guidelines

NIST 800-34, § 3.1 calls for the organization to create an overall continuity planning framework that will be used to establish the organizational responsibilities for continuity planning.

International Standards Organization Guidelines

ISO 17799, § 4.1 calls for the establishment of a management framework to initiate and control the implementation of information security within the organization.

Section 4.2.1 calls for the establishment of a framework for setting objectives and direction when creating an information security management system.

Section 11.1.4 calls for the establishment of a business continuity framework in order to ensure that all plans are consistent and to identify priorities for testing and maintenance.

General Guidance Guidelines

CobiT 4 ME3.1 calls for an organization to implement a process ensuring timely identification of local and international legal, contractual, policy and regulatory requirements that are related to information, information service delivery and IT processes and infrastructure.

ME3.2 recommends that an organization review and optimize its IT policies, standards and procedures, including legal and regulatory requirements.

The BCI Good Practice Guidelines 1.1 Process says to review and if necessary challenge the scope set out in the BCM Policy.

CERT OCTAVE App A: Contingency Planning/Disaster Recovery (SP6.4) Pg A-10 says contingency, disaster recovery and business continuity plans should be periodically reviewed, tested and revised.

Commentary

You can't properly scope your information management framework until you've analyzed your organizational objectives, functions, and activities [UCF ID 00598]. The scoping process will involve your analysis of rules that govern information technology in *your* environment [UCF ID 00611], and then identifying the information processes and applications that are significant to the organization [UCF ID 00688]. Once you understand the rules that you fall under and the significant processes and applications that you are using, you can create the compliance and assurance framework to protect those processes and assets in a way that meets the rules you must follow.

Notice what the guidelines *don't* say. They *don't* say that your organization has to follow one or the other framework. Nor do you have to follow any particular framework *in whole*. What they do say is that your organization should use the frameworks that exist as a template and choose the parts that fit *your* circumstances and *your* needs.

Defining rules that govern information technology

In defining the rules that govern information technology within an organization, care should be taken to ensure appropriate standards are complied with, and the size and complexity of existing systems have been taken into account. Generally speaking, organizations should be sure to comply with privacy, intellectual property, transborder data flows, and cryptographic regulations applicable to IT practices of the organization.

> The organization will determine IS management's level of awareness and compliance with laws and regulations, especially as they pertain to confidentiality, integrity, availability, and accountability. The organization will also collect, organization, and incorporate compliance with third party mandated contracts, Service Level Agreements, and Memorandums of Understanding. [UCF ID 00611]

This section discusses in detail what types of rules ought to govern information technology as well as what categories of rules an organization must be aware of.

Sarbanes Oxley Guidelines

SAS 94 ¶ 8 does not specifically mention the rules governing information technology, however, it does have this to say about defining objectives, which can be applied to information and information services rules. "*There is a direct relationship between objectives, which are what an entity strives to achieve, and components, which represent what is needed to achieve the objectives. In addition, internal control is relevant to the entire entity, or to any of its operating units or business functions.*"

Banking and Finance Guidelines

The FFIEC Information Security Handbook Pg 3 states that financial institutions that are developing or reviewing their information security controls, policies, procedures, or processes have a variety of sources to draw on. These include federal laws and regulations, security industry best practices from outside auditors, consulting firms, and information security professional organizations.

Also, international standard-setting organizations are working to define information security standards and best practices for electronic commerce. There is no list of formally accepted standards. Instead, there are several regulations and standards institutions can draw on to define the rules that govern information technology.

Healthcare and Life Sciences Guidelines

HIPAA 164.306(b) says that in designing rules and security measures, the approach the organization uses should be flexible while taking into account standards that must be complied with and the size and complexity of existing systems. It suggests a set of steps to use to determine whether a new rule or security measure is feasible for the organization.

US Federal Security Guidelines

FISMA § 11331 discusses compliance with the National Institute of Standards and Technology Act as mandatory but advises that the heads of agencies have the discretion to apply stricter standards.

§ 303b states that there should be standards available categorizing information and information systems used by the organization, and there should be guidelines that recommend what types of information and information systems to include in each category. Minimum security requirements for information and information systems in each category should also be provided.

NIST 800 Series Guidelines

NIST 800-14 § 3.2.1 recommends creating a central security program with guidelines that describe the stable program management function, existence of policies, published mission and functions statement, long-term computer security strategies, compliance programs, intraorganizational liaisons, and liaisons with external groups.

NIST 800-53 recommends that organizations use the document as the minimum standards for the organization and a starting point for information security controls and plans for information systems. Specifically, NIST 800-53 § 1.3 states that *"building a more secure information system is a multi-faceted undertaking that involves the use of: (i) well-defined system-level security requirements and security specifications; (ii) well-designed information technology component products; (iii) sound systems/security engineering principles and practices to effectively integrate component products into the information system; (iv) appropriate methods for product/system testing and evaluation; and (v) comprehensive system security planning and life cycle management."*

General Guidance Guidelines

CobiT 3 PO8.4 states that management should ensure compliance with privacy, intellectual property, transborder data flow, and cryptographic regulations applicable to IT practices of the organization.

CobiT 4 PO4.1 suggests that an organization define an IT process framework that includes an IT process structure, relationships, ownership, maturity, performance measurement, improvement, compliance, quality targets and plans to achieve each of these things. The framework should be defined in such a way that it executes the IT strategic plan.

ME3.1 says the organization should define and implement a process to ensure timely identification of local and international legal, contractual, policy and regulatory requirements related to information, information service delivery-including third-party services- and the IT organization, processes and infrastructure. Consider laws and regulations for electronic commerce, data flow, privacy, internal controls, financial reporting, industry-specific regulations, intellectual property and copyright, and health and safety.

ME4.1 requires an organization to define and establish an IT governance framework that includes leadership, processes, roles and responsibilities, information requirements, and organizational structures that ensure the organization's investment programs.

Commentary

In order for you to define the external rules that govern information systems, information management, and information technology within your organization, you need to understand the *types* of rules that you might fall under. Their general classifications are Regulations, Standards, Guidelines, and Best Practices.

Aᵥ Regulations are rules of law that, if not followed, can result in penalties. Regulations state *that* something must be done.

Aᵥ Standards are rallying points created by well organized groups or are generally accepted within the industry. Standards rally the governed body around *what* must be done.

Aᵥ Guidelines are detailed outlines and plans for determining a course of action. Guidelines *prioritize and direct* the course of action.

Aᵥ Best practices are programs, initiatives or activities which are considered leading edge, or exceptional models for others to follow. Best practices *set the example of how to do something* the best way.

Organizations **do** have to follow regulations, but they **don't** have to follow standards, guidelines, and best practices.

Contractual agreements are also important to the organization. Contracts per se, Service Level Agreements (SLAs), and Memorandum's of Understanding (MOUs) might contain language directing the information services group to uphold certain commonly accepted standards, guidelines, or best practices. Some of these agreements might also specify *their own* standards, guidelines, or best practices that might have to be upheld. Therefore, it is imperative for the information services group to understand any and all organizational agreements that bind them to certain process and performance criteria.

Identify information processes and applications significant to the organization

The purpose of describing your organizational functions is to develop a conceptual model of what the organization does and how it does it by examining the business activities and purposes. The objective of this step is to establish the model representation of the business activities that are carried out by the organization.

> The organization will identify and map all information process and applications that are significant to the organization. The organization will regularly conduct application reviews to identify unique products and services delivered by network-based applications and any required third-party access requirements. [UCF ID 00688]

The simplest representation will come in the form of a tree structure that begins with the organizational goals and structures and then develops out through the functions, activities, and transactions of the organization. It doesn't matter if that tree structure is a simple table or an elaborate Visio diagram or relational database.

Sarbanes Oxley Guidelines

Thanks to the **Institute of Internal Auditors' Generally Accepted IT Principles (GAIT)** document, we finally have some solid guidance as to how to properly scope the information processes, systems, and assets. Section 3 of GAIT is entitled "What in IT must be controlled," and since there are over ten pages of solid information there, backed by another twenty or so pages of supporting information, it is best to turn to the document itself for more detail because there is a wealth of it. In short, however, GAIT defines a set of principles surrounding the belief that there exists a set of IT assets, and that changes are made to those assets according to organizational entitlement policies (or because of exceptions). GAIT further links these entitled changes (and their exceptions) to the assertions that the business process assets are supporting. In other words, the validity of the business process is tied to the validity of the system being scoped.

Banking and Finance Guidelines

The FFIEC Information Security Booklet, pages 8 and 9, detail the information gathering steps necessary for understanding systems' risks. A key part of this information gathering is the listing of all information systems and breaking those systems down by their IT assets classifications (documents, applications & databases, OSes, storage, system, network, power & cooling, facilities).

Exam Tier I Q 2.2 says unique products and services and any required third-party access requirements should be identified.

The FFIEC Operations Booklet goes into more detail on Pg 6 through 11 where they cover gathering information system information under the rubric of an environmental survey and technology inventory. The operations material actually blends into another control objective we cover about gathering system specific information.

US Federal Security Guidelines

FISCAM Appendix VI.1.1 states the need for organizations to identify computer applications significant to the financial statements of the organization. Significant applications are those with auditable line items and accounts under investigation or that are material to the organization.

Records Management Guidelines

DIRKS § B.4 suggests two types of analysis; hierarchical (top down) and process-based (bottom up). Whichever method is used, DIRKS suggests that the interview identify:

- "your organization's goals and the strategies to achieve these goals;
- the broad functions the organization undertakes to support its goals and strategies;
- the activities that contribute to the fulfillment of the organization's functions; and

♠ the groups of recurring transactions or processes that make up each of these activities."

Section B.4.2 of DIRKS further defines the differences between function, activity, and transaction as such:

♠ Functions are the largest unit of business activity in an organization. They represent the major responsibilities that are managed by the organization to fulfill its goals. Functions are high-level aggregates of the organization's activities.

♠ Activities are the major tasks performed by the organization to accomplish each of its functions. Several activities may be associated with each function.

♠ Transactions are the smallest unit of business activity. They should be tasks, not subjects or record types. Transactions will help define the scope or boundaries of activities and provide the basis for identifying the records that are required to meet the business needs of the organization. The identification of transactions will also help in the formulation of the records description part of a records disposal authority.

In order to create a common language that everyone in the organization can use when talking about what it is they do all day and how they are going to categories what they do, DIRKS suggests in § B.4.2.1 to assign specific terms to functions and activities. The choice of terminology should depend upon the way in which the organization has defined its functions, activities, and transactions. By choosing and documenting terminology, you will be able to create an unambiguous and integrated business classification scheme.

Section B.4.2.2 of DIRKS takes this further and then asks the analyst to create a glossary entry for each of the terms, much like the glossary entry used for writing purposes. DIRKS would have the analyst produce much the same thing, using documentary sources or interviewees as the authority sources and the interview or research material as the basis for the definition of the term being described.

Section B.4.2.3 of DIRKS takes this one step further by asking the analyst to document dates for functions and activities. These dates "establish a time frame, which will be useful for the development and application of the linked recordkeeping tools such as a thesaurus and disposal authority" states DIRKS. In practical terms, it provides more metadata that you can feed into your recordkeeping system.

NIST 800 Series Guidelines

NIST 800-14 § 3.3.1 states that prior to conducting a risk assessment, the system under consideration must be identified and analyzed, documenting the system's level of detail and formality.

NIST 800-18 § 2.1 states that information resources should be clearly assigned to an information system – which directly supports business processing and therefore supports the business functions, activities, and tasks. Doing this creates clear boundaries for all information systems. Methods for grouping resources are provided. Generally, a group of resources should serve the same function or meet the same objective and reside in the same general operating environment.

§ 2.2 gives a definition for major applications in an organization. They are applications that are critical to an organization's success and require special management in order to be properly maintained. System owners should be notified if they oversee a major application and provided with a copy of the application's system security plan. The plan should contain a reference to the general support system security plan.

§ 2.3 defines a general support system as an interconnected set of information resources under the same direct management control that shares common functionality. It often includes hardware, software, information, data, applications, communications, facilities, and people and provides support for a variety of users and applications.

§ 2.4 defines minor applications as those applications not selected as major applications. It is important to be sure that security controls are covering these applications and that the minor applications are documented in the system security plan as an appendix or a paragraph.

General Guidance Guidelines

ISACA Guidelines for Auditing Control § 2.1.1 says that prior to conducting a risk assessment, the organization should identify and prioritize their business objectives and ensure that identification of objectives is consistent across all levels of the organization.

Carnegie Mellon's **CERT OCTAVE** approach is a 1200+ page document that centers almost entirely on the methodology of identifying information processes and information systems as well as their threats and vulnerabilities. Process 1 of CERT's OCTAVE defines how to document information processes and information systems. Process 6 defines how to evaluate those processes and systems and is therefore a good read as well since the two tie directly together.

Section B.5.a(i) and (ii) of the **Business Continuity Institute's Standards of Professional Competence** point out that a key to defining business continuity is being able to identify and confirm the processing and documentation critical to the organization's key business activities. Their point is that you can't determine which processes and systems should be replicated off site unless you can place them into their context within the organization's day-to-day business activities.

United Kingdom and Canadian Guidelines

BS 15000-2:2003 § 5.6.1 documents the need for a service provider to maintain an inventory of the information assets that are necessary to deliver services such as information processing, and that those assets should be classified according to their level of criticality. Section 8.1.1 deals with configuration management planning, but also stresses the need to understand the configuration of information processes as those processes are the key to integrating the system overall.

Asia and Pacific Rim Guidelines

The Australia BCM Guide Pg 34-35 requires that key business processes be identified and ranked. When determining how to rank each process, consider what would happen if any of the following happened:

✦ Failure to meet statutory obligations for service delivery

✦ Failure to meet key stakeholder expectations

✦ Loss of cash flows essential to business operations

✦ Degree of dependency on business processes by internal business units or clients

Concerns of executive and senior management should also be obtained before determining a rank. For each business process to be ranked, determine the activities that constitute that process. Then match resources to the activities. Resources include people, buildings and property, equipment and consumables, and finance. To ensure all key business processes, activities, and resources are identified use this checklist:

✦ Document and confirm organizational objectives and outputs

✦ List key business processes that underpin achievement of objectives and delivery of outputs

✦ Review the functional organization chart to identify general areas of operational responsibility

✦ Interview managers responsible for key business processes to confirm understanding of activities (complex organization only)

✦ Document the activities and resources essential to each key business process

✦ Formally communicate the list of key business processes and supporting activities and resources to the project steering committee

Commentary

Wherein UCF ID 00598 asks that we analyze organizational objectives, functions, and activities, this control asks that we go beyond that initial scope and identify those information processes and applications that are **significant** to the organization.

The first question we have to ask is, what does "*significant*" mean in this instance? In this instance, we are looking for any processes that have supporting applications that are **unique**. In other words, business processes that are supported by common off the shelf software products like Microsoft Office would not be unique enough to be significant to the organization. However, information processes that depend upon custom-designed applications that require special attention *are* significant to the organization because they are unique enough that if the application suffered a loss of confidentiality, integrity, or availability, the solution would not be quick or inexpensive.

Remember that the validity of the business process is tied to the validity of the system supporting it. Any system that falls outside the boundaries of common protection techniques is therefore significant in some way regarding the effort it will take to ensure the system's compliance.

Any application that is deemed a **major application** (as opposed to a minor application or a general support system) is going to be a significant application supporting significant information processes.

If you haven't gotten far enough into your planning phases to document which processes and their supporting applications are major, minor, or supporting, you can rely upon the rules and regulations you have to support, turning to any Service Level Agreements, contracts, or Memorandums of Understanding wherein your organization made warranty assertions regarding an information processes' operational availability, operational integrity, or operational confidentiality. It's a good bet that if your organization had to make assertions of those kinds, then the process or application in question is a significant or major application and falls within this discussion.

The next step is to determine whether or not the validation of the warranties can be accomplished as a whole without validating the technology involved, or whether validating the technology involved is necessary. The IIA GAIT documentation is outstanding in their explanation of this process. Checks and balances of many record keeping systems *can* be accomplished without the use of the application that input or manipulated the data. On the other hand, databases that consolidate and automatically place orders *must* be relied upon if the process in question is ordering automation.

The final question to ask when determining if the application is in scope or out of scope for being significant is whether or not a *change in the application* would invalidate the warranty assertion. In other words, if the application's integrity, confidentiality, or availability status were changed – would this affect the warranty of the *process*? If the answer is yes, then the application is indeed significant to the organization.

Defining systems by identifying their boundaries and assigning them to a category

This is a *core* step that you'll need for most every other control, policy, and procedure that you will encounter within the Unified Compliance Framework. This answers the question "what is in and what is out" of the discussion for protection.

> The resources necessary for delivery of the key business processes need to be identified and their boundaries documented. These are the resources required by the operational areas to support the activities that deliver the outputs or results. Without these resources, the business processes would not achieve their goals. [UCF ID 00695]

While most of the regulations and standards reference the system documentation or system boundaries, only a handful of guidelines actually cover *how* to define the boundaries of a system and then how to categorize and document that system properly.

Sarbanes Oxley Guidelines3/1/2007

The **Institute of Internal Auditor's Generally Accepted IT Principles (GAIT)** focuses both on the scoping of information processes as well as the scoping, or defining the boundaries of, the systems that support those processes. GAIT defines a set of principles surrounding the belief that there exists a set of IT assets, and that changes made to those assets must be made according to organizational entitlement policies or explicit exceptions to those policies. Their point is that the validity of the business process is tied directly to the validity (or integrity) of the asset supporting the process. Hence, the boundaries of the asset *must* be properly defined.

Healthcare and Life Sciences Guidelines

CMS System Security Plans Methodology, § 1.3 defines their methodology for determining systems boundaries. This requires an analysis of both technical system boundaries and organizational responsibilities. Constructing physical and logical boundaries around a set of processes, communications, storage, and related resources, as defined by this document, identifies a system. The set of elements within these boundaries constitutes a single system requiring a security plan. Each component of the system must:

- Be under the same direct management control (i.e., one system owner even though the MA may cross several business lines
- Have the same general business function(s) or business objective(s)
- Have essentially the same operating characteristics and security needs
- All components of a system do not need to be physically connected.

Section 1.4 discusses the different categorizations for these systems and basically follows the same definitions as does FIPS and NIST by defining Major Applications, General Support Systems and *other systems* (the same as Minor Applications).

NIST 800 Series Guidelines

NIST 800-18, § 2 defines the methodology for identifying the boundaries of information systems. Before the system security plan can be developed, the information system and the information resident within that system must be categorized based on a FIPS 199 impact analysis. Then a determination can be made as to which systems in the inventory can be logically grouped into major applications or general support systems. The process of uniquely assigning information assets to an information system defines the security boundary for that system. While there is no set rule for a strict definition of which assets should be included, NIST 800-18 does give a few guidelines:

- Each asset should generally be under the same direct management control. Subsystems typically fall under the same management authority and are included within a single system.
- Each asset should have the same function or mission objective and essentially the same operating characteristics and security needs.
- Each asset should reside in the same general operating environment (or in the case of a distributed information system, reside in various locations with similar operating environments).

The process of establishing boundaries for agency information systems and the associated security implications is an agency-level activity that should include careful negotiation among all key participants—taking into account the mission/business requirements of the agency, the technical considerations with respect to information security, and the programmatic costs to the agency.

The categories that a system should be assigned to are **Major Application, General Support System**, and **Minor Application**.

Certain applications, because of the information they contain, process, store, or transmit, or because of their criticality to the agency's mission, require special management oversight. These applications are Major Applications. Major Applications are systems that perform clearly defined functions for which there are readily identifiable security considerations and needs (e.g., an electronic funds transfer system). A Major Application might comprise many individual programs and hardware, software, and telecommunications components. These components can be a single software application or a combination of hardware/software focused on supporting a specific, mission-related function. A Major Application may also consist of multiple individual applications if all are related to a single mission critical function (e.g., payroll or personnel).

A General Support System is an interconnected set of information resources under the same direct management control that shares common functionality. A general support system normally includes hardware, software, information, data, applications, communications, facilities, and people and provides support for a variety of users and/or applications. Common general support systems include:

- The organizational backbone network (WAN/MAN)
- The facility LAN
- The facility VoIP system
- The data center and MDF/IDFs
- Shared storage or shared application systems
- The backup or replication system

Minor Applications are those applications that neither fall into the Major Application nor General Support Systems Categories.

NIST 800-18, Appendix A, lists all of the key information that must be recorded for a system within the System Security Plan:

1. Information System Name/Title: Unique identifier and name given to the system.

2. Information System Categorization: Identify the appropriate FIPS 199 categorization.

3. Information System Owner: Name, title, agency, address, email address, and phone number of person who owns the system.

4. Authorizing Official: Name, title, agency, address, e-mail address, and phone number of the senior management official designated as the authorizing official.

5. Other Designated Contacts: List other key personnel, if applicable; include their title, address, e-mail address, and phone number.

6. Assignment of Security Responsibility: Name, title, address, e-mail address, and phone number of person who is responsible for the security of the system.

7. Information System Operational Status: Indicate the operational status of the system. If more than one status is selected, list which part of the system is covered under each status.

8. Information System Type: Indicate if the system is a major application or a general support system.

9. General System Description/Purpose: Describe the function or purpose of the system and the information processes.

10. System Environment: Provide a general description of the technical system. Include the primary hardware, software, and communications equipment.

11. System Interconnections/Information Sharing: List interconnected systems and system identifiers (if appropriate), provide the system, name, organization, system type (major application or general support system), indicate if there is an

ISA/MOU/MOA on file, date of agreement to interconnect, FIPS 199 category, C&A status, and the name of the authorizing official.

12. Related Laws/Regulations/Policies: List any laws or regulations that establish specific requirements for the confidentiality, integrity, or availability of the data in the system.

13. Minimum Security Controls: Provide a thorough description of how the minimum controls in the applicable baseline are being implemented or planned to be implemented. The controls should be described by control family and indicate whether it is a system control, hybrid control, common control, if scoping guidance is applied, or a compensating control is being used.

14. Information System Security Plan Completion Date: Enter the completion date of the plan.

15. Information System Security Plan Approval Date: Enter the date the system security plan was approved and indicate if the approval documentation is attached or on file.

NIST 800-26, § 2.1 covers the same topic as does NIST 800-18, but not in as much detail.

General Guidance Guidelines

Carnegie Mellon's **OCTAVE Method Implementation Guide**, Process 5 covers the identification of key components. Process 5 identifies the key components of the infrastructure that should be examined for technological vulnerabilities for each critical asset. The analysis team, along with additional IT staff members, considers the organization's various systems and their components. The team looks for the systems of interest for each critical asset, identifying specific instances of the components selected for evaluation.

The EU Guidelines

The **Information Technology Security Evaluation Criteria (ITSEC)** which is a "harmonized" document that France, Germany, the Netherlands, and the United Kingdom have all agreed to, defines, in § 1.4 the boundaries for an IT system is as a specific IT installation with a particular purpose and known operational environment. Section 1.5 goes on to state that from the point of view of security, the main difference between systems and products lies in what is certain about their operational environment. A system is designed to meet the requirements of a specific group of end-users. It has a real world environment which can be defined and observed in every detail; in particular the characteristics and requirements of its end-users will be known, and the threats to its security are real threats which can be determined. A product must be suitable for incorporation in many systems; the product designer can only make general assumptions about the operational environment of a system of which it may become a component. It is up to the person buying the product and constructing the system to make sure that these assumptions are consistent with the actual environment of the system.

Commentary

The question at hand right now is what defines "a system." And then more in-depth, how do you classify these systems into major and minor applications or general support systems? Let's tackle the overarching question of "system" first. We'll use the three most common rules for defining system here, that all products (applications and assets).

1. Are under the same direct management control (i.e., one system owner even though the MA may cross several business lines.

2. Have the same general business function(s) or business objective(s).

3. Have essentially the same operating characteristics and security needs .

Checking for the first rule is very much like what a surveyor does when he or she draws the lines for the boundary of a yard or other physical location. By that we mean, the best place to start is the question of **ownership**. When dealing with land ownership, a person lays claim to a certain amount of land saying "this is mine." Same basic principle with information systems. When Danny Dingledimer down in accounting says "this suite of three applications all work together to support our process," what he is doing is laying claim to the limits and boundaries of that particular accounting system in terms of their objectives or functions.

As far as rule two goes, more explicitly for us, those three applications (or products) have been incorporated to form a single system as warranted by the system's owner.

And then rule three follows nicely because we can then question the system's owner and ask pointedly whether or not each of the applications in question all have roughly the same operating characteristics and security needs. If the answer is yes, then we are home free.

That's easy enough for major applications, but becomes more tricky when you get to minor applications and even trickier when you get to general support systems.

Minor systems in many organizations are many times what Paul Strassmann would call "stealth" systems - systems that haven't made it onto the radar screen of upper management. Working with one of our clients a few years back, we encountered a woman with an *incredible* spreadsheet and Access database application on her desktop computer. This spreadsheet/database was used monthly to pull down all of the key performance indicators from the mainframe accounting systems, in order to cross-reference the numbers. Those numbers were then turned into management reporting tables and charts that were used for the CEO's management executive committee. The information was then archived into the database for future reference. Should this be considered a minor application that should be warranted for protection? *Absolutely*! The CEO, along with most of the management executive team, *counted* on this information and *made critical business decisions* based upon this information. Had this been documented as a system? No - because nobody knew about it until we just happened to ask what it did. Was this system under "direct management control" - yes and no. It was under the *user's* control, but not management's control. Figuring out whether or not minor systems have the same function and security needs is usually much easier than with major systems because there are fewer products you have to think through. In this case, the two applications (the spreadsheet and the database) both shared the same function and security needs.

Then there are the general support systems that all of our organizations have in place – our local and wide area networks, our Voice over IP telephone systems, our shared storage systems, our backup and archiving systems, and our user authentication and directory systems. Without these key general support systems, our other systems could neither communicate nor share information, nor could they even allow user access. The problem you'll face when documenting general support systems is initially determining ownership. For instance, let's look at the local area network(s) that might be in your network. You'll have the border router and firewall and then a series of switches and hubs and maybe a few WiFi access points. If you have a small network, no doubt there is a single owner for all of this. But who owns all of the networking gear for a larger network? And what about the networking gear that extends into the data center? Does the same person own that? This is where ownership as a definitive rule for assigning assets to a single system can get tricky. When there are multiple owners, you might need to defer to rule two, that of a single function.

For general support systems — especially your local area network if it is large enough — invoking rule two in order to determine your scope is usually the best way to go. If the assets in question support the same business objective and function (local connectivity in this instance) they can be considered to be a part of the same general support system.

With general support systems, again focusing on your local area network segments, rule three can be a bit tricky. Different network domains and security segments will have different security needs. Your DMZ will have different security needs than your general network segment. And that will have different security needs than your data center's segment. Does this mean that these are three different supporting systems? No. They all should fall under a single authority and they all support the same overarching function of providing connectivity to the organization as a whole.

Establish an organizational framework of policies, standards, and procedures

It is imperative for all organizations to ensure that they have created a framework of policies, standards, and procedures. In this world of regulatory mayhem, it is just as imperative that those policies and procedures are harmonized across all of the authority guidelines that the organization must follow.

> The organization will harmonize all of the rules that apply to governing information management for their environment into a coherent set of organizational controls by establishing effective policies, standards, and procedures. [UCF ID 01406]

While the regulatory bodies don't directly mandate the creation of a framework for policies and procedures, a few of the guidelines suggest methods for going about the task.

Sarbanes Oxley Guidelines

The IIA's **Global Technology Audit Guide**, § 5.3.1, states that all organizations needs to define their aims and objectives through strategic plans and policy statements. *"Without clear statements of policy and standards for direction, organizations can become disoriented and perform ineffectively. Organizations with clearly defined aims and objectives tend to be successful."* The section further states that for some smaller organizations a single policy statement might suffice, but for larger organizations there will most likely be a need for multiple policy statements.

Healthcare and Life Sciences Guidelines

HIPAA Pg 8337 in a response says that it is critical for each covered entity to establish policies and procedures that address its own unique risks and circumstances.

NIST 800-66 § 4.7 recommends that the organization establish the organizational framework, roles and responsibilities for this area.

NIST 800 Series Guidelines

NIST 800-34 § 3.1 states that an organization should have a contingency planning policy statement that defines the organization's overall contingency objectives and establishes the organizational framework and responsibilities for IT contingency planning.

Pg C-2 says the organization should establish the organizational framework and responsibilities for IT contingency planning. The policy statement should also address roles and responsibilities.

General Guidance Guidelines

Page 37 of the **ISF Security Audit of Networks** guide suggests that control questionnaires be used to assess the extent to which controls have been implemented in a communications network. It goes on to further state that the control questionnaires are normally grouped by subject or theme with the respondents being required to indicate if they are complying with each control listed, or according to a certain degree of compliance or maturity.

Commentary

There isn't much guidance for the creation of a robust, harmonized set of policies and procedures.

But that doesn't mean that the task should be ignored, because the Unified Compliance Framework currently tracks over 1,300 controls that have been harmonized from a list of over 12,000 total controls. That's almost a ten to one reduction ratio.

Would your organization rather support a larger number of controls, or have a process to harmonize controls into a manageable framework?

Say what you Do

PRODUCTS AND SERVICES TO HELP YOU ALONG

We always like to include a tools section in our books to refer you to products and services that can help you in your efforts.

Our approach is an unbiased approach. You *will not* find a section in here detailing which product or service we think is best. What you will find in here are several products and services that have been brought to our attention through input from our esteemed field editors.

If you don't see a product or service in here that you'd like to see, one of two things have happened; 1) we didn't know about the product or service, or 2) the organization wouldn't let us put the product or service through its paces.

In the book, we'll only list those products and services we've run through the paces. The reason for this decision is simple – once we finish the book, the book is "out there" and we can't retract what we've written. Therefore, we want to ensure that we know what we are writing about when we talk about tools and templates.

But the web is different. We'll list *all* of the products and services we've heard about on our website, annotating which ones we haven't tested. We'll allow open comments from you, our readers, as to what you think about the products, services, and templates we have listed there. By allowing more openness on the web, we can increase our scope of coverage by providing direct feedback from the most important people in the world to us, our readers.

If you like to see other products or services covered, send an e-mail to Dcougias@netfrontiers.com, and we'll make every effort to include your recommendation.

3RD PARTY TEMPLATES

One of the things we'll try to do as often as possible, is to post templates on line for registered users to have access to. While we are building up a library of templates for you, we've also discovered a few template providers that you might want to look into.

Altius risk management policies

Altius Information Technologies (http://www.altiusit.com/riskpolicies.htm) can provide your organizations with policy and procedure template, or, they can work with you to customize their templates to fit your needs.

The sample policies that Altius provides don't fit the format that we espouse, but that doesn't mean that they can't or shouldn't be used. It just means that you'll need to take the policies and provide extra formatting for them. No big deal.

Altius' sample policy

They also provide the following security solutions: Network Security, Security Assessments, Security Policies, Firewall Security, Business Continuity, Intruder Detection, and Security Quizzes.

Bizmanualz pre-written procedures

Bizmanualz (http://www.bizmanualz.com) offers pre-written policies and procedures solutions for a wide range of business processes as well as training for process improvement and policy and procedure writing. Their Computer, Network and IT Policies and Procedures Manual, includes 40 IT Procedures, 70 IT Forms, a sample IT Manual, and an IT Security Guide. Their Disaster Recovery Policies, Procedures and Forms include:

- How to Manage Disaster Recovery Planning
- How to Manage Emergency Services and Agreements
- How to Manage Operations Centers
- How to Manage Emergency Notifications
- How to Manage Office and Department Recovery

There is *no* management software. They provide pure, clearly written procedures that follow the outline we espouse.

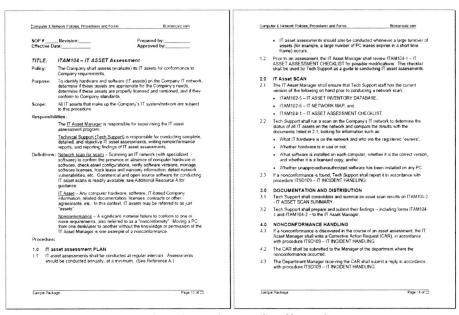

A sample procedure page from Bizmanualz

RUsecure information security templates

RUSecure (httpwww.information-security-policies.com) provides a set of information security policy templates in Microsoft Word and PDF format. These policies are fully editable and can be changed or added to with ease. Each policy also contains:

- Explanatory notes providing background for each policy
- Some of the key information security issues which should be considered when implementing the individual policy in question
- The related ISO17799 reference(s) for the policy.

Note that these are *not* procedures, that they are policies only.

Sample RUSecure policy

SAMPLE COMPLIANCE FRAMEWORK

Information and the systems that process it are among the most valuable assets of our organization. Therefore, our organization will create and maintain a program to 1) assure that systems and applications operate effectively and provide appropriate confidentiality, integrity, availability, and accountability according to our need for compliance with both external and internal rules and regulations; and 2) protect information commensurate with the level of risk and magnitude of harm resulting from loss, misuse, unauthorized access, or modification.

This policy and procedure framework (referenced from now on as the Framework) provides a method for agency officials to 1) determine the current status of our compliance programs relative to existing policy and 2) where necessary, establish a target for improvement. It does not establish new compliance requirements. The Framework may be used to assess the status of compliance controls for a given asset or collection of assets. These assets include information, individual systems (e.g., major applications, general support systems, mission critical systems), or a logically related grouping of systems that support operational programs, or the operational programs themselves. Assessing all asset compliance controls and all interconnected systems that the asset depends on produces a picture of both the compliance condition of the component and of the entire organization.

This Framework comprises five levels to guide organizational assessment of compliance programs and assist in prioritizing efforts for improvement. Coupled with a self-assessment questionnaire, the Framework provides a vehicle for consistent and effective measurement of the compliance status for a given asset. The compliance status is measured by determining if specific compliance controls are documented, implemented, tested and reviewed, and incorporated into a cyclical review/improvement program, as well as whether unacceptable risks are identified and mitigated. The questionnaire provides specific questions that identify the control criteria against which organizational policies, procedures, and compliance controls can be compared.

The Framework is divided into five levels: Level 1 of the Framework reflects that an asset has documented controls and rudimentary compliance processes. At level 2, the asset also has documented policies and procedures to implement the policy. Level 3 indicates that policies and procedures have been implemented. Level 4 shows that the policies and procedures are tested and reviewed. At level 5, the asset has policies and procedures fully integrated into a comprehensive program. Each level represents a more complete and effective compliance program. The organizational goal is to bring all assets and their surrounding policies and procedures to level 4 and ultimately level 5.

Framework description

The organizational framework identifies five levels of IT security program effectiveness as shown in the following list. The five levels measure specific management, operational, and technical control objectives. Each of the five levels contains criteria to determine if the level is adequately implemented. For example, in level 2, all written policies should contain the purpose and scope of the policy, the individual(s) responsible for implementing the policy, and the consequences and penalties for not following the policy. The policy for an individual control must be reviewed to ascertain that the criteria for level 2 are met. Assessing the effectiveness of the individual controls, not simply their existence, is key to achieving and maintaining adequate compliance. In addition, there are six areas of developmental concern that must be addressed for each control. These areas are awareness, policies and procedures, tools and automation, sills and expertise, responsibility and accountability, and measurement. Each area of developmental concern has five levels of maturity, as listed below.

Awareness

1. Recognition of the need for the process is emerging
2. Management are firmly aware of the need to act
3. Formal communication from management exists
4. Management are leveraging communication tools and techniques
5. Management are proactively communicating

Policies and Procedures

1. The approach to processes and practices are ad hoc
2. Informal processes exist
3. Policies and procedures are defined
4. Policies and procedures are fully disseminated
5. Policies and procedures are becoming automated

Tools and Automation

1. No planned approach to tool usage

2. Some users are leveraging tools

3. A plan has been created for tool usage

4. Tools are being related and implemented according to plan

5. Tools are fully integrated and related

Skills and Expertise

1. Required skills are not identified

2. Minimum skill sets are identified for key areas

3. All skill requirements are defined and a training plan has been developed

4. Mature training techniques are being applied

5. Continuous improvement training is underway

Responsibility and Accountability

1. Ownership is based upon personal pride

2. Informal responsibility has been assigned

3. RACI (or similar) charts have been defined

4. Process owners have full authority to exercise initiative

5. Process owners are taking charge and making their own decisions

Measurement

1. No trusted metrics

2. Metrics are binary

3. Tolerances of change for metrics are defined

4. Metrics are now statistically valid

5. Metrics are being used adaptively

A compliance program may be assessed at various levels within the organization as a whole. For example, a program could be defined as an organizational asset, a major application, general support system, high impact program, physical plant, mission critical system, or logically related group of systems. The Framework refers to this grouping as an asset. The Framework describes an asset self-assessment and provides levels to guide and prioritize agency efforts as well as a basis to measure progress.

Authority guidance criteria

The Framework approach begins with the premise that all organizational assets must meet minimum compliance requirements as established by the list of regulations, contracts, SLAs, MOUs, letters of agreement, and other legal and contractual documentation defined by the list that follows.

Document	Importance

Compliance control criteria source documents

It is within the purview of the organization to limit, through a scoping process, the controls *necessary* for compliance. The guidance that this organization will follow when selecting controls is based upon six categories of considerations that are related to: technology, infrastructure, public access, risk, and common control.

Technology related considerations

Controls that refer to specific technologies (e.g., wireless, cryptography, public key infrastructure) are only applicable if those technologies are employed or are required to be employed within the information system.

Controls are only applicable to the components of the information system that typically provide or support the capability addressed by the control. In other words, if the system in question doesn't have the processing capability dealt with in the control, the control can be ignored. As an example, a single user system wouldn't need any networking controls because they don't apply to that system.

For off the shelf products, if an automated mechanism isn't built in to support a control, it doesn't need to be developed. In other words, if the control states that after three failed password attempts the user should be kicked out of the off-the-shelf application, but the application doesn't have that capability already built into it, you can ignore the control for that application because there's nothing you could develop to make the control work.

Infrastructure related considerations

Controls that refer to organizational facilities (e.g., physical controls such as locks and guards, environmental controls for temperature, humidity, lighting, fire, and power) are applicable only to those sections of the facilities that directly provide protection to, support of, or are related to the information system (including its information technology assets such as electronic mail or web servers, server farms, data centers, networking nodes, controlled interface equipment, and communications equipment) under consideration.

Public access related considerations

Controls associated with public, customer, or third party access information systems should be carefully considered and applied with discretion since some controls (e.g., two-factor identification and authentication, personnel security controls) may not be applicable to users accessing information systems through public interfaces. For example, you might not want users to have to sign in when obtaining certain publicly available information while ensuring that they do so in order to change their account information.

Scalability related considerations

Controls must be scalable to match the system under consideration's size and complexity as well as its level of impact to the organization. Organizations should use discretion in scaling the controls to the particular environment of use to ensure a cost-effective, risk-based approach to control implementation. In other words, don't spend $10,000 protecting a $1,000 system. See risk related considerations for downgrading controls.

Risk related considerations

Controls that uniquely support the confidentiality, integrity, or availability objectives may be downgraded to the corresponding control in a lower baseline (or appropriately modified or eliminated if not defined in a lower baseline) if, and only if the downgrading action: 1) is consistent with the categorization for the corresponding objectives of confidentiality, integrity, or availability before moving to the high water mark; 2) is supported by an organizational assessment of risk; and 3) does not affect the relevant information within the information system.

Common control related considerations

Controls designated by the organization as common controls should be managed by an organizational entity other than the information system owner. As an example, access controls that support the entire network and all systems in it should *not* be managed by an information system manager responsible for a single system. Organizational decisions on which controls are viewed as common controls may greatly affect the responsibilities of individual information system owners with regard to the implementation of controls in a particular framework. This does not exempt the organization from implementing the control (i.e., letting it fall through the cracks). Every control in the framework must be addressed either by the organization *or* the information system owner.

Certification of process maturity levels

The organization will conduct both ad hoc, and regular reviews of all controls, policies, and procedures. Each identified control will be assigned a level of maturity, and that level of maturity will be reported to organizational management. The goal of the person responsible for each control will be to raise the level of maturity from the existing level to the next-higher level (e.g., level 1 to level 2) according to an acceptable timetable. The levels of maturity and their criteria are listed as follows:

Level 0 - Ignored

There are no recognizable processes that fit this particular control, nor does the organization recognize that there is an issue to be addressed regarding this control.

Criteria for documenting acceptance of level 0 certification

❏ All authority guidance has been properly documented in the framework.

❏ Through the organizational scoping process, a defined set of controls has been established.

❏ The organization has documented that the controls in question either 1) do not apply and the organization is willing to take the risk, 2) the organization has implemented alternate controls, or 3) are duplicates of controls called for by other authority documents.

Level 1 - Initial

There is evidence that the organization has recognized that the issue exists and needs to be addressed. Without standardization, there are ad hoc approaches to each issue that are either applied person-by-person or situation-by-situation. In other words, processes are unpredictable, poorly controlled, and reactive.

Awareness and communication – recognition of the need for the process is emerging, but there is sporadic communication of the issues.

⚡ *Policies, standards and procedures* – There are ad hoc approaches to processes and practices and policies are as yet undefined.

⚡ *Tools and automation* – While tool usage might exist, there is no planned approach to tool usage.

⚡ *Skills and expertise* – Required skills are not identified and no training plan exists.

⚡ *Responsibility and accountability* – Ownership is based upon personal pride without any definition of accountability and responsibility.

⚡ *Measurement* – At this point, metrics cannot provide a trusted baseline because the baseline is being developed.

⚡ *Goal setting* – The overall goal is to be able to perform the base practices without any real measurement.

    o *Identifying and involving relevant stakeholders*

    o *Perform and document the base practices*

Criteria for completing level 1 certification

❑ The process team has been established and has agreed on a documentation methodology.

❑ All stakeholders have been defined and are participating in the process documentation development.

❑ The team agrees on what the control is supposed to accomplish and has documented this as the process goal.

❑ The team has documented if any other supported or supporting processes, policies, and procedures link to this one.

❑ A rough cut of the process flow diagram has been created and approved.

❑ Problems in the process flow diagram have been examined and solutions documented. The process flow has been re-written as necessary.

❑ The scope of all IT assets in relation to the process flow has been analyzed and documented.

❑ The scope of involvement of all internal and external staff has been analyzed and documented.

❑ The necessary tools and prerequisite knowledge have been analyzed and documented.

❑ The final step, or "success" has been documented and all after-action reporting to support this step have been documented.

❑ The process has been "field tested" and signed off (or revised as necessary) by at least 1 person not on the writing team.

Level 2 – Repeatable

The process is used repeatedly. Similar procedures are followed by different groups or people when undertaking the same task. There is no formalized standardization, documentation, communication, or training of procedures. All intellectual property of the process is locked inside each person's mind.

⚡ *Awareness and communication* – Management are aware of the need to act and are able to communicate their issues.

⚡ *Policies, standards, and procedures* – Informal documentation and understanding of policies and procedures exist. Intuitive common processes are emerging based upon individual expertise.

⚡ *Tools and automation* – Individuals within the organization have created tool based automated solutions that may or may not have become common usage.

⚡ *Skills and expertise* – For critical areas, minimum skill requirements have been identified. On the job training is provided in response to specific needs only without a formal training plan being developed.

⚡ *Responsibility and accountability* – There is confusion about responsibility when problems occur, leading to the pointing of fingers and blame. Individuals are assuming responsibility and are being held informally accountable.

⚡ *Measurement* – At this point metrics are binary – either the process is being performed or not. Baselines are now being established and defined.

⚡ *Goal setting* – The overall goal for this phase is to institutionalize a managed process through

   o   *Establishing an organizational policy*

   o   *Documenting processes and procedures*

o   *Providing the necessary resources*

   o   *Assigning responsibility*

   o   *Training the staff*

   o   *Managing configurations*

o   *Monitoring and controlling the process*

   o   *Objectively evaluating adherence*

   o   *Reviewing the status with higher level management*

Criteria for completing level 2 certification

❏   A defined organizational policy based upon the procedure documented in level 1, and written according to the organizational policy format manual, has been created, reviewed, edited, and approved.

❏   All necessary procedures to carry out the organizational policy in the previous step have been written according to the organizational procedure format manual. These procedures are based upon the process documented created during level 1 certification. In addition, these procedures have been reviewed, edited, and approved.

❏   All necessary configurations for assets associated with the above-mentioned policies and procedures are documented and managed appropriately.

❏   The above policy, procedures, and configuration management is being monitored for compliance and reported to organizational managers on a routine basis.

Level 3 - Defined

The process is defined/confirmed as a standard business process. Existing practices have been formalized into policies that have been documented and communicated. Procedures that carry out these policies have been standardized, documented, communicated, and staff trained. However, there is no continuous monitoring and measurement that the processes are being followed according to procedure.

- *Awareness and communication* – Management is formal and structured in its communication of their understanding of the need to act.

- *Policies, standards, and procedures* – The policies, procedures, and processes are defined and documented for all key activities. Usage of good practices has emerged.

- *Tools and automation* – A plan has been defined for the use and standardization of process automating tools. However, they may not be integrated with each other.

- *Skills and expertise* – Skill requirements are defined and documented for all areas. A formal training plan has been developed, but the actual training that takes place is based upon individual initiative.

- *Responsibility and accountability* – Process owners have been identified with process accountability and responsibility defined and documented. However, process owners are unlikely to have full authority to exercise their initiatives.

- *Measurement* – Tolerances of change for metrics are being established.

- *Goal setting* – The overall goal for this phase is to institutionalize a defined process through

  o *Ensuring full dissemination of defined procedures and processes*

  o *Collecting improvement information*

Criteria for completing level 3 certification

❏ All policies and procedures are fully disseminated throughout the organization.

❏ All affected staff and third parties have been properly trained on the policies and procedures.

❏ Improvement information for the regular usage of the policies and procedures is being collected as a part of the ongoing policy and procedure control plan.

Level 4 - Managed

Process management and measurement takes place. Through the monitoring and measurement of compliance with organizational policies and procedures, the organization is able to intervene and take actions where processes are not effective.

↝ *Awareness and communication* – Management is able to maturely use techniques and tools to communicate their understanding of the full requirements.

↝ *Policies, standards, and procedures* – All aspects of the process are documented and repeatable. Policies are approved by management and documented. Standards for developing policies and procedures are adopted and followed.

↝ *Tools and automation* – Tools are implemented according to a standardized plan and some have been integrated with other related tools. Tools are being used in main areas to automate management of processes, as well as monitor critical activities and controls.

↝ *Skills and expertise* – Skill requirements are routinely updated for all areas with proficiency being ensured for all critical areas. Mature training techniques are applied according to a training plan with knowledge sharing being encouraged. Internal domain experts are involved in training. Effectiveness of the training plan is routinely assessed.

↝ *Responsibility and accountability* – Process owners have full authority to exercise their initiatives with accountability and responsibility fully accepted by management. A reward culture has been put into place.

↝ *Measurement* – Metrics are now statistically valid with an increase in their breadth and interconnectedness.

↝ *Goal setting* – Effectiveness and efficiency are linked to business goals and the overall IT strategy. Root cause analysis is being standardized through institutionalizing a quantitatively managed process by

   o   *Establishing quantitative objectives for the procedures and processes*

   o   *Stabilizing sub-process performance*

Criteria for completing level 4 certification

❑ Quantitative objectives for the measurement of procedures have been established.

❑ Reporting methods to higher-level management of quantitative objectives have been established and approved.

❑ Sub-performing procedures are being analyzed, documented, and stabilized.

Level 5 - Optimizing

Process management includes deliberate process optimization/improvement. Processes are being continuously refined to a level of best practice.

- *Awareness and communication* – Management is able to integrate tools and techniques when proactively communicating their forward-looking understanding of issues and requirements based upon trend analysis.

- *Policies, standards, and procedures* – Process documentation has evolved into automated workflows. Policies and procedures are standardized and integrated to enable end-to-end improvement.

- *Tools and automation* – Tools are fully integrated with other related tools to enable end-to-end support of processes, automatically detect control exceptions, and improve the process. Standardized toolsets are used across the enterprise.

- *Skills and expertise* – Based upon organizational goals, continuous improvement of skills is formally encouraged. Training and education support best practices and use leading-edge concepts and techniques. Knowledge sharing and knowledge-based systems have been formalized.

- *Responsibility and accountability* – Process owners are encouraged to make their own decisions and take action on their own accord. The acceptance of accountability and responsibility has been cascaded throughout the organization in a consistent manner.

- *Measurement* – Metrics are used adaptively, depending upon the current need.

- *Goal setting* – An integrated performance measurement system links IT performance to business goals. Exceptions are globally and consistently noted by management through root cause analysis. Continuous improvement has been inculcated into organizational culture through

  o *Ensuring continuous process improvement*

  o *Correcting root cause analysis of problems*

Criteria for establishing level 5 certification

❑ The organization has formalized documentation of root cause analysis techniques and process improvement methodologies.

SAMPLE POLICY AND PROCEDURE FOR CREATING POLICIES AND PROCEDURES

Here's a policy and procedure we've created to go along with the framework document. Again, like the other documents, this is available to registered users.

Creation and approval of organizational policies and procedures	Control ID	**UCF ID 01406**
	Effective Date	
	Revision Date	
	Revision Number	
	Approved By	

1. Policy Statement

The organization will harmonize all of the rules that apply to governing information management for their environment into a coherent set of organizational controls by establishing effective policies, standards, and procedures.

2. Description

This process is designed to assist policy and procedure owners as they formulate and review new or existing policies and procedures. This document outlines 1) the areas of responsibility for all involved in the process of creating, editing, and managing policies and procedures, 2) the steps required to formulate and revise policies and procedures, and 3) the components of policy and procedure documents.

3. Purpose

The purpose of this document is to set the organizational standard for a common policy and procedure lifecycle.

4. Compliance

Sarbanes Oxley Guidelines The IIA's Global Technology Audit Guide, § 5.3.1, states that all organizations needs to define their aims and objectives through strategic plans and policy statements. *"Without clear statements of policy and standards for direction, organizations can become disoriented and perform ineffectively. Organizations with clearly defined aims and objectives tend to be successful."* The section further states that for some smaller organizations a single policy statement might suffice, but for larger organizations there will most likely be a need for multiple policy statements.

Healthcare and Life Sciences Guidelines HIPAA Pg 8337 in a response says that it is critical for each covered entity to establish policies and procedures that address its own unique risks and circumstances.

NIST 800-66 § 4.7 recommends that the organization establish the organizational framework, roles and responsibilities for this area.

NIST 800 Series Guidelines NIST 800-34 § 3.1 states that an organization should have a contingency planning policy statement that defines the organization's overall contingency objectives and establishes the organizational framework and responsibilities for IT contingency planning.

Pg C-2 says the organization should establish the organizational framework and responsibilities for IT contingency planning. The policy statement should also address roles and responsibilities.

General Guidance Guidelines Page 37 of the ISF Security Audit of Networks guide suggests that control questionnaires be used to assess the extent to which controls have been implemented in a communications network. It goes on to further state that the control questionnaires are normally grouped by subject or theme with the respondents being required to indicate if they are complying with each control listed, or according to a certain degree of compliance or maturity.

Creation and approval of organizational policies and procedures	Control ID	UCF ID 01406
	Effective Date	
	Revision Date	
	Revision Number	
	Approved By	

5. Scope

a. Coverage

This policy and procedure covers *all* organizational process, policy, and procedure development as well as policy and procedure lifecycle management.

b. Assignment

R = Responsible A = Accountable C = Consulted I = Informed	Policy owner	Subject expert	LOB contact	Client contact	Policy reviewer	Policy approver	Policy Coord Gp	Training Team
Identify the need to formulate or to revise new or existing policies and procedures.	RA	C	C	I				
When formulating or revising policy/procedure, check for existing policies, procedures, and responsible individuals.	RA						C	
Ensure that new or revised policies or procedures are consistent with existing policies or procedures and with the organizational mission and objectives.	R				A		C	
Identify cognizant organizational office(s)/officer(s) with formal delegated responsibility for the policy/procedure area(s) under consideration.	RA		C					
Identify those directly affected by the changes, consult with them and consider their views.	RA	I	I	I			C	
Ensure that approved policies and procedures are simple, consistent, and easy to use.	C				R	A	C	
Ensure that written documents meet the standards for layout, language, and formatting.	C				R	A	C	
Review final draft of policy/procedure with Owner and cognizant organizational officer(s).	C	C	C		R	A		
Review final draft with Policy Coordinating Group and cognizant organizational officer(s).	C					A	R	
Complete the Policy and Procedure Transmittal Sheet; submit the policy/procedure for final review by the policy and procedure review team.	RA							

Creation and approval of organizational policies and procedures		Control ID	**UCF ID 01406**
		Effective Date	
		Revision Date	
		Revision Number	
		Approved By	

	Policy owner	Subject expert	LOB contact	Client contact	Policy reviewer	Policy approver	Policy Coord Gp	Training Team
Designate policy and procedure "experts" for interpretation and problem resolution.	R	A						
Prepare training program for new or revised policies or procedures, as needed.								RA
Disseminate policy/procedure; notify affected parties.							RA	
Post approved policy or procedure to the on-line intranet policies and procedures system.							RA	

c. Prerequisite Knowledge

	Policy owner	Subject expert	LOB contact	Client contact	Policy reviewer	Policy approver	Policy Coord Gp	Training Team
Existing policies and procedures	X	X			X	X	X	X
Organizational style guide for policies and procedures	X	X			X	X	X	X
Familiarity of standard usage of Microsoft Word, including spell and grammar checking	X	X			X	X	X	X
Usage of transmittal form, and filling out forms in Acrobat	X				X	X	X	

d. Prerequisite Tools

	Policy owner	Subject expert	LOB contact	Client contact	Policy reviewer	Policy approver	Policy Coord Gp	Training Team
Policies and procedures manual	X	X			X	X	X	X
Organizational style guide	X	X			X	X	X	X
Microsoft Word	X	X			X	X	X	X
Adobe Acrobat	X				X	X	X	

6. Extended Definition

a. Procedure Goals

To create simple, clear, and effective policies and procedures, the organization must follow a standard lifecycle development methodology. The goal of this document is to lay out that methodology.

	Control ID	**UCF ID 01406**
Creation and approval of organizational policies and procedures	Effective Date	
	Revision Date	
	Revision Number	
	Approved By	

b. Supporting and Supported Procedures

None

c. Procedure Triggers

When new processes, policies, and procedures need to be created.

When processes, policies, and procedures need to be reviewed and edited.

When policies and procedures need to be disseminated and staff and clients training on them.

d. Potential Mishaps & Reaction Steps

Symptom	Possible Cause	Solution
The policy and procedure formatting isn't working correctly	Your document isn't linked properly to the organizational template	In Word, select **Tools** menu > **Templates and Add Ins...** and then navigate to the "PandP_policy.doc on the Sharepoint server.
You can't find a good example policy or procedure document that fits your situation		Contact the Policy Coordination Group for assistance
You don't understand the possible exceptions to an existing policy or procedure	The applicability and authority section of the document in question is not clear	Re-check the applicability and authority section of the document, or call the Policy Coordination Group for assistance

e. Successful Execution

When finished, the completed policy and procedure will be

- Reviewed

- Approved

- Trained

- Disseminated

- Posted to the intranet

351

Creation and approval of organizational policies and procedures	Control ID	UCF ID 01406
	Effective Date	
	Revision Date	
	Revision Number	
	Approved By	

f. Reports

All rough drafts and editing notes will be attached in an e-mail to the Policy Coordination Group for entering into the policy knowledgebase system and will be retained for 14 months from the time of final approval of the document.

All final versions of processes, policies, and procedures will be stored in both Word and PDF (certified document) format on the internal Sharepoint server and also replicated off site for secure, available storage.

7. Procedure Steps

Initial process documentation

The check list for process owners is quite different from policy and procedure creation in that it focuses solely on creating rough draft process flow and process documentation that will *become* policies and procedures in the future.

a. Create the process development team by coordinating with the Policy Coordinating Group for assignment:

   1. Identify all of the potential activities involved in the process.

   2. Identify the key roles (or key staff, but identify this as a role) assigned to those activities.

b. Determine the process documentation methodology:

   1. Agree on one, or all, of the following: narrative outline, playscripting, FAQ, troubleshooting tables, or simple flowcharts or UML diagrams.

c. Document the process objective.

d. Check for existing policies and procedures that this process must coordinate with.

e. Create a rough cut flow diagram of the process and:

   1. highlight any potential problems in the flow,

   2. create a rough cut description that follows the flow,

   3. analyze the scope of IT assets affected by the flow,

   4. analyze the scope of personnel affected by the flow,

   5. determine the prerequisite tools needed to accomplish the flow,

   6. determine the prerequisite knowledge needed to accomplish the flow, and

   7. determine what the final outcome should produce.

f. Create the "success" after-action reports.

Creation and approval of organizational policies and procedures	Control ID	**UCF ID 01406**
	Effective Date	
	Revision Date	
	Revision Number	
	Approved By	

g. Have a subject matter expert, and then an amateur, run through the process:

    1. Identify short term improvements with the control process.

Policy

A detailed diagram/flow chart illustrating the policy formulation and approval process steps appears as Attachment I. The following check list, however, can serve as a guide to the policy owner:

a. Check for existing policies and responsible individuals:

    1. Check policies and procedures manuals system-wide.

    2. Check delegations of authority (or unit with operational responsibility).

    3. Check with Policy Coordinating Group (if existing policy and/or responsible office cannot be located from other sources).

b. Identify cognizant administrative office/officer and policy gap:

    1. Work closely with Policy Coordinating Group to research policy context and to identify related policies and procedures.

    2. If the policy has business process implications, check with LOB director for the affected group on the need for further consultation.

    3. If the policy affects specific groups for which explicit consultations are required, check with the appropriate principal officer or unit manager for additional instructions e.g., policies with labor relations implications must follow a specific process).

c. Develop new or revised policy by engaging in appropriate consultation and review.

    1. Work closely with Policy Coordinating Group to identify affected parties and appropriate review bodies.

    2. In the early policy development stages, consult with/consider the views of those who will be directly affected by the new or revised policy.

    3. Draft new or revised policy. When drafting a new policy, ensure that it includes the following sections:

        i. Policy statement

        ii. Policy description

        iii. Policy purpose

        iv. Compliance

    4. Review near-final draft of policy with Policy Coordinating Group and reviewing authority (for clarity, readability, and consistency with other policies and procedures).

    5. Review near-final draft of new or revised policy with cognizant policy reviewing officer (per delegation of authority or

	Control ID	**UCF ID 01406**
Creation and approval of organizational policies and procedures	Effective Date	
	Revision Date	
	Revision Number	
	Approved By	

operational responsibility).

    6. Disseminate policy for full review process.

d. Working closely with the Policy Coordinating Group, conduct additional review/consultation as appropriate.

    1. Complete an initial version of the Policy and Procedure Transmittal Sheet (Attachment II) and forward it along with the final draft policy to the Policy Coordinating Group.

    2. Take final draft to appropriate senior administrative officer(s).

    3. Concurrently, submit (via the Policy Coordinating Group) the final draft to the policy and procedure review team.

    4. Engage in additional review/consultation (as may be suggested).

    5. Revise policy as necessary (and engage in another round of review/consultation, if appropriate).

    6. Finalize the policy, get the appropriate signatures on the Policy and Procedure Transmittal Sheet, and submit it to the Policy Coordinating Group.

e. Ensure that existing procedures affected by the new or revised policy are updated or that new procedures are developed. Contact Policy Coordinating Group for assistance.

f. Disseminate policy.

    1. Provide notice to affected population.

    2. Provide training/orientation (as appropriate).

Procedure

The check list for procedure owners is quite similar except for some of the details of the review process. Note that with procedures, the review process is less formal although it is expected that procedure owners will incorporate the principles of "customer voice" into their process:

a. Check for existing policies, procedures, and responsible individuals:

    1. Check policies and procedures manuals system-wide.

    2. Check delegations of authority (or unit with operational responsibility).

    3. Check with Policy Coordinating Group (if existing procedure and/or responsible office cannot be located from other sources).

b. Identify cognizant organizational office/officer and need for procedure:

    1. Work closely with Policy Coordinating Group to research procedure context and to identify related policies and procedures.

    2. If the procedure requires the development of new policies, follow the steps in the policy formulation and approval process.

Creation and approval of organizational policies and procedures	Control ID	**UCF ID 01406**
	Effective Date	
	Revision Date	
	Revision Number	
	Approved By	

c. Develop new or revised procedure.

   1. In the early policy development stages, consult with/consider the views of those who will be directly affected by the new or revised procedure.

   2. Review the principles and objectives for process redesign and ensure that they are achieved as new or revised procedures are developed.

   3. Draft new or revised procedure. When drafting the procedure, ensure that it includes the following sections (in addition to those already included in the policy):

      i. Scope and coverage

      ii. Assignment

      iii. Required knowledge

      iv. Required tools

      v. Procedure goals

      vi. Supporting and supported procedures

      vii. Procedure triggers

      viii. Potential mishaps & reaction steps

      ix. Successful execution

      x. Reports

      xi. Procedure steps

      xii. Procedure checklists

      xiii. Revision history (if it is not being automatically tracked by the software)

   4. Review final draft of new or revised procedure with cognizant organizational officer (per delegation of authority or operational responsibility).

   5. As appropriate, consult with Policy Coordinating Group.

d. Conduct additional review/consultation as appropriate.

   1. Complete an initial version of the Policy and Procedure Transmittal Sheet and forward it along with the final draft procedure to the Policy Coordinating Group for final review by the policy and procedure review team.

   2. Engage in additional review/consultation (as may be suggested).

Creation and approval of organizational policies and procedures	Control ID	**UCF ID 01406**
	Effective Date	
	Revision Date	
	Revision Number	
	Approved By	

  a. Review the procedure for a valid format and valid process steps.

  b. Review the procedure for editorial checks and balances.

  c. Review the procedure for appropriate style guide usage.

 3. Revise procedure as necessary (and engage another round of review/consultation, if appropriate).

 4. Finalize the procedure, get the appropriate signatures on the Policy and Procedure Transmittal Sheet, and submit it to the Policy Coordinating Group.

e. Disseminate procedure.

 1. Prepare training program for new or revised procedures.

  a. Assign responsibility for training the staff

  b. Create a procedure quiz for opting out of training

 2. Provide notice to affected population.

 3. Hold training workshops/orientation (as appropriate).

f. Manage any necessary configuration changes.

g. Monitor and control the usage of policies and procedures.

8. Procedure Checklists

☐ Do you have the right people on the process team?

☐ Do you have the right tools for documentation?

☐ Do you have access to currently existing policies and procedures?

☐ Do you have the correct templates and applications for process, policy, and procedure documentation?

☐ Do the review teams have the appropriate reviewer's guides, editorial markup guides, and stylesheets?

☐ Do you have access to the current version of the transmittal form?

SOFTWARE TOOLS

There are several well designed policy and procedure tool management packages out there.

These are the packages that we've tested so far.

They are widely varied in their focus. Some focus on the routing of the policies and procedures during their lifecycle. Others focus on the interactivity of the policies and procedures with the everyday life of the end users.

Pathworks

Pathworks, from Ambient Software (http://www.ambientsoftware.com/), helps your team easily capture, *use*, and manage procedures. It is either sold as a web-based ASP service or as an enterprise server product. The reason that I italicized the word *use* is that Pathworks takes an extra step that we've not seen other applications take. It allows managers to direct the use of a procedure to individuals as an activity that must be performed by a certain date. This means that not only does Pathworks manage the policy and procedure lifecycle, it can produce reports showing which procedures have been run as activities, when, and by whom. Very nice.

Pathworks *does not* follow the compliance outline for policies and procedures as documented in the Unified Compliance Framework. Their procedure editor has three sections; Description, Prerequisites, and Steps.

Procedure creation

Creating a new procedure brings up a very intuitive interface that allows the user to fill out the procedure template. All of the writing tools that the user needs are located within this window.

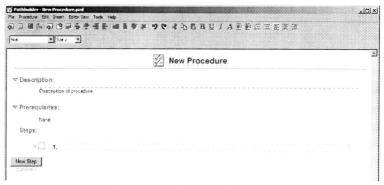

Procedure creation and editing window

To edit a section of the procedure, the user clicks into the field and starts typing. Within the steps portion, the user can re-arrange the order of each step through the use of an icon-based toolbar within the window.

Moving steps up, down, in, out

Adding information other than straight text is also simple through the use of the icon bar within the window. Users have the option of adding pictures, attachments, links, and even form fields that can be validated.

Additional information tools

In addition to the above, pre-existing procedures can be added to the steps, creating a linked set of hierarchical procedures that can walk users through an entire complex procedure grouping.

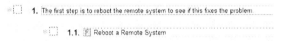

Adding link to an existing procedure

Once the user is finished writing a procedure, it can be published to the procedure site.

Approval routing

Once a reviewer or editor has made changes to the procedure, upon saving the changes and checking the procedure back in, Pathworks asks the editor to provide comments on what was changed within the procedure.

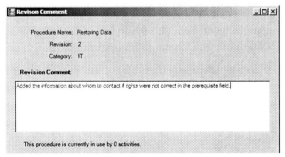

Procedure comment

The one thing missing is that Pathworks doesn't have routing and approval in the formal sense. The software allows the administrator to configure which groups have "approval" authority to publish a procedure in a given category. If a procedure owner or somebody with "Edit" permission revises a procedure and wants to publish it, they will be asked if they want to submit a request that it be published. Anyone with publish permission will be notified, and can then review the changes and publish the newer revision of the procedure.

Public and private comments

Pathworks' collaboration feature keeps comments and feedback in-line with the step and procedure it belongs to and uses proactive reminders to alert authors to new feedback. Pathworks allows both public and private feedback notes to the author, allowing comments to be sent back and forth freely.

 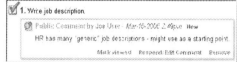

Private (left) and public (right) comments

Notation for continuous improvement

Notes provide valuable feedback to the procedure owner and to other users of the procedure. The more the procedure is used, the better it gets. Activity Notes add information to the Activity Log for tracking.

An *Activity Note* is created on a specific Activity and is tracked in the Activity Log. There are two types:

Informational: used for informal information. It will be logged in the Activity Log.

Variance Reason: used for entering errors messages, work-arounds, and other information related to the non-standard completion of a step. This information is logged in the Activity Log and a report can be run to display all Activities containing a variance. This is often important for compliance.

Feedback to Owner note is used to send private feedback to a procedure owner. The owner uses this feedback to update and improve the procedure.

A *Public Comment* on a procedure is similar to sticking a Post-It note on a document. These comments are viewable by any user that views the procedure. Although you might not have permission to edit the "master copy" of the procedure, you might have permission to add public comments, which are viewable by other users.

Revision control

While only the most current version of a document appears in the Library, older versions can be accessed. As documents are updated, Pathworks stores previous revisions. Authors can open previous revision and compare any revision to any other revision.

Revision history

If a procedure has changed since the last time a user has run it, Pathworks alerts the user with a pop-up message and new steps are highlighted. If a step has changed, the step is highlighted and the user can choose to display and compare the old version of the step to the current version of the step.

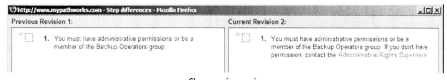

Changes in versions

Categorization and searching

Because everything is database driven, categorization is a snap. Procedures are categorized into a hierarchical library, where each level of the hierarchy specifies permissions for create, edit, publish, and add comments according to group and role. Each procedure's categorization can be inherited from a parent category, or over-ridden at each level.

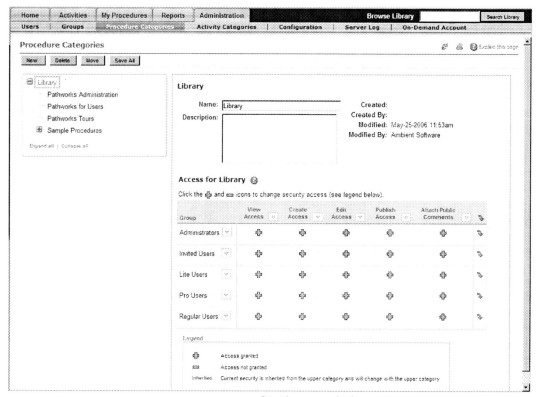

Procedure categorization

Full text search capability

A powerful full text search capability lets users search for activities or procedures, including the contents of any attached documents (PDF, Word, Excel, PowerPoint, etc.). All procedures and activities are automatically indexed by Pathworks. For example, searching the procedure library for *+"Expense*

Report" attachments:Form will find procedures that contain the phrase "Expense Report," and will give extra weight to procedures containing the word Form in an attached document.

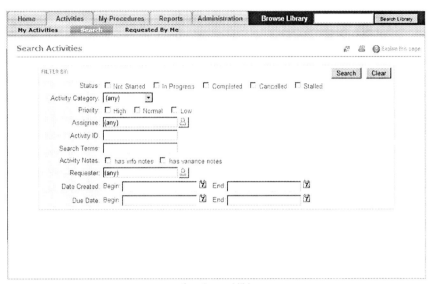

Search capabilities

Creating templates

Users can certainly publish a library category that "Everyone" can see which contains templates. Users can then start from these procedures, and publish their finished procedures to any library category to which they have been given "Create" permission.

Turning procedures into activities

Once you are using (or "running") a procedure Activity, it becomes interactive. When working with a procedure activity, the user can mark steps and add notes.

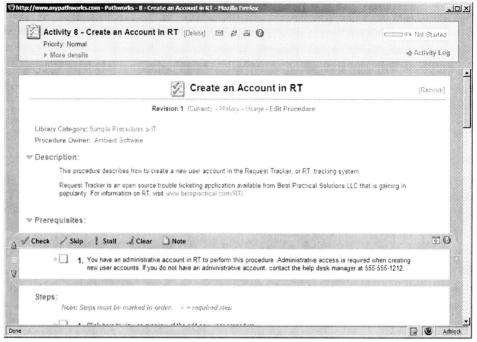

An onscreen procedure with the copyholder showing the current step

As the user moves through the procedure from top to bottom, the system tracks the status of each step as well as the overall activity status. Activity reports provide visibility into who did what and when. Policy and procedure usage is automatically tracked and can be accessed via reports or by displaying Usage data. An example of usage data for the procedure "Add a User to the Domain" is shown in the following diagram:

Revision ▽	Assignee	Activity	Date Created	Activity Status
2	Mary Manager	14 - Add a User to the Domain	Mar-16-2006 4:00pm	100% Completed
2	Helen Smith	13 - Add a User to the Domain	Mar-16-2006 3:59pm	100% Completed
2	Joe User	7 - Add a User to the Domain	Mar-10-2006 11:32am	46% Stalled

Procedure reporting

Full reporting

One of the things that we think is so fantastic about this product is its reporting capability. What makes it so neat? Simple. As people *use* the procedures, their usage is logged continuously. Turning a report over to an auditor that shows who was running which procedures, and when, ends all arguments about following the compliance guidelines. You now have *proof* that you are complying (or not). Nice.

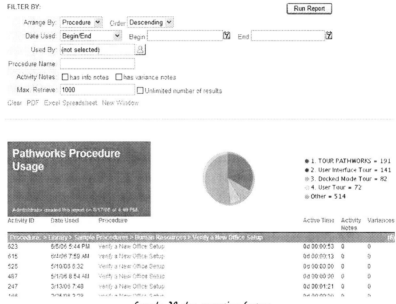

Sample 30 day reporting feature

One of the things that you can use this type of reporting for, is to test an entire plan *one procedure at a time*. By testing individual procedures, spread across several weeks, and in order, you can distribute the time away from normal procedures over a longer period of time to ensure less impact on day to day operations. And with the reporting and continuous feedback provided, you can ensure that each procedure tested will be able to form a complete plan, such as a continuity plan, change management plan, privacy management plan, etc.

Integration with helpdesk systems

The Pathworks integration with Remedy provides the following features:

- The ability to find Pathworks procedures from within the Remedy Help Desk application.

- All data from Pathworks obeys the Pathworks security rules - a user viewing Pathworks data from Remedy sees exactly what they could see from the Pathworks interface itself.

- The ability to select a procedure from within Remedy, and then run it using checklist or docked mode in Pathworks. The procedure is associated with the Remedy Help Desk ticket.

- The Pathworks activity log is copied to the work diary in Remedy, with the correct user names and timestamps matching the names and timestamps in Pathworks.

- Single-Sign On: A user signed in to the Remedy client (native or web/mid-tier) does not need to login to Pathworks separately. The Remedy Connector for Pathworks supports single-sign-on by accepting a unique 128-bit single-sign-on token from Remedy, and validates that against the Remedy server to determine if it is valid.

- The name of a procedure used is automatically copied to the Solution Summary field on the Help Desk ticket.

Policy & Procedure Manager

Policy & Procedure Manager from Policy Technologies International (http://www.policytech.com) is a database driven, Windows-based, policy lifecycle management application. The application runs on a Web server. Users access the application through a Web browser running on their workstation computers.

Policy & Procedure Manager moves the user through a built-in policy lifecycle management process. The publishing process consists of the following stages:

1. **Draft** – A document enters the draft stage at creation. It remains in draft stage until the document owner submits it for review. A document is returned to draft stage whenever a reviewer or approver revises or declines it.

2. **Review** – A document enters the review stage when the document owner submits it for review. It remains in review stage until all designated reviewers have accepted, revised, or declined it. If all reviewers accept the document, it is moved to the approval stage. If one or more reviewers revise or decline the document, it is returned to draft stage for editing.

3. **Approval** – A document enters the approval stage after all reviewers have accepted it. It remains in approval until all designated approvers have accepted, revised, or declined it. If all approvers accept the document, it is moved to the approved (or published) stage. If one or more approvers revise or decline the document, it is returned to draft stage for editing.

4. **Pending** (optional) – After a document is accepted by all approvers, it enters the pending stage (instead of the approved stage) if the document owner designates a date that the document will become effective. The document remains in the pending stage until the effective date, at which time it is moved to the approved (or published) stage.

5. **Approved** (or Published) – A document enters the approved (or published) stage after all approvers have accepted it. The document remains in the approved stage until it is replaced by a new version or archived. Emails are sent to employees that are required to read the approved document.

6. **Archived** – A document enters the archived stage when a new version of that document is approved, when it is replaced (made obsolete) by a different document, or when it is manually archived. A document remains in the archived stage indefinitely.

In addition, because the software is web and server based, Policy & Procedure manual support the four key roles of the document lifecycle (owner, reviewer, approver, control administrator).

Creating a new policy

When creating a new policy, the software walks the user through a set of wizard screens, starting with the document setup screen. In the first screen the software asks for the document's title, version number, document review date (as months from the document's effective date), whether or not the document should be available to internal users, and the effective date of the document.

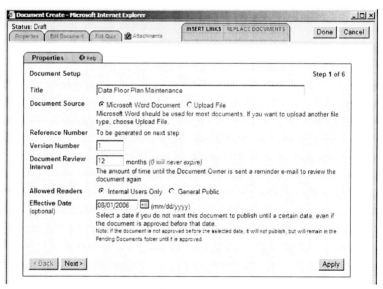

Document setup

The next step, show in the diagram that follows, asks the document creator which departments this document affects. This step depends upon the user having entered organizational sites, departments, and groups ahead of time.

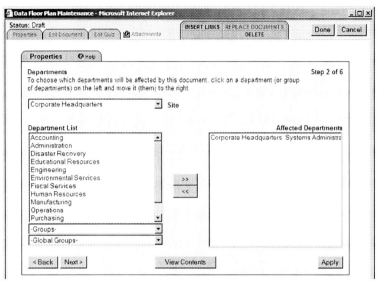

Affected groups

The third step is to select the template to be used for the document, assign an owner, and assign keywords to the document for meta tagged searching.

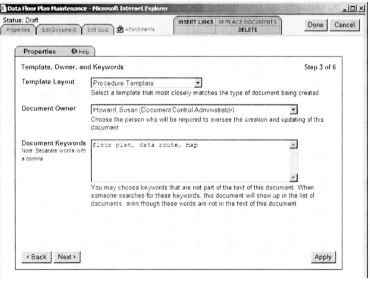

Assigning a template owner and template type

A note about the templates. Templates are set up by the document control administrator, and can be *highly* tailored. Each site and department can have its own templates. And each template can have its own lifecycle stewards assigned to each step of the process. For instance, the headquarters group can have their own policy template with certain headquarters staff assigned to the roles of document owner, reviewer, and approver. And another group can have a completely different template with completely different owners, reviewers, and approvers.

The next step is to assign the document a predefined category and document type (in our case, the document type is a pre-defined procedure template).

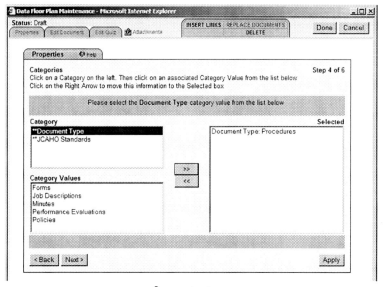

Document category

Once the document has been assigned to a category, the next step is to select from the predefined list of reviewers and approvers. This list can be different for every site, and each list of reviewers and approvers can be hierarchically ordered. Once the person is assigned to the role, they will *automatically* be notified when it is their turn to take part in the document's lifecycle.

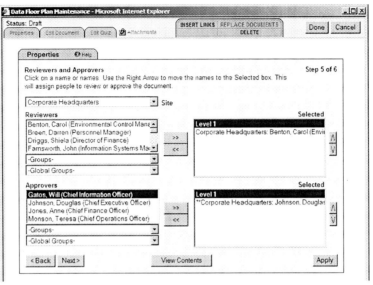

Selecting document reviewers

The final step is assigning readership. There are *required* readers who can be assigned a repeating timeframe, and allowed readers for general access.

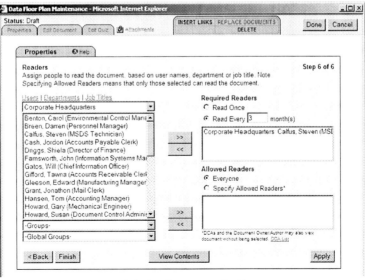

Assigning document readership

Editing a document

The application uses ActiveX to open up a browser window with Microsoft Word embedded into the browser. Process owner names and dates are all database driven and are therefore interactive with the database that powers the software – a real nice touch. All changes within the document are automatically tracked for revision editing purposes.

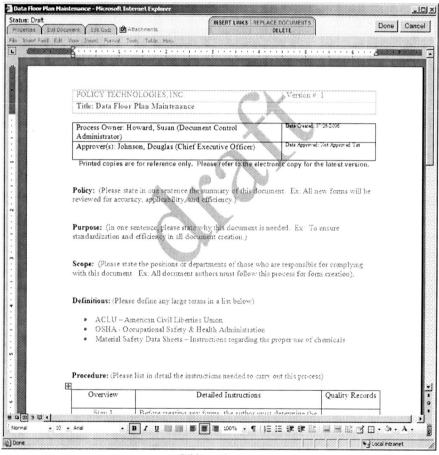

Editing a document

Once the document has been edited by either the reviewer or the approver, the document is then automatically forwarded to the next person in the review cycle. The submission window that follows on the left shows that the document will be routed to the next person and that a review by that person is required. The window that follows on the right shows a reviewer's options upon receiving the document. According to standard industry practices, the reviewer or approver has the option of editing the document, approving the document, sending it back to the draft status for major revision, or approving it as is.

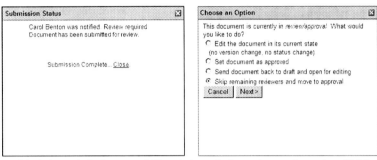

Submitting a draft document (left) and the reviewing and approving options (right)

Reports and document viewing

Because this application is SQL database driven, it is a *very robust* tool. Reports can be generated for documents at every step of the document lifecycle. Reports about which documents have been read can also be generated. Which brings me to another feature of Policy & Procedure Manager – the ability to create quizzes to test and ensure that the end user *has* read and *does* understand the document. The quizzes are multiple-choice, fill in the blank, or true-false.

Because the application is web-based, all documents in all phases of the lifecycle are always available on the website. As long as the website is running. Which is why you'll want to have a policy and procedure for ensuring that in case of an emergency you are backing up the server to an off site website so that your emergency policies and procedures are stored off site.

Systems Continuity Plan Pro

Systems Continuity Plan Pro, from Palo Alto Software (http://www.paloalto.com/ps/sc/), is a combination auditing and policy & procedure creation and management tool.

While the audit section focuses almost primarily on systems continuity questions, the policy and procedure creation and management portion can be used to create, edit, and manage *any* type of policy and procedure.

The creation or editing of a policy or procedure is done through a wizard interface with explicit instructions for every step of the process built into the application.

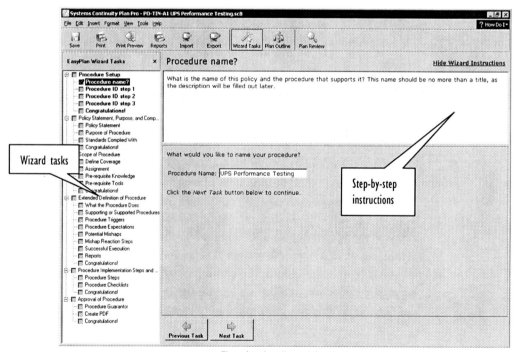

The wizard tasks and instructions

Or, if you'd rather work in an outline format, SCPP can switch from the Wizard Task view to the Plan Outline view with a click of a button. The checkboxes for completion of all of the tasks are then replaced with a hierarchical outline numbered in legal fashion (1.1, 1.2, etc.).

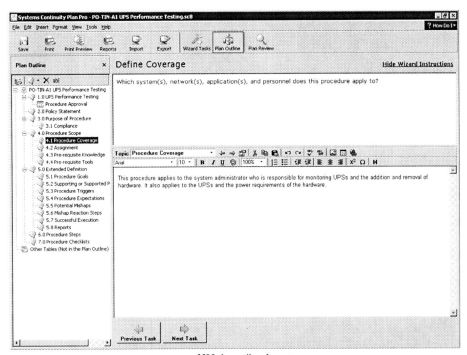

SCPP in outline format

In addition, the software provides a collaboration tool that allows the user to distribute for editing anything from a single item to the entire procedure. The great thing about the collaboration wizard is that it doesn't take any special software (other than the team members having a copy of SCPP). It distributes the sections that need to be written through regular e-mail, or places editable files within the organization's document repository. Even table options, plan settings, and activities can be distributed within the team. Nicely done.

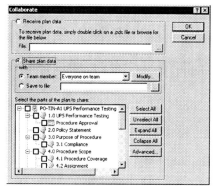

Collaboration wizard

It is the most flexible product we've found in terms of creating re-usable templates, as either whole documents can be turned into templates, or individual sections can be turned into templates.

Exporting completed procedures as a template

When finished, policies and procedures can be exported to a Palo Alto provided secure website, PDF, intranet, Word, or other format file.

The formatting of the templates is relatively simple, but don't let that fool you. The application is built upon an XML and CSS foundation. This enables the end user to create their own styles and XML schema so that the exported information can be shared with *any* type of system (such as databases, XHTML, OpenDoc format, etc.).

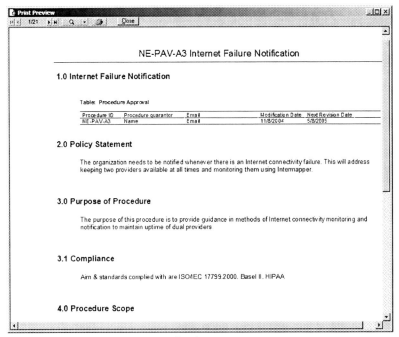

Sample output

One more bonus is that Systems Continuity Plan Pro also includes LANsurveyor from Neon Software for configuration management reporting. Incredibly, the price for Systems Continuity Plan Pro, including LANsurveyor, is the same price as LANsurveyor itself if purchased directly from Neon Software. We don't quite get how that works, but we aren't complaining.

While Systems Continuity Plan Pro is installed on a per computer basis, its built in distribution methodology allows both large and small teams to work together during a document's lifecycle.

NetiQ VigilEnt Policy Center

VigilEnt Policy Center is a database driven policy management tool that helps organizations control the complete lifecycle of policies. With VigilEnt Policy Center, organizations can ensure the regulatory compliance of their policies and procedures by using the extensive workflow capabilities to create, distribute, verify, and publish policies throughout all departments. For later reference or immediate use, VigilEnt Policy Center keeps a library of all policies and procedures from the draft status over the approved ones to retired documents.

The ample set of security features and access control lists in VigilEnt Policy Center guarantees that every department is provided solely with the policies that concern them. Reports can be run at any time to check the organization for compliance.

To add to the broad range of features, policy administrators can send out quizzes to assure that the executors fully understand the policies.

VigilEnt Policy Center presents itself through two interfaces. The administrative interface is used to set up users, groups, roles, send out policies and many other administrative tasks. The users' interface is for reading, commenting, approving, and releasing policies.

Administration

The screenshot that follows displays the wide arrange of administrative tasks that can be performed around the creation and distribution of policies.

- **Access Control Lists** define how documents can be handled by whom,
- **Groups** define users in operational groups,
- **Mail** allows the setup of automatic e-mail notification,
- **Quiz Reports** let the administrator evaluate how the users did in the quizzes, just to name a few of the options.

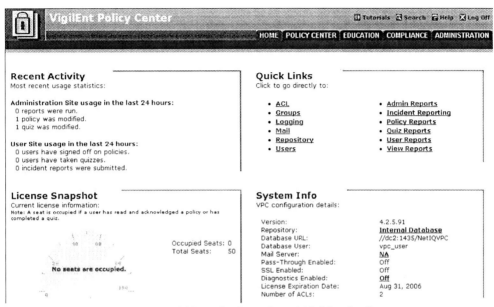

VigilEnt Policy Center General Administration Site

Security structure

One of the strongest features of VigilEnt Policy Center is the detailed security structure that lets the administrator assign users to groups, assign roles to users and/or groups and assign access rights to each of the above. The screenshot below demonstrates the administrative depth of which VigilEnt Policy Center is capable.

Setting Access Rights for the Users

Compliance

VigilEnt Policy Center contains a **Compliance** module that gives the administrator various tools for checking the current level of compliance of the organization.

- **User Reports** creates reports by single users or by groups, detailing, which documents have been reviewed and which quizzes have been taken
- **Policy Reports** gives detailed information about the status of a policy
- **Quiz Reports** generates a report about what users have taken which quizzes
- **View Reports** allows you to view any stored report
- **Incident Reporting** allows you to report, manage and track incidents

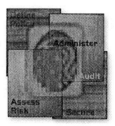

Compliance

The Compliance tab allows you to quickly verify which users in the organization have read and understood your policies, as well as measuring who has completed your quizzes. You can also use this area to report and track incidents.

User Reports allow you to track policy compliance by each user. You can select individuals or groups of users and determine if they have read published policies or taken published quizzes.

Policy Reports allow you to view compliance for a particular policy document.

Quiz Reports allow you to view information on what users have taken each quiz, along with summary and detailed scores on each quiz.

View Reports allow you to view any stored user, policy or quiz reports.

Incident Reporting allows you to report, manage, and track incidents in your enterprise. The incident reporting allows you to track critical details about your incidents and produce management reports.

The Compliance Module

Creating policies and procedures

In many cases one does not need to create a new policy or procedure from scratch. To this VigilEnt Policy Center boasts an extensive library of pre-defined policies plus several policy templates; and as you probably already have several policies and procedures in place, lets you import policies in XML-Format.

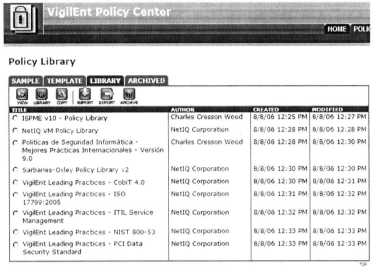

The VigilEnt Library

The process of editing and assigning a policy, or multiples thereof, is very straightforward. You can create a new policy or use an existing one, alter it, and then assign it to a user or a group of users.

To create a new procedure from the templates, you would select the template and create an empty copy.

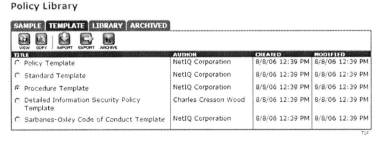

Templates in VigilEnt Policy Center

VigilEnt Policy Center then transfers you directly into the **Edit** mode where you can fill the procedure with appropriate content. The writer only needs to fill in all necessary fields and add or remove categories or subcategories according to the organization's policy.

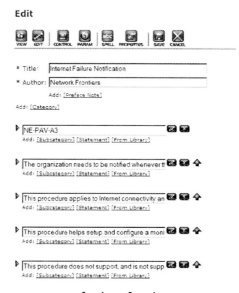

Creating a Procedure

As a next step you assign the access control list so that this procedure is routed correctly, and sent out for review, which automatically places it into the **Review** tab and makes it accessible to the reviewers. Ideally, the e-mail notification functionality of VigilEnt Policy Center should be setup to notify the concerned parties of the availability of policies and procedures.

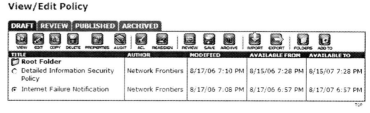

Sending a Procedure to Review

The User Experience

When users are connected to VigilEnt Policy Center, they see a list of all documents that are currently assigned to them and need to be processed according to the predefined access rights and roles. In our example, there is one procedure assigned to the reviewer. When reviewing or editing the procedure, the user clicks on the assigned document and performs all necessary action.

A user's list of Assigned Documents

In this case, the policy spells out the assigned task for the user: "Read the policy." The user can now add a comment to the policy, or just read the policy and acknowledge by checking the checkbox that it has been read. After clicking the Submit button the policy is marked as approved and is published.

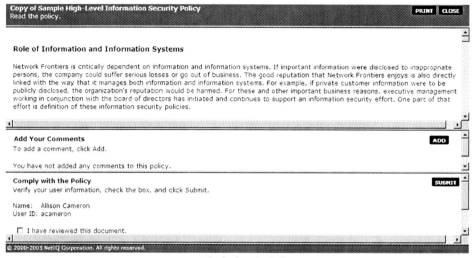

Reviewing the Policy

The acknowledgement of the reviewer triggers an e-mail alert to the administrator, who then publishes this procedure. It will now appear in the Published section on the administrator's site and on each user's home page as an approved procedure.

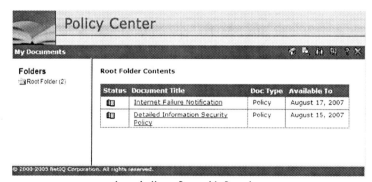

A user's Home Page with Procedures

SmartDraw business graphics software

SmartDraw (www.smartdraw.com) offers a very nice drawing package that is in some respects much better than its competitor Visio. We used their application when writing our material and found it *very* easy to work with. We also like that it exports directly to PDF, Word, and Excel.

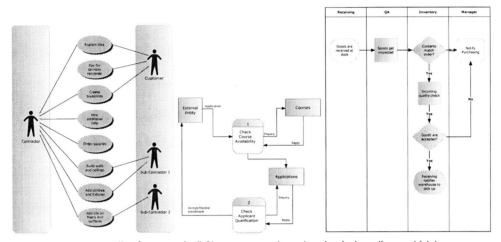

Use Case scenario (left) process map (center) and swim-lane diagram (right)

Another aspect that we like *a lot* is that the folks at SmartDraw offer great content for business process improvement (through proper documentation), templates, and a great support center for flowcharting, and business graphics best practices (www.smartdraw.com/resources/process/index.htm).

Seeing as how business process mapping is the *key* to effective procedure writing, you really should invest the time and effort into learning a good business graphics software package and how to apply that package when documenting your IT compliance practices.

Make your life easier

By ordering the Say What You Do forms set! The forms set contains all of the forms mentioned in this book – over a **dozen of them**, including the 19 page policy and procedure lifecycle plan, policy and procedure review forms, and a sample template policy and template procedure.

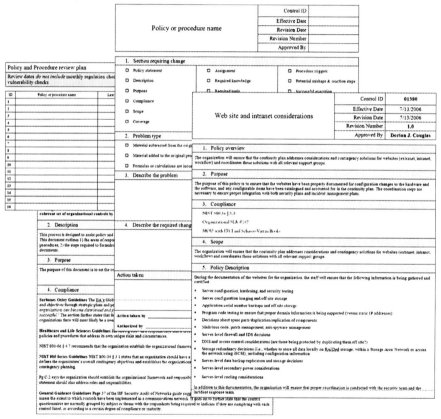

Sample policies and forms

Our competitors are selling these forms for more than one hundred dollars. You can't beat our price at $34.95 – with forms updates available to you for two full years! That means that as we develop new forms, you'll be notified and you can pick them up online where they will be ready and waiting for you. http://saywhatyoudo.unifiedcompliance.com/buy_now/templates.php

The Language of Compliance

A glossary of acronyms, terms, and extended definitions, version 1.0. The Language of Compliance is the biggest (3,000+ entries), and the best (the only glossary endorsed by the Unified Compliance Framework) resource for acronyms, terms, and extended definitions. Authored by the internationally acclaimed and award winning authoring team of Dorian Cougias and Marcelo Halpern, this is the glossary that more IT professionals turn to than any other. It covers the terms found in HIPAA, SOX, GLB, CobiT, ISO 17799 and 27001, BCI, BSI, ISSF, and over 100 other regulatory bodies and standards agencies.

The Language of Compliance

Buy the e-book online at our site and receive two years worth of updates for free! And it's only $29.95 — the price that Amazon charges *without* the updates! http://glossary.unifiedcompliance.com.com/buy_now/ebook.html

The IT Compliance Institute

THE PRIMARY AUTHORS

Dorian J. Cougias, swc

Dorian J. Cougias is the founder and CEO of Network Frontiers, a company that focuses on systems continuity, regulatory compliance, and IT infrastructure consulting, training, and publishing.

Over the last fourteen years, Dorian has overseen the establishment, sale, and re-launch of Network Frontiers, has authored significant portions of multiple IT certification programs, has served as CIO of two of the leading Ad Agencies in the world, launched multiple successful IT products, and has served as CEO of an international software company. He has written and spoken extensively on all matters of information technology, has become a leading expert witness, and has won numerous writing and speaking awards.

He is also an Adjunct Professor of Technology, lecturing and serving on the board of advisers for the University of Delaware; College of Human Services, Education, and Public Policy.

Dorian has authored hundreds of articles and dozens of books, including the award-winning Backup Book: Disaster Recovery from Desktop to Data Center, and most recently the Unified Compliance Series.

As the primary architect of the Unified Compliance Framework, Dorian and his research partner, Marcelo Halpern of the international law firm Latham and Watkins, have created the first independent initiative to exclusively support IT compliance management. By focusing on commonalities across regulations, standards-based development, and simplified architectures, the UCF supports a strategic approach to IT compliance that reduces cost, limits liability, and leverages the value of compliance-related technologies and services across the enterprise.

Dorian and his team continue to consult to clients with significant data management requirements. He works extensively with application and hardware developers such as NetIQ, CommVault, Quantivate, Symantec, Emerson Network Power, Computer Associates, LXI, Scalable, Quantum, and SonicWall.

Dorian also serves as an adviser, research fellow, or working group member to the Financial Technology Forum, IT Compliance Institute, NetFocus, Hospitality Law, the National Association of Convenience Stores, and the Hospitality Financial & Technology Professionals.

Contact Information

Tel: **+1 (510) 835-2415, ext 112**
E-mail: dcougias@netfrontiers.com

And if you are wondering what the "swc" stands for after Dorian's name, that's simple; "scholar without credentials." He's the only one on the primary team without all of those funny initials behind his name, so we thought we'd make up a set just for him. If you know of anyone who'd like to give this poor fellow an honorary PhD, we're sure he'd be more than happy to receive it.

Marcelo Halpern, esq

Marcelo Halpern is a partner with Latham & Watkins LLP, global law firm with more than 1,900 attorneys in 24 offices. Marcelo is resident in the firm's Chicago office and serves as Chair of the firm's Global Technology Transactions Practice Group.

Marcelo has provided representation and advice to global "Fortune 100" companies, start-up and emerging growth companies, charitable and not-for-profit organizations as well as domestic and foreign governments. His experience includes structuring and negotiating technology-based strategic alliances and joint ventures; domestic and international outsourcing transactions; software, database, intellectual property and content licensing; counseling on digital strategy concerns including internet security, data acquisition, data privacy and regulatory compliance issues; ISP, ASP, hosting, and software services agreements; internet advertising and sponsorship agreements; technology development and co-development transactions; ERP implementation transactions; private labeling, co-branding, and other marketing and distribution strategies; venture capital investments; and mergers and acquisitions involving technology companies or intellectual property assets. Marcelo also provides general corporate representation to software, consulting, internet, e-commerce and technology companies.

Mr. Halpern has been recognized as an industry leader in *Chambers USA – America's Leading Business Lawyers*, *The Best Lawyers in America*, and in *Illinois Leading Lawyers Network*. He currently serves on the Board of Editors for *The Internet Newsletter* and for *The E-Commerce Law Report* and formerly served on the Board of Directors, and as Secretary and Treasurer for the MPEG-4 Industry Forum, a nonprofit international organization dedicated to the promotion of technological standards in digital media. He has also served as an Adjunct Professor of Computer Law at The John Marshall Law School in both its JD and LLM programs. Marcelo is a member of the American Bar Association (Section of Science and Technology), the Illinois State Bar Association, the Chicago Bar Association (Computer Law Committee), and the Computer Law Association.

Marcelo also serves on the Diversity Scholars Program Committee, Technology Committee and Security Committee.

Prior to attending graduate school, Marcelo served as vice president of a software development and consulting firm and worked as a software systems developer and manager.

Education

J.D., Columbia Law School, 1992
Harlan Fiske Stone Scholar; Associate Editor, *Columbia Business Law Review*
M.B.A., Columbia University Graduate School of Business, 1992
Beta Gamma Sigma
B.A., Wesleyan University, 1985

Contact Information

Tel: **+1 (312) 876-7723**
E-mail: marcelo.halpern@lw.com

Rebecca Herold, CISSP, CISA, CISM, FLMI

Rebecca is an information privacy, security and compliance consultant, author and instructor with her own company since mid-2005, Rebecca Herold, LLC. Rebecca has over 16 years of privacy and information security experience, and assists organizations in all industries throughout the world of all sizes with all aspects of their information privacy, security and regulatory compliance programs. Rebecca was instrumental in building the information security and privacy program while at Principal Financial Group, which was awarded the 1998 CSI Information Security Program of the Year Award. Rebecca is also an Adjunct Professor for the Norwich University Master of Science in Information Assurance program.

Rebecca has served as a board and council member of various organizations, and is currently on the Norwich University Journal of Information Assurance Board of Review. Rebecca is frequently interviewed and quoted in diverse publications such as *Consumer Financial Services Law Report, hcPro Briefings on HIPAA, SC Magazine, SearchSecurity, Information Security, Business 2.0, Disaster Resource Guide, The Boston Herald, Pharmaceutical Formulation and Quality, IT Business Edge, Fortifying Network Security, IT Architect, CIO Strategy Center, Physicians Weekly,* IEEE's *Intelligent Systems, Cutter IT Journal* and others, including the "Privacy Piracy" California radio broadcast.

Prior to owning her own business, Rebecca served in key privacy and security roles. She was Vice President, Privacy Services and Chief Privacy Officer at DelCreo, Inc., Chief Privacy Officer and Senior Security Architect for QinetiQ Trusted Information Management, Inc. (Q-TIM), the Global Security Practice Central Region Security Subject Matter Expert for 2 years at Netigy. Prior to joining Netigy, Rebecca was at Principal Financial Group (PFG) where she was responsible for the corporate information security and privacy program.

Rebecca authored many books; some of them include **The Privacy Papers (Auerbach)** in 2001, co-authored **The Practical Guide to HIPAA Privacy and Security Compliance** (Auerbach) in 2003, **Managing an Information Security and Privacy Awareness and Training Program** (Auerbach) in 2005, the **Privacy**

Management Toolkit (Information Shield) in 2006 and co-authored *Say What You Do* in 2007. Rebecca has also authored chapters for dozens of books along with over one hundred other published articles. She has been writing a monthly information privacy column for the CSI Alert newsletter since 2001 and contributes articles to other publications regularly. Rebecca has a B.S. in Math and Computer Science and an M.A. in Computer Science and Education.

Contact Information

Tel: **+1 (515)491-1564**
E-mail: rebeccaherold@rebeccaherold.com

Index

Printed in the United States
109606LV00005B/31-34/A

9 780972 903967